From Corner Shop to Corner Shop in Five Generations

A History of William Jackson & Son plc

Written by
Alan Wilkinson

Researched by
Katharine F. Beedham

HUTTON PRESS
1994

Published by

The Hutton Press Ltd.,
130 Canada Drive,
Cherry Burton, Beverley,
East Yorkshire HU17 7SB

Typeset and printed by
Image Colourprint Ltd.,
Willerby, Hull.

ISBN 1 872167 65 9

DEDICATION

*To All our Staff and Customers
who have helped build this Company.*

CONTENTS

ACKNOWLEDGEMENTS

We would like to thank the following former employees of William Jackson, their families, and a number of members of the public for their invaluable assistance in the researching of this book. Their anecdotes and reminiscences, as well as their capacity for remembering minute details of long-ago events, have contributed to what we hope is an accurate history of the company, its staff and its relationship with its customers. Current employees, not listed here, have given us their time, their co-operation and the benefits of their experience. We would therefore like to thank the staff, management and board of William Jackson & Son for the courtesies accorded to us. Due to limitations of space we have unfortunately not been able to make use of all the informative, illuminating and often hilarious anecdotes. But we would like to express our gratitude for the insights and entertainment they have afforded us.

Jack Allen, Jack Allerston, Wilfred Appleby, L.E. Armitage, Esther Baker, Molly Baker, Bill Bark, Jim Bark, Ron Boult, A. Boynton, Leslie Bland, Kathleen Calland, Harry Cappleman, Eileen Carmichael, Sidney Charlton, Herbert Cockerill, Mrs J. Cook, G.H. Connell, Ray Critchley, F. Cuttill, John Davis, Jess Dodson, Brenda Dyke, Mrs Fallon, Brian Fenner, Mabel Fenton, Flo Fletcher, John Flew, Archie Flynn, Jack Gallant, Freda Gould, Alex Hatfield, Edward Hewson, Adrian Horsley (Gelder & Kitchen), Mrs M. Hughes, Molly Hunter, Joan Hutchinson, Thomas Jackson, Allan Jewsbury, Gladys Johnson, Les Johnson, Rene Johnson, Christopher Ketchell (Local History Archives Unit), Audrey King, Kingston upon Hull Record Office, Margaret Kirk, Local Studies Library, Hull, Ann Los, Muriel Lusby, Mrs Mainprize, Cyril Marshall, Agnes Matthewman, Mrs I. McWilliams, Hellick Millson, Geoff Nurse, Mr L. Oliver, Vera Owen, Muriel Panther, Tom Pearson, Vincent Pearson, Ken Porter, Leonard Pounder, Frank Reed, Maree Riches, Betty Richmond, Brian Robinson, Margaret Robinson, Norah Russell, Dorothy Scholefield, S.R. Shearsmith, Sid Slater, Ernest Smee, J. Smethurst, Peter Smith, Fred Standing, Norah Tasker, Frank Taylor, C.R. Taylor, Clive Telfer, Cyril Terry, Ian Thomson, E. Timm & Son Ltd, Jenny Tinker, Fred Todd, Donald Woodward (The Corporation of the Hull Trinity House), Alf Turner, Mrs M.N. Turner, Robert Tyson, Walter Varney, T.C. Waite, Audrey Weightman, Iris & George White, Kenneth Williams.

Photographic, pictorial and documentary contributions have come from a wide variety of sources. We are particulary grateful to the following for their kind assistance:

Hull Daily Mail, Harry Abba, Molly Baker, Herbert Balland, Bill Bark, Leslie Bland, Kenneth Bright, Norman Burnitt, Kathleen Calland, Herbert Cockerill, Ray Critchley, Paul Cross, F. Cuttill, Walter Fussey, Mike Igoe, Donald Innes, Allan Jewsbury, Gladys Johnson, Mrs Lister, Ian S. McLaren, Mr L. Oliver, Muriel Panther, Geoff Parvin, Jean Pattison, Photo Mayo Ltd, David Rennardson, Dorothy Scholefield, S.R. Shearsmith, A. Sissons, Ernest Smee, Nigel Snowden, C.R. Taylor, Frank Taylor, E. Timm & Son Ltd, Jenny Tinker, Fred Todd, Walker Studios, Audrey Weightman, Kenneth Williams.

Foreword

We have been considering writing a history of Wm. Jackson & Son PLC for some time and have been gathering material with that in mind over a number of years. Many of our pensioners have been able to contribute a great amount of detail of their experiences in the Company, the trading concepts of earlier years and the personality of Company employees, senior staff and directors between and after the two World Wars. We are greatly indebted to them.

The differnt patterns of trade over the years are very evident. The Company has changed course several times to keep abreast and indeed ahead of events. Many new ventures not allied to the food trade have been instigated and pioneered with considerable success. Now it seems that to some extent we are returning to our core business of food manufacturing and the smaller retail stores - almost a full cycle of events.

Jacksons has always been a Hull-based organisation. The family involvement has been continuous; I am myself a great-grandson of the founder. Many other families have similar long-term connections and commitment with the Company. Very often there have been three or four members of a family working for the Company at the same time. Their loyalty and their memories are now chronicled. So although this book is a history of events in the Company since its inception in 1851, it is also a saga of people and life in Hull over the intervening years. That is why we feel that it is important it should be on record for posterity

Peter B. Oughtred
September 1994

The Founder, William Jackson (1828-1912).

William Jackson and his wife Sarah (1828-1902).

Chapter One

WILLIAM JACKSON & HIS SON

William Jackson, the son of a farmer, was born in October 1828 in the village of Elstronwick, some eight miles to the east of Hull. No record remains of his early days, but it can be surmised that he somehow acquired a knowledge of the tea trade, for one September day in 1851 he opened a shop at number 28, Scale Lane in the heart of Hull's old town, trading as a grocer and tea dealer at a site today occupied by a Greek take-away restaurant. That same September day he married Sarah Brown, five years his junior. For a man who was throughout his life a staunch 'no beer and no baccy' Methodist she was an appropriate choice, coming as she did from the heart of Wesley country, the Lincolnshire village of Epworth. The couple had six daughters and two sons, two of the girls and one boy surviving beyond infancy. In one dreadful outbreak of scarlet fever three infants died within four months of each other.

Throughout his life Jackson was closely associated with the Nonconformist church, devoting all his spare time to spiritual matters, and preaching regularly at an old chapel in George Yard. Indeed, he gave the last sermon ever heard there before it was demolished, and was presented with the keys as a memento. His religious concern evidently governed his business practice too, for it was said that each new assistant who worked for him would be asked where he or she worshipped. The applicants apparently learned to point to whichever chapel was nearest to the branch at which they were to work.

For the next thirty-seven years William's business would remain more or less a one-shop operation, albeit

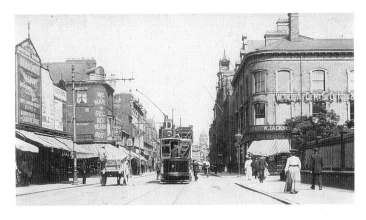

The Carr Lane Shop, opened in 1861. Jackson's head office was here until Paragon Street was opened in 1929.

one which appears to have enjoyed a modest growth. A second shop was opened in 1860 or '61 at 72 Carr Lane, next to the Jacksons' home, and for two or three years Scale Lane remained open. After it closed, probably in 1863, Jackson continued to trade from various premises in Carr Lane for the rest of his life. His first offices were there - and his warehouse - until the early 1930s, some twenty years after his death.

In 1865, four years after the first Carr Lane shop opened, Jackson bought two houses further along the street at number 65, between the Black Horse Inn and the Mariners' Almshouses, property owned by Trinity House from whom he had rented the shop at number 72. In 1877 the Town Improvement Committee required these houses in order to widen the street, so he moved his growing business into new premises at 37 and 38 Carr Lane on the corner of Anne Street. This establishment, known as the West End Tea Mart, was purpose built by Trinity House.

By this time William's only surviving son George had been some years in his father's company, having started with him in 1878 as a lad of fifteen. In April 1887 George Harry Hall joined the firm. He was a

The original plaque from the Scale Lane Shop, 1851.

Spring Bank branch, run for a time by Mr. Bentham - until he went into politics.

time-served grocer, formerly with the local firm of Cusson's. He was a country boy, son of a Howden market gardener. When, at his interview with William Jackson, wages were discussed, Hall, who had been on a meagre fifteen shillings at Cusson's, asked for the grand sum of thirty shillings a week. Jackson then displayed either a subtle sense of humour or an idiosyncratic bargaining technique. "That's far too much," he told the applicant - and thereupon offered him twenty-eight. However, Hall - who has been described as "a marvellous carver who could cut a currant into three" - so impressed as first counter-hand at Carr Lane that he was granted his extra two shillings the very next week. In 1891 he would become the first manager of Jackson's third shop, Bright Street.

1888 saw the opening of a new grocery store at 127 Spring Bank, on the corner of Clarendon Street, initially managed by W.E. Cooper, later by the twenty-five-year-old George. This move heralded the start of a steady and sustained expansion: a confectionery shop was added by 1891, and a bread and confectionery works opened around the corner in Clarendon Street. And, just as the business expanded so it broadened its scope. Whereas Jackson's 1882 notepaper was headed "Grocer and Tea-dealer" the 1889 version read "Tea dealer and coffee roaster, general grocer and provision dealer, vendor of household and toilet requisites".

According to Christopher Oughtred, Jackson's great-great-grandson and currently Managing Director of the firm, the tradition within the family has been to cast the old man as a founding father and somewhat visionary character, his son George as something of a black sheep. There are reasons for this but it now seems as though William was, quite simply, the tea

The founder's son George, later to become George Jackson Bentham, M.P.

dealer and grocer he described himself as in 1851, and his son George a prime mover in the expansion that took place later. William was past sixty when the Spring Bank shop was opened, George not yet thirty. In the years to William's death the company did expand considerably but this was probably due to the younger man's prompting than to the ambitions of his ageing father. One of the few recollections of the old man which come down to us today is offered by a lady whose parents used to shop at Carr Lane. For their extreme caution in weighing out dry goods for a customer the proprietor and his wife were, it appears,

George Harry Hall, known as 'Bompy'. He was instrumental in the firm's expansion from its two branches in 1888 to over fifty in 1930.

The first Mrs. Ada Bentham, mother of Doris and Phyllis.

known to the community as Mr. and Mrs Split-Currant! Perhaps, then, it is fair to see William as the man who carefully laid the foundations on which later generations were to build.

By 1912 the company had around seventeen shop units, as well as a bakery, jam factory, warehousing and stables. Up to 1904 the individual premises were owned either by the father or the son, in at least one case jointly. In that year, however, the firm became a limited company and each sold his own properties to William Jackson and Son Limited.

While the founder thus fades into history his son has to be considered not only as head of the company presiding over a huge expansion, but also as a public and political personage, and finally in terms of his private life. George Jackson became, in 1897, George Jackson Bentham. A number of reasons have been put forward for this change, which was done legally by deed poll. One is his undoubted admiration of the great Liberal Jeremy Bentham and the fact that George would have considered it politically a more acceptable - and more electable - name than plain Jackson. A second reason is that the father, upon hearing that his son intended to stand for Parliament, feared that half his customers - the Conservative element - would desert him, and thus suggested a `nom de guerre'. The probable reason, however, is rather more prosaic: as his public activities increased George found that some of his mail was going astray, there being apparently too many Jacksons in the city of Hull. Nevertheless, the actual choice of name suggests an opportunism worthy of one of the area's up-and-coming entrepreneurs.

Bentham was an energetic and committed Liberal in an age when, prior to the emergence of the Labour party as an effective force, campaigners for social reform were constantly at odds with a conservative establishment. He entered the political ring in 1893 as a Hull City councillor, lost his seat in 1895, but regained it three years later. He sat on the Council for a total of thirteen years, his particular interests being in gas and water and general town improvements. He was also interested in education, being a strong advocate of a national system of schooling, and further involved himself in the work of the free churches. From 1908 he was a Justice of the Peace and was for some time deputy chairman of the Hull Watch and chairman of the Licensing Committee.

He first attempted to enter Parliament in 1906 when he stood as Liberal candidate for Central Hull. He lost to the Conservative Sir Seymour King but reduced his majority from 3000 to just over 1000. In 1910 he was adopted by the Gainsborough, Lincolnshire, constituency and won the seat, holding it until 1918 when the Lloyd George Liberals split with the Asquith faction and joined the Conservatives in a coalition government. Bentham was to oppose the Welshman vigorously for the remainder of his political life.

Bentham was not a notably active speaker in the House of Commons, making about half a dozen speeches a year, mostly on issues affecting his constituency. As befitted a man of his background, he sat on the Catering Committee. Indeed, on the occasion of a strike which disrupted payment of wages to the House caterers, it was the Jackson's chairman who came to the rescue. He took the Hull express, collected the company's takings for the week and hurried back to London to pay the distressed staff in person. In a few letters which have survived from his

Three generations of William Jackson's descendants at Swanland House: (standing) Jack Oughtred and Mrs Ada Bentham, (seated from left) Phyllis, Peter Oughtred on G.J. Bentham's knee, Norman Oughtred holding Jean Oughtred who was to marry Ron Mountifield.

regular correspondence with his daughters at boarding school in Eastbourne we can gain a more intimate portrait of his parliamentary life. He refers constantly to the late sittings and lengthy debates, and talks of the "end of term" and the "holidays" with evident anticipation. In one or two of these faded documents he speaks to his girls of current issues. To Phyllis, who evidently had to write a piece of work on the subject, he outlines his views on absolute freedom of the press. It's fine in principle, he says, but in the reporting of crimes it can without doubt lead to `copycat' acts. War scares can be inflamed by publishers with an axe to grind, and industrial booms set up by unscrupulous businessmen.

Where his father had been an active preacher and churchman, Bentham was thus evidently more concerned with secular matters, he held strong views on the monarchy and occasionally caused something of a stir when at public functions he refused to stand to toast the king. Outside of Westminster Bentham was something of a philanthropist, involving himself in a number of charitable affairs. An example is the Victoria Hospital for Sick Children in Park Street in the city of Hull. In a 1920 handbook for that institution he is listed as having made seven separate donations amounting to £429. At that price he was one of its leading benefactors.

With Bentham thus engaged in a very active public life it is perhaps to 'Bompy' Hall that much of the credit for the firm's expansion should go. Certainly that is the view of some of his heirs and descendants. The name 'Bompy', by the way, comes from the time a young grandchild of his visited him at work. Unable to pronounce 'Grandpa' she came out with 'Bompy' - and it stuck. Very early on in his career with the firm

Hall had been chided by Mr. William Jackson. "You're too ambitious," he was told. "We shall never be another Cusson's." There is an irony in the remark. Until 1900 Cusson's, with a total of two dozen shops in the Hull area, was well out in front, Jackson's having half that number. And both in any case were to be outstripped by the Co-op who, by 1920, had well over thirty stores. But by 1929 Jackson's, now on forty-two, had squeezed ahead of Cusson's on forty-one, and would just about double their number in the next two decades.

Throughout this period of rapid growth Hall was very much at the helm. He was made a director of the firm in 1913, shortly after the death of old Mr. Jackson, with specific responsibility for the shops. His grand-daughter Margaret Kirk not only insists that 'Bompy' was the man who built up the retail arm of the company but is quite unequivocal in asserting that Bentham held him back. He it was, in the 1920s, who held out against expansion beyond the city's boundaries. When Margaret was growing up Bentham was spoken of as a 'bogey-man'. She recalls that 'Bompy' never got a decent salary until after Bentham's death, and puts down what she regards as his rather shabby treatment to the fact that he was not of the family. However, he did have allies, and they would later serve him well.

Bentham has also been considered as a less than savory character by the Oughtred family who head the firm today. In part this is almost folklore, but it all goes back to Bentham's personal life. He certainly had a reputation as a womaniser. Molly Hunter and Rene Johnson, who worked in the Carr Lane offices in the late 1920s, shortly before Bentham's death, recall how whenever he sent for a girl to perform some task in his office upstairs there would be consternation as to who would be delegated. Generally a girl would try to get a colleague to accompany her. Failing that the youngest or most obviously innocent would be sent up. Apparently there was even a couch in his inner sanctum where he was believed to entertain young women from time to time.

It was Bentham's liaison with a raven-haired young widow, Mrs Ada Green, however, which caused the greatest scandal. She was manageress of one of the confectionery shops. Her husband had been killed in the War. The affair was evidently no great secret. Perhaps Mrs Bentham herself - also named Ada - knew about it. Certainly Bentham's daughters Phyllis and Doris were outraged. They had by this time married the brothers Jack and Norman Oughtred, and become with their new husbands major share-holders in the company. On the death of the company secretary W.E. Cooper in 1925 Jack - that is, Captain John Alwyn Oughtred, M.C. - would take over that post.

The animosity between Bentham, his daughters and his sons-in-law was probably aggravated when he married Mrs Green in January 1926, his first wife having died in October 1924. Her death, although following a spell of ill health, appears to have happened in rather tragic circumstances. She died alone, locked in her room, her body being found after a ladder had been fetched and the window forced.

Norman Oughtred had little real influence within the company, preferring to concentrate his energies and entrepreneurial skills on the shipping business he had set up with Herbert Harrison after his return from the war. His brother Jack who had joined Jackson's in 1919 as cashier, had by 1925 become secretary and was obviously at the heart of things. In June 1928, however, he resigned his post, presumably because of friction between himself and Bentham, and went to work for Norman as company secretary at Oughtred and Harrison.

Two documents from this period are revealing. One is from one of Bentham's sisters - probably Annie - resident in the south of France, and is quite prophetic, being written in late 1927, several months before Jack's departure. "Mr. Bentham's intention is evidently to freeze you out," it reads. "He knows if he dismissed you he would be up against public opinion, so realising that he is already unpopular he will not risk that, but hopes to make you leave." The letter goes on to speak of his fickle nature, of an unnamed woman with whom he is fascinated, and of a hope that he will soften as he gets older. The second document is a receipt, Bentham receiving from his daughter Phyllis certain sums of money: £1175 for a house named "Studlea" in Davenport Avenue, Hessle; £278 4s 4d being half the cost of a motor car; £352 10s 0d being seven and a half years' interest on the £1175, less income tax at four shillings in the pound. What it seems to add up to is Bentham receiving back gifts - although they might have been loans - made to Phyllis and Jack at the time of their wedding just over seven and a half years before.

The Oughtreds had married into the Jackson family, entered the business, and then been frozen out. But Bentham did not long survive their departure. He died suddenly late in October 1929 as he boarded a train at York station, the five minutes past five for Hull. The event was widely reported in the newspapers. What they did not report, however - in those far-off days of press restraint - was that he was in the company of a young lady, not his wife. She is rumoured to have been a confectionery assistant from the Carr Lane shop. Only one press report, in the Eastern Morning News of November 5, contained the slightest hint of a reference to this matter. In its report on Bentham's funeral - he was, incidentally, cremated - it gave a resumé of the minister's address: "In a moment of tragic suddenness he had been taken away from us, and in connection with that tragic departure words have been used that might have cut some people to the quick."

The Hull Evening News, however, reporting from the Police Court on the day after the death, reports Mr. W. Rippen, the Chairman of the Bench, offering a nicely balanced view. Many things might be said of Mr. Bentham, he remarked, but "some time ago I was visiting the Institute of the Blind and I saw twenty or thirty people under rather sad conditions. They were exceedingly happy, however, and pointed to a wireless set in the room and remarked how kind it had been of Mr. Bentham to provide them with the means of pleasure. One likes to think of these kindly actions."

William Jackson, then, is a vague and distant character, his son a man of controversy. But this is the story of a business, and it is through the growth of the business and the actions of those engaged in it, that the prime movers are best revealed.

Chapter Two

THE SHOPS

When Christopher Oughtred, great-grandson of George Jackson Bentham, son of the present Chairman, and himself Managing Director of the company, first saw the 1935 film "Food For Thought" which contained footage of Jackson's bread in production he remarked, "We haven't really come all that far, have we?"

It is true that bread, the staff of life, is still made with the same ingredients and by the same basic process as it has always been made. The plant is more sophisticated, the process a little quicker, and the operatives have different haircuts - in 1935 they all had the look of new recruits to the armed forces.

But the same cannot be said of Jackson's shops. To compare the flagship Paragon Street branch of the 1930s with a Grandways of the early '60s or the new "Jackson's Of..." Convenient Neighbourhood Supermarket is to see three distinct and dissimilar establishments.

The earliest reliable descriptions of Jackson's grocery stores come from interviews with retired staff whose working lives reach back into the post-World War I era. It is fair to assume that the typical shop of the 1920s was not a great deal different from that of the late nineteenth century. Indeed, one former apprentice grocer, later a Jackson's manager and training supervisor, Mr. Ted Hewson, evoked the spirit of Charles Dickens in describing his early days in the trade. He harks back to a passage in A Christmas Carol in which Dickens offers a minutely detailed

description of a grocery store, listing the items stocked and even the smells that enticed a bustling crowd of customers to jostle at the counter. That description, Mr. Hewson says, "is true in the minutest detail to the grocery trade as I knew it, and which - alas - has gone forever."

Ted Hewson left school early in 1922, aged fourteen, and spent some six months tramping the streets of Hull, calling in at every joiner's shop in the hope of finding an opening in that trade, for that was his ambition. Fate, however, brought him to Linsley's Grocery, Provision and Wine Store on Anlaby Road, at the corner of South Parade - and a career of fifty-one years in food retailing. Ted's account of his early days - it would be some six or seven years before Jackson's would entice him to their Paragon Street branch - is a beautifully evocative description, but by virtue of his seniority we ought perhaps to begin with

We have been unable to identify this shop. Was it 249 Anlaby Road which was closed in 1955?

HOLDERNESS ROAD, 3, HULL

"East Park" branch on the corner of Southcoates Avenue and Holderness Road. Opened in 1912 this store was the first managed by 'Bompy' Hall.

the career of C.R. 'Roy' Taylor, who took up an apprenticeship with Jackson's in 1920.

C.R.'s father was a manager at the Goole Steam Shipping Company before it was taken over by the Lancashire and Yorkshire Railway. His family were modestly well off, his older brothers and sisters attending boarding school. But by the time Roy was of an age to join them there simply was not enough money for his fees. He attended instead Hull Grammar School, and upon leaving there went along to the Labour Exchange. He was sent to Jackson's to be interviewed by 'Bompy' Hall. He remembers arriving fifteen minutes early and going to play in East Park, finally showing up for his appointment five minutes late - and still in his school cap and short trousers.

He was engaged by the company and sent first to the Carr Lane shop where Mr. Charles Leaf was manager. He remembers Mr. Leaf standing outside the store each morning with his watch in his hand checking all the staff as they arrived. Leaf, who had joined the firm in 1886, retired in 1939 as senior grocery manager and apparently spent most of his time thereafter in the Paragon Street shop, coming and going as it suited him.

Roy was next sent to Newington branch under Mr. Bolton. Here all the staff would arrive and wait outside until eight o'clock struck. Then the first hand would enter, followed by the rest of the staff in descending order of rank. He spent two years at Newington, until he mentioned to one of the directors that "a move would suit me", hinting that he was an ambitious lad, and was sent to Carr Lane on a permanent basis. Carr Lane was, of course, headquarters: the offices were above the shop and it

was the place to be if you wanted to be noticed. And Roy was noticed all right: he recalls the occasion when Mr. Bentham himself came down to the shop and stood watching him for two full hours, finally asking Mr. Leaf, "Who is that young man?" Evidently the boss was impressed.

It was during his time at Carr Lane that Roy first experienced the generosity and loyalty for which so many past and present employees have had cause to be grateful. He was unable to work for six months, being ill, but received his full wages throughout that time.

A number of promotions soon came his way after he had completed his apprenticeship: a move to Gipsyville (821 Hessle Road) as first provision hand; to Chanterlands Avenue which he opened as first hand in April 1928; to Prince's Avenue; and then to Inglemire Lane which he opened as provisions manager in September 1932. These regular moves - and there would be plenty more - were typical. Jackson's were keen to promote promising staff and to test them out in new environments, to stretch them. Occasionally an assistant might be moved with alarming regularity. This, according to one former assistant, was the company's way of reminding wayward employees to buck their ideas up or move on. The constant upheavals would soon enough have one effect or the other. Gladys Naylor remembers making several moves in the two wartime years she spent with the firm - sometimes for no more than a few days at a time. Whether these were due to emergency staff shortages or whether she was failing to meet the required standards, she doesn't remember. But she finally quit in exasperation, going to work for the rival firm of Reed and Mackman. "The money there was much better," she says.

Hessle Square branch, the first outside the city's boundaries, was opened in 1927. Here it is decked out for the 1937 Coronation. Manager Mr. Allington is in the dark coat.

A publicity shot for Burroughs Adding Machines, taken in Inglemire Lane branch, Roy Taylor behind the counter, manageress Miss Dalton seated. The customer's chair was a fixture in most shops until the coming of self-service.

As a provision hand C.R.'s work was not all behind the counter. At Gispyville, a new shop with no established trade to build on - only a reputation attached to the name - he went out canvassing, door to door, as far as Hessle. After he had obtained his first order - it was for twelve shillings and seven pence (63p) he sent an errand lad out along the foreshore with a barrow. Later he acquired enough custom in what was, for Jackson's, *terra incognita*, to make it worth sending the boy out with a horse and cart, and on this, as Christmas drew near, he would send samples of the firm's seasonal wares.

Being a counter-hand in those days required true salesmanship: you had to find your customers, woo them, and hang onto them. And in a time when most shoppers would come into a shop with a prepared list of items and a strict budget to adhere to, it was up to the assistant to 'push' new lines or specialities. And if hanging on to your customers meant sending out a delivery boy from Chanterlands Avenue to Sunny Bank at five o'clock with an order for two tomatoes, or a quarter of potted meat - "and right away please" - for an Avenues resident, then you did it. You'd even send the lad out to an afternoon card school in some drawing-room whence an order had come by 'phone for five shillings' worth of halfpennies. You might mutter and curse, but you'd do it - for your valued customers.

Many of C.R.'s customers in those days were idiosyncratic, to put it mildly. There was the doctor on Princes Avenue to whose house an ounce of yeast was delivered daily - not for bread baking, but for each member of the household to take as a daily supplement to a healthy diet. At Newington there was the elderly Miss Jackson, the founder's daughter, probably Lizzie,

who died in 1929. It was C.R.'s task to go across to her house at ten each morning to collect her order. He had to go up to her bedroom, trying hard not to look at her bedside table where she kept an old china teacup as a spittoon. Occasionally she might give him the leash and have him exercise her Pomeranian dog in the park. One time it slipped away and Roy, fearing retribution, slunk back to the shop to tell his boss what had happened. He was advised to go and face the music, and went back with palpitating heart only to find the dog awaiting him on the porch.

One bitterly cold winter's morning Miss Jackson told Roy, "Tell Mr. Bolton I'll be bringing up a jug of hot soup for the staff." The shops, of course, had no heat at that time. Moreover, most managers insisted that the door remained open to welcome customers in. More than one former employee can recall hoping and

Bright Street, 61-65 Holderness Road. The young ladies would be from the confectionery department.

A group of young shop assistants. Mr. Bentham had an eye for the confectionery girls!

Beverley branch staff: Miss Bratley (2nd right), Audrey Weightman, Miss Wilson (squatting).

praying that a customer might comment upon the weather and close the door for them. If a customer closed it it might remain shut. Otherwise staff were expected to suffer in silence. One assistant recalled crying with the cold. So a jug of hot soup was going to be more than a little welcome. C.R. could hardly wait - until the venerable Miss Jackson walked in and produced his steaming portion in her spittoon!

Miss Jackson, by the way, had her own way of warding off the winter chill, along with any other discomforts. She would have one of the lads bring across what she referred to as her daily dose of 'medicine'. It was, in fact, whisky - presumably bought in from a neighbouring vintner's and charged to her account.

C.R. had made the grade of manager in 1932 at the age of twenty-seven or thereabouts. Many staff, notably women, were managing shops at a considerably younger age. Jackson's shops, as they expanded, frequently comprised as many as five departments, distinct and separate: provisions, grocery, bread and confectionery, greengrocery, and a butchery. These would be individual shop units operating side by side under their own managers with no inter-connecting doors, perhaps just a hatch through which to pass messages, orders or small items. Some shops were integral, however. Bean Street, at 130-134 Hessle Road, opened in 1919 as Jackson's first 'department store', all units open to one another so that customers might buy everything they required without having to go out and come back in through another door.

As a branch won custom, properties next to a shop might be bought up, or rented, in order for a butchery or greengrocery to be added. An example of the way in which shops expanded was the family grocery shop at 127 Spring Bank, the one originally managed by Bentham. By 1891 a confectionery had been added, by 1912 a greengrocery, and shortly after that a pork butcher's. The Bright Street grocery, actually 61 Holderness Road, was open by 1891, a bakery and confectionery department added at number 63 in 1899, and a fruiterer's at number 65 by 1912. The Eton Street branch at 280 Hessle Road opened in 1913 as a bakery and confectionery; a grocery was added at number 282 in 1916, a pork butcher at 278 in 1919. Similar growth took place at the East Park shop, 614-620 Holderness Road.

Most of these shops would have been managed by men. Women managers were almost exclusively employed on the bread and confectionery side. Typical of the kind of career a young woman might have expected to follow is that of Freda Marshall (later

485a Anlaby Road (Newington branch). The staff entered at eight o'clock sharp in strict order of rank.

Gould). She began work in the Spring Bank confectioner's in 1923 at the age of fourteen. She earned eight shillings a week, later raised to ten shillings, or fifty pence. Spring Bank at that time consisted of four separate shops - the confectionery under Miss Tindall, fruit under Miss Heelas, a butchery, and the grocery under Mr. Robert Hall, brother of General Manager 'Bompy' Hall. Robert later married Miss Palmer, one of his assistants. Freda's day began with washing the glass plates and shelves in the shop itself. (Washing the marbled base of the facade with ammonia to deter the local dogs from cocking their legs against it was probably the special privilege of one of the errand lads!) Then she would wash the marble tiled walls and swill out the yard. Each morning she would have to cycle down to the Carr Lane offices to take the previous day's sales figures to Eric Soulsby, the grocery buyer who would succeed Jack Oughtred as Company Secretary when he resigned from the firm. Eric Soulsby, born in 1897, was a great-nephew of the founder. He had joined the company in January 1914 as a Carr Lane apprentice. He left during the war and on his return went into the offices under W.E. Cooper to learn buying. He would eventually become a director in 1928.

Freda soon progressed to serving behind the counter full-time and found herself going out to other shops as relief assistant: to Washington Street at 430 Beverley Road, to the Park Estate shop at 1022 Anlaby Road or to Brunswick Avenue, perhaps. At the age of seventeen she was made a manageress, and two years later went to manage the confectionery department of the newly opened Marlborough Avenue branch on Chanterlands Avenue.

The reason for this kind of rapid promotion - any number of girls became manageresses before they attained the age of twenty - was that staff would generally be getting married in their late teens or very early twenties. And in those days Jackson's would not employ married women. It is notable that the only women to have reached any kind of position within the company - the shops' supervisors - were single: Miss Bratley, for example, the formidable Miss Gash, and later on such people as Vera Owen and Dorothy Scholefield, Miss Fenton or Miss Lusby.

The affection with which former staff recall the pre-war Jackson's shops is remarkable. The wages were poor, the discipline strict, the premises cold, and the hours seemingly unending. Before the 1914-18 war a typical working week would be sixty-two and a half hours, less lunchtimes: from eight o'clock until six-thirty, with an eight o'clock finish on Friday and ten o'clock on Saturday. Thursday would be a half-day for most staff, with a one o'clock finish. From 1919 a six o'clock finish was the norm, eight o'clock Friday and nine on Saturday. Yet Jackson's, with their Liberal tradition behind them, were proud to let it be known that their staff worked shorter hours than were the norm in most other shops. However, the closing time of the shop did not always mean going-home time for the staff. Clearing the shelves, cleaning and preparing for the next day was all supposed to be done after the last customer had been served. Stock-taking every quarter required those responsible to stay behind long into the night.

Yet despite all this one former assistant has said, "I wish William Jackson's could rise from the ashes of the Second World War and show the world how we made the firm what it was in those now lost years." Another, remembering the former glory of the flagship branch, states, "Paragon Street: I cannot go in. It upsets me to see it now."

So what were those fabled shops like? In what ways were they superior to today's clean, convenient and well-stocked supermarkets? Ted Hewson began, as we have seen, with a rival firm, but the picture he paints - of the shop fitments, the goods for sale, and the methods of storing and packaging these wares - might apply to any quality provisions merchant of the day.

Hewson began as an errand-boy, although he would soon succeed in pestering his manager into taking him on as an apprentice. Like the typical delivery lad of the popular imagination he soon became wise to the sort of tricks whereby he might supplement his ten shillings a week wage. For example, nearly all the goods at that time were delivered in non-returnable wooden boxes or crates and he would leave these with certain customers for firewood, being tipped as much as twopence or threepence a time. His errands took him out in all weathers and of course the company provided no protective wear. Instead he would take a two-hundredweight sugar sack from the warehouse and fold it in such a way as to fashion a kind of hooded cape, tied around his middle with a length of twine.

When he was offered the apprenticeship he had sought, starting on February 23 1923, his wages went down from the ten shillings plus tips he had been making. From the paltry sum he now earned he had to purchase white coats and aprons and launder them each week at a cost of sixpence for the coats and twopence for the aprons, the coats being changed every Tuesday, the aprons daily. Net cost: 2/6 - or twelve and a half pence - out of his new wage of eight shillings, or forty pence. His wages did rise, however, by increments of three shillings for each year of time served.

The grocery department in which he served was fitted out with polished oak counters and fixtures, with oak display tables and plated glass shelving. The provisions side had Italian white polished marble counters with marble mosaic floors. A grocery department in those days sold such items as tea, coffee, sugar, dried and canned fruits, spices, biscuits, hardware. The provisions, as the marbled counters suggest, consisted of bacon, ham, cheese and cooked meats, lard, butter and so forth. Handling any of these required specialist skills and knowledge picked up on the job by observation and practice, as well as through regular attendance at night classes.

Whereas lads from many local firms were sent - and paid for - by their employers (Ted would meet boys from such companies as Cusson's, the Co-op, Lamberts, Fields and, of course, Jackson's). Hewson had to find his own fees. He soon noted that this singled him out as one of the more highly motivated scholars. He would have been a couple of years behind Roy Taylor who graduated with honours, receiving a copy of Samuel Smiles' Self Help signed by the Institute of Grocers' president Lord Leverhulme.

For those who sat the Institute's exams, the motto - "Promotes Education for the Grocery and Allied Trades" - was not to be taken lightly. Mr. Herbert Cockerill, who was apprenticed to Jackson's in Withernsea before the Second World War - he later opened his own shop in the town - still has a copy of the preliminary exam paper he took in 1938. Some of the questions reveal the general scope of the education he was receiving: it wasn't all tasting tea and boning bacon joints. (See copy opposite).

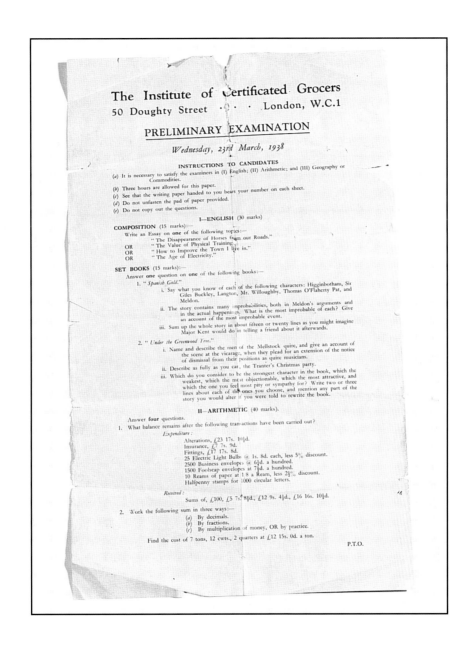

The Institute of Certified Grocers
50 Doughty Street · · · London, W.C.1

PRELIMINARY EXAMINATION

Wednesday, 23rd March, 1938

INSTRUCTIONS TO CANDIDATES

(a) It is necessary to satisfy the examiners in (I) English; (II) Arithmetic; and (III) Geography or Commodities.

(b) Three hours are allowed for this paper.

(c) See that the writing paper handed to you bears your number on each sheet.

(d) Do not unfasten the pad of paper provided.

(e) Do not copy out the questions.

I—ENGLISH (30 marks)

COMPOSITION (15 marks):—

Write an Essay on **one** of the following topics:—

"The Disappearance of Horses from our Roads."
OR "The Value of Physical Training."
OR "How to Improve the Town I live in."
OR "The Age of Electricity."

SET BOOKS (15 marks):—

Answer **one** question on **one** of the following books:—

1. "*Spanish Gold.*"

   i. Say what you know of each of the following characters: Higginbotham, Sir Giles Buckley, Langton, Mr. Willoughby, Thomas O'Flaherty Pat, and Meldon.

   ii. The story contains many improbabilities, both in Meldon's arguments and in the actual happenings. What is the most improbable of each? Give an account of the most improbable event.

   iii. Sum up the whole story in about fifteen or twenty lines as you might imagine Major Kent would do in telling a friend about it afterwards.

2. "*Under the Greenwood Tree.*"

   i. Name and describe the men of the Mellstock quire, and give an account of the scene at the vicarage, when they plead for an extension of the notice of dismissal from their positions as quire musicians.

   ii. Describe as fully as you can, the Tranter's Christmas party.

   iii. Which do you consider to be the strongest character in the book, which the weakest, which the most objectionable, which the most attractive, and which the one you feel most pity or sympathy for? Write two or three lines about each of the ones you choose, and mention any part of the story you would alter if you were told to rewrite the book.

II—ARITHMETIC (40 marks).

Answer **four** questions.

1. What balance remains after the following transactions have been carried out?

   Expenditure :

     Alterations, £23 17s. 10½d.
     Insurance, £7 7s. 9d.
     Fittings, £17 17s. 8d.
     25 Electric Light Bulbs @ 1s. 8d. each, less 5% discount.
     2500 Business envelopes @ 6½d. a hundred.
     1500 Foolscap envelopes at 7½d. a hundred.
     10 Reams of paper at 1 8 a Ream, less 2½% discount.
     Halfpenny stamps for 1000 circular letters.

   Received :

     Sums of, £100, £5 7s. 8½d., £12 9s. 4½d., £16 16s. 10½d.

2. Work the following sum in three ways:—

   (a) By decimals.
   (b) By fractions.
   (c) By multiplication of money, OR by practice.

   Find the cost of 7 tons, 12 cwts., 2 quarters at £12 15s. 0d. a ton.

P.T.O.

The Institue of Grocers was keen to promote a general education for its apprentices.

One of the observations Ted Hewson makes in comparing shops then with shops now is the very obvious - but overlooked - point that customers nowadays willingly purchase goods without actually seeing them, such is the sophistication of modern packaging - and the power of marketing. In the old days commodities arrived at the retailers in bulk quantities and had to be weighed and measured - or cut or sliced - often before the customer's very eyes.

Flour, arriving from the mill in ten-stone sacks (140 lbs), was kept out of sight in a special room containing a large bin with a capacity of fifty stone, or about a third of a ton. In here the assistant had to weigh the meal into packs of one stone, half a stone or a quarter of a stone. Sugar came in two-hundredweight sacks from the beet factory or, if from America, in one hundred pound 'pockets' with linen liners inside the hessian. These liners would be carefully separated and sold to the customers at sixpence apiece for use as pillow cases. At the counter the sugar would be weighed into 'spun cups' which the assistant made from blue sugar paper by the hundred. Sugar, incidentally, sold at twopence halfpenny a pound.

Bacon came in many varieties: Harris' Wiltshire - which might be pale ('green' to some people) or smoked; Danish, pale or smoked; Irish rolls, flat shoulders, rolled shoulders, American bellies, and so on. The American bellies were extremely fat, the eye of the loin having been removed in the States. But they were very cheap. Ted recalls that the bacon sides were all hung from racks in the shop window for the customers to view and select at leisure. An assistant would be required to take down whichever side the customer wished to buy from, cut it to order, and replace the side in the window. One busy morning, with some twenty or thirty women in the shop, a particular assistant failed to replace one of the American sides. The manager, appearing in the doorway, yelled out, "Get your bellies back to the window!" to the consternation and subsequent amusement of the assembled clientele.

Ham too came in a number of varieties. Hanging from the high ceilings would be a selection of Irish, American or Danish gammon, Irish rolls, Danish fore-ends, Spencers (which were Wiltshire cut sides minus the gammon), three-quarter sides, flat fores, rolled fores and picnic ham. Picnic hams were not true hams but rather trimmed fore-hocks. In addition there were the American hams - salt-cured long cut and pickle-cured short-cut. These arrived in quarter-ton wooden crates constructed of satin walnut, beautiful knot-free timbers all of an inch thick, the crates themselves measuring four feet by three by three. Not surprisingly, a number of joiners and handymen with furniture to make would pester the shops for this 'scrap' - and get it at a shilling apiece!

Butter came in one hundredweight casks, much of it imported from Denmark. Someone from the offices would have to be despatched to the docks to release it from customs. Each cask was emptied onto the butter block at the end of the counter. This had a slate bed to keep the butter cool, and was additionally sprinkled with salt water from a bucket kept under the counter. The butter itself had to be moulded into half-pound and one-pound blocks with wooden slicers and beaters, then decorated with wooden prints.

While the slicing, weighing and measuring of these various goods was something of an art, it was a precise art. It had to be, for Weights and Measures Inspectors

On these sturdy scales anything from a half ounce of pickling spice to a joint of bacon might be weighed.

A 1951 display celebrates the company's centenary, and recalls its roots in the tea business.

from the Corporation would make regular visits to check-weigh all commodities on display as well as the actual scales. These were checked annually, being verified and given the official validating stamp.

Tea and coffee were two further commodities requiring great expertise, and these would be studied at night school. As we have seen, Jackson's began as grocers and tea-dealers and had become by 1904 "Grocers, Tea-Dealers, Provisions Merchants, Italian Warehousemen, Bakers and Confectioners". By the time of the firm's 1920 re-organisation this description read:

> Tea Dealers, Italian Warehousemen, Bakers, Confectioners,Dairymen, Market Gardeners, Cattle Dealers and Butchers,Dealers in Drugs, Chemical and other articles and commodities of personal and household use and consumption, and generally of and in all Manufactured Goods, Materials, Provisions and Produce Whatsoever.

Can it have been that the Grandways concept was already on the Board's mind? The point is that stores like Jackson's did deal in a wide variety of goods and services, and in some of their larger branches shopping might well have been close to a one-stop affair with same-day delivery.

A number of former employees who worked in the Carr Lane offices before the death of Mr. Bentham recall the firm's tea-tasters at work. Muriel Lusby remembers Eric Soulsby and Mr. Conyers, the assistant buyer, undertaking the task. Rene Johnson, who was a telephonist and Mary Singleton (later Hunter), a clerk, remember "a couple of very old men"

Interiors were frequently dressed for special promotions in this case Tik-Tak firelighters.

ceremoniously taking out their false teeth before sipping the contents of a row of little round cups without handles. The men savoured each brew in turn, eyes closed, lips smacking, and spat the sample out into a bucket. To Miss Singleton, the junior hand, fell the task of washing up afterwards - cups, bucket and all. Jackson himself and a Mr. Walker had been the original tasters, often having as many as four sessions a day. Indeed, on the day before his death in October 1912, Jackson had been in Carr Lane at 9.45, having walked from his Prince's Avenue home, and spent a full two hours at his craft.

Common teas, such as Assam and Ceylon, were kept behind the counter but below the fixtures in huge metal bins holding a hundredweight apiece. Special varieties were kept in twenty-pound black-japanned canisters above the fixtures at customers' eye-level. These would contain Darjeeling, Flowery Orange Pekoe or Lapsang Suchong. In small oak drawers were the green, or unfermented teas: Hyson, Young Hyson and Gunpowder, any of which might be blended to suit an individual customer's taste.

Fresh coffee was not widely consumed then - most people would settle for 'Camp' coffee essence from the jars still available to this day. Fresh beans had to be ground to the required specification, flat wrapped with extreme care so as not to allow any spillage, and tied with tea twine. Ted Hewson recalls one elderly lady who came in and asked him for "A quarter of white coffee, please." Quite undeterred, Ted brought her a sample of two or three different types of bean and told her the prices. The lady looked dubiously at the dark roasted beans and said, "No, I want white." It turned out that the customer had been to a friend's house where she was offered a choice of black or white. Unused to coffee, and happening to go for the white, she had enjoyed it. She understood that she might get some at this shop: she rather fancied some more of this *café au lait*. When Ted explained to her as tactfully as he could that black coffee, with added cream or milk, became white, the lady gave him a rather doubtful look and left.

In another row of small drawers with brass handles were the various spices for sale: stem and root ginger, ground ginger, allspice, black and white pepper, nutmeg, mace, pickling spice, caraway seeds, chillis, cinnamon, cloves, turmeric.

A second major change which has taken place since before the war is the effective passing of the strictly seasonal goods. Today one can buy most fruits and vegetables, for example, all year round - albeit at fluctuating prices. In the 1920s and '30s not only fresh produce but certain dried or processed goods appeared only at certain times, and the smooth running of the shops required all staff to be aware of this. As an example there is the note in the directors' minute-book for September 1937: new fixtures for the East Park fruit shop were ready for installation but would have to wait until the end of the soft fruit season to minimise inconvenience.

The year started in earnest in February after the clearance of the Christmas items with the Seville orange crop and the marmalade season. Post-cards would arrive from the eastern Mediterranean, from growers and exporters announcing the readiness of "mountain bitter oranges, lemons in cases, and peels in brine". The fruit would be displayed around the shop, and small machines were hired out for slicing the hard-skinned, bitter fruit - at sixpence a day. Stocks of preserving nibs (sugar) were bought in. There would be elaborate displays on the counters and in the windows of ready-made marmalade in jars, lit from behind to show them to advantage, the thinly-cut peel suspended in a golden jelly.

In March and April came the Spring Cleaning sales - of wash leathers, floor cloths, dishcloths, dusters,

Paragon Street's elegant interior. Staff who worked here were considered 'demi-gods'.

Paragon Street, opened Tuesday October 8th 1929 as a high-class shop and offices. The office staff were soon moved out and a restaurant and cafeteria opened.

mops, buckets, shovels, carpet-sweepers, real hair sweepers, flue-, nail-, shoe- and paint-brushes; and along with them the various cleaning agents such as soda, whiting, distemper, loose starch, loose soap flakes, Hudson's wash powder, Acdo tablets and Preservene soap which the housewife would cut up into small pieces and feed into the copper boiler.

As summer came on - the season for picnics and parties - jellies, custard powders and canned fruits would be promoted. Surprisingly, the range of canned fruits was then far wider than now. In peaches alone there would be a number of types: fancy, extra fancy, choice, extra choice, standard and seconds. For pie-making there was a selection of bottled fruit. Jackson's bottled their own fruit at the Derringham Street works, employing extra staff on a seasonal basis, particularly in strawberry time. Jars - with money back on the empties - came in twenty-six, forty and eighty-ounce sizes, the fruit unsweetened. An eighty-ounce jar of black-currants cost 3/9 - that is, 19 pence, the same quantity of Victoria plums 1/8, or 8 pence.

In June massive displays of new strawberry jam would adorn the windows and counters. But jars full of luscious whole fruit were not to everyone's taste. "I don't want that," a lady once told Mr. Hewson, returning to the shop and banging a jar of strawberry jam onto the counter. "It's all fruit. My kids'll polish it off at one sitting. Can't you find one with more syrup in, to go further?"

In October the dried fruit came in: it was time to bake the cakes, puddings and pies for Christmas, or make up the mincemeat. At this time the staff would work well into the evening, not just on their regular late nights, but midweek as well - and all for no extra pay. After closing the shop they would all have a cup of tea and then split into teams of three: a filler, a weigher and a wrapper - of currants, sultanas, dried mixed peel. Again, the variety is astonishing to the modern consumer. Prunes, for example, would come in half a dozen or more sizes: 10s to 20s, 20s to 30s, 40s to 50s and on up to 90s to 100s, being that many to the pound. The wealthier customer bought the large Bosnians, perhaps as few as six to the pound, the poorer happy to settle for the smallest at six to the ounce. That way a mother would at least be sure that there were a few fruit in every child's bowl at tea-time.

In addition to the prunes there were the dried peaches, apricots, pears, fruit salad, two varieties of fig - layer or flat, apple rings, and dates. Raisins might be the seedless variety from California, large Lexias from Australia, or Valencias. Currants ranged from ordinary Greek, to Australian, which had to be sieved to remove the stalks, to Greek Vestizzas, the finest of all with the delicate blue bloom still on them. Sultanas from Australia alone came in five grades - from one crown to five - and then there were the Californian and the very choicest fruits from Smyrna.

In addition to all these were half caps of orange or lemon peel, cut thick or thin; Valencia almonds, Jordan almonds - a dessert variety to go with Muscatels; crystallised rose petals or violets, glacé cherries, silver cashews, angelica, crystallised stem ginger, and any number of other delights. "What joy," Ted noted in his record of his days at the counter, "to see these wonderful commodities!"

While Ted was arming himself with this storehouse of knowledge, these various skills and broad experience, he was unhappy where he was. He

Staff pose for a publicity shot at newly-opened Paragon Street.

watched with great interest as Jackson's built what was to be their prestigious Paragon Street store through 1929. He had written at various times to a number of local firms such as Cussons, the Co-op, Lamberts, but nothing had come up. Finally, as the Paragon Street shop neared completion, he wrote to Mr. Hall, now joint Managing Director with Mackman.

Within a matter of days Mr. Hall, and young Gordon Russell, had called at Ted's lodgings to ask him to report to Paragon Street in his lunch hour. The interview was inconclusive. He was told that should a situation arise they would contact him. At the end of the week came what he calls "the bombshell". His boss called him into the office to say that a Mr. Hall of Jackson's had 'phoned and tendered Ted's notice for him!

Shocked as he was, Ted's answer to the question, "Is that what you want?" was a firm "Yes". He then had to admit to his boss that he had told Mr. Hall that he earned £2 5s 0d a week, whereas he only actually earned £1 17s 6d But in this little deception he was quite safe: Linsley's would not have dared admit that they were paying so little for the services of a fully qualified Associate of the Institute of Grocers. And naturally Jackson's had to improve on that. They came up with the lordly sum of £2 8s 0d, a net rise of half a guinea a week. No wonder Ted was "walking on air" when the news sunk in.

The Paragon Street shop, opened on Tuesday October 8th 1929, was to be the jewel in the Jackson's crown for the next three decades or so. Certain of their shops already had acquired reputations, especially for the kind of staff they turned out. Miss Barker, who went on from management to become a supervisor, produced a succession of very able girls at the Grafton Street shop on Newland Avenue, all of whom went on to become manageresses with a particular skill in window-dressing. And there was Miss Jules, who insisted on a well turned-out staff, her girls all wearing a white blouse and a navy tie. Dorothy Scholefield, who worked under her in the 1930s before going off to a munitions factory and returning to manage Grafton Street, recalls, "If you were 'a Miss Jules girl' you were the creme de la creme".

Paragon Street, and the staff who worked there, were held in awe. They were, in the words of one former retail manager, "looked upon as demi-gods". If you were good enough to be asked to work within its hallowed portals you were without doubt "a cut above other mortals". The first manageress on the confectionery side was the renowned Miss Hilda

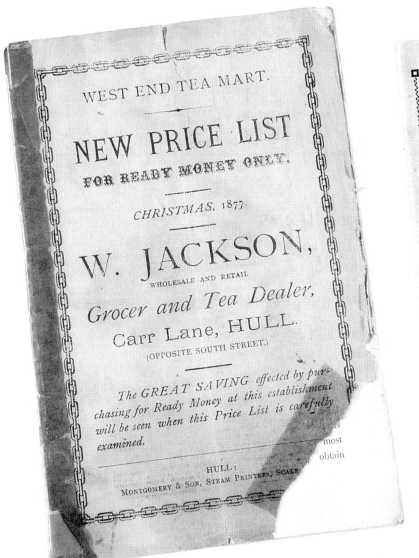

WEST END TEA MART.

NEW PRICE LIST

FOR READY MONEY ONLY.

CHRISTMAS, 1877.

W. JACKSON,

WHOLESALE AND RETAIL,

Grocer and Tea Dealer,

Carr Lane, HULL.

(OPPOSITE SOUTH STREET.)

The GREAT SAVING *effected by pur-chasing for Ready Money at this establishment will be seen when this Price List is carefully examined.*

most

obtain

HULL :

MONTGOMERY & SON, STEAM PRINTERS, SCALE

A very early price list from Jackson's Carr Lane shop.

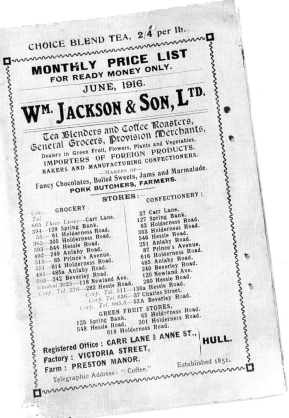

CHOICE BLEND TEA, 2/4 per lb.

MONTHLY PRICE LIST

FOR READY MONEY ONLY.

JUNE, 1916.

WM. JACKSON & SON, LTD.

Tea Blenders and Coffee Roasters,
General Grocers, Provision Merchants,
Dealers in Green Fruit, Flowers, Plants and Vegetables,
IMPORTERS OF FOREIGN PRODUCTS.
BAKERS AND MANUFACTURING CONFECTIONERS.

—MAKERS OF—

Fancy Chocolates, Boiled Sweets, Jams and Marmalade.

PORK BUTCHERS, FARMERS.

STORES :

GROCERY :	CONFECTIONERY :

Cor.
Tel.
665 *Three Lines*—Carr Lane.
394—129 Spring Bank.
55— 61 Holderness Road.
305—305 Holderness Road.
593—544 Hessle Road.
492—249 Anlaby Road.
515— 85 Prince's Avenue.
551—614 Holderness Road.
485—485a Anlaby Road.
603—242 Beverley Road.
Central 3025—118 Newland Ave.
Corp. Tel. 576—282 Hessle Road.

37 Carr Lane.
127 Spring Bank.
63 Holderness Road.
303 Holderness Road.
546 Hessle Road.
251 Anlaby Road.
87 Prince's Avenue.
616 Holderness Road.
485 Anlaby Road.
240 Beverley Road.
120 Newland Ave.
280 Hessle Road.

Corp. Tel. 511—136a Hessle Road.
Corp. Tel. 636—37 Charles Street.
Corp. Tel. 665A—52A Beverley Road.

GREEN FRUIT STORES.

125 Spring Bank.
548 Hessle Road.
618 Holderness Road.

65 Holderness Road.
301 Holderness Road.

Registered Office : CARR LANE & ANNE ST., HULL.
Factory : VICTORIA STREET,
Farm : PRESTON MANOR.

Telegraphic Address : "Coffee."

Established 1851.

A monthly price list with Jackson's 32 stores and the wide range of products sold in them.

Gash. A number of members of her family worked elsewhere within the company: her sister Alice managed Severn Street on Holderness Road and her brother Stan managed Preston Road. Her nephew Ron Gash and his wife Connie also worked for the firm. Hilda herself joined at the age of fourteen, towards the end of the First World War. By the time she was thirty she had risen to shops inspector, a formidable lady with a reputation for being something of a law unto herself. Certainly the delivery drivers who went to the Doncaster branch above which she had her flat had to tread lightly on their early morning rounds or she would be down in her night gown telling them not to wake up the neighbourhood!

While in the early days the staff were evidently hand-picked, there were a number who might get the chance to work for brief spells at Paragon Street, often for special or seasonal events. Mrs Muriel Panther (neé Stevenson) who had become a manageress at the age of nineteen, remembers going in for a few days over the Easter period to serve. And from the confectionery works at Derringham Street staff might be sent out to pipe customers' names onto Easter eggs.

It was for many a privilege to work at Paragon Street. The three-storey premises, designed by Hull architects Gelder & Kitchen, featured an elegant ground-floor shopping area, above which there were a cafeteria and restaurant. After the war, when the fire-damaged property was repaired, a third floor was added as a ball-room. This was to become one of the city's most popular night-spots for many years.

Ted Hewson was not the only person who was walking on air when Jackson's offered him a job. Mr. Vincent Pearson, who was engaged in February 1934,

had set his stall out to work for the company because of what he had heard of them. He knew they were a caring company, that they encouraged the pursuit of education at night school, and that they dealt compassionately with instances of sickness. Vincent had been at Southcoates Lane branch less than a week when he found out just how understanding his new employers were. He collapsed behind the counter, a victim of influenza, and had to be assisted home by two of his new colleagues. "For three successive weeks," he says, "Dorothy Bennett came to my house with my full wages. In those days this really was incredible, and my father said, 'If you leave this company you'll be a fool'. And he was right. I stayed for forty-seven and a half years."

Like Ted Hewson, Vincent has vivid memories of the various seasons - the Christmas displays with rows of turkeys, geese, ducks and chickens, the rabbits too, suspended from the arms that supported the exterior blinds. He stresses the point that prices were remarkably stable during the early to mid-thirties. There might be two or three amendments a week, those generally in goods such as bacon, butter or cheese. Historians have noted elsewhere that prices at the outbreak of the First World War were more or less identical to what they had been in 1750! - and that after a period of steep inflation to 1920 they fell in the next decade, sustaining a level to the end of the second war which was barely 50% up on those eighteenth-century prices. And the customers were very mindful of these facts. Dry and processed items never seemed to change. HP sauce, Vincent recalls, was fourpence halfpenny year after year, John West salmon tenpence halfpenny a tin for as long as he could remember. If an item rose by so much as a halfpenny a customer would in all probability refuse to buy it.

As will become evident, retail staff had little to do with the bakery. Later we will see that at boardroom level there was - and until relatively recently still was - a degree of competition, leading at times to friction - between the two sides. Former shops supervisor Vera Owen is quite unequivocal in her judgement of the bakery side as she remembers it: "The management up there didn't know what day it was," she says. For the other side Les Johnson at Stockton bakery insists that shop staff never knew how much bread to order. One regular point of contact between the two divisions was through the men who delivered the bakery goods to the shops. Vincent Pearson recalls in particular bakery driver Billy Thacker. Thacker was one of a number of professional Rugby League players, mostly from Hull F.C., who worked for the firm. Mr. Mackman, the bakery director, was also on the board of the Airlie Birds and helped find work for such players as Bob Taylor and Billy Stone who, along with Thacker, toured Australia with the Great Britain side before the war. Danny Wyburn and Tommy McGee also worked at the bakery, as did Fred Todd, who had turned out for the Armed Forces international side during and just after the war. Fred in fact signed for Hull K.R. but his career was cut short by an injury. Not surprisingly, Ted Hewson remembers these as well-built men with phenomenal strength. It was nothing, he recalls, to see one of them carry three full bread trays on his head. Bob Taylor, along with another 'giant', Danny Wardle, regularly delivered warehouse stock to the branches. Each of these two had the knack, according to Ted, of lifting on his own the five-hundredweight puncheon of treacle onto its gantry in the store-room.

From these huge puncheons metal containers holding about one hundred pounds were filled, and it was from these that the customers' own jars or tins were replenished. Many good stories are told about mishaps with the treacle or syrup - the sort of things which are laughed at now but which had catastrophic effects at the time. Treacle is fairly thin and easy to pour in the warmer months of the year, thick and obstinately slow in the winter. In the cold weather an assistant might take a customer's glass jar, place it under the spigot and leave it for five or ten minutes while he attended to the rest of an order. The results of misjudging - or of forgetting that the tap was open - may be imagined. But it wasn't always the forgetful grocery hand who caused the problem: once in a while it was the customer. Ron Boult, who after the war became slaughterhouse manager at the firm's Inglemire Lane meat division, recalls the time in the mid-thirties when his mother sent him down to Jackson's for some treacle. She handed him the clean jar and three pennies, warning him not to lose them.

"What can I get for you, young man?" the assistant in the shop asked.
"I want a jar of treacle, please."
"We have no treacle, I'm afraid."
"Well, golden syrup, then."
Ron handed over the container, waited for a few minutes until the assistant returned with the jar.
"That'll be threepence, please. Where's your money, son?"
"In a safe place," Ron replied. "At the bottom of the jar."

Ron got a thick ear for his trouble, which shows that while the customer may always have been right in those days, some were righter than others.

The payment of weekly wages was, in one employee's words, "an uncomplicated thing". Wages were made up in the attic at Carr Lane, later at the subsequent office sites at Paragon Street or Spring Bank. Sometime between lunch and tea on a Friday Miss Appleyard, accompanied by Miss Barker or Miss Fenton, would arrive at a shop by car and deliver the pay packets to the manager. The flat weekly sum very rarely had any additions, and the deductions were minimal. Overtime was not an issue; the humble shop-worker did not earn enough to qualify to pay income tax; and the small contribution towards health insurance never seemed to change. Once in a while someone might get a silver crown - and that might mean good news or bad, for it meant either a move to another branch - or the poor recipient had received his cards!

The chance to earn any extra money came around rarely, if at all. Those who were especially well thought of might be fortunate enough to go to one of the branches which required extra assistance in the summer months. Vincent Pearson remembers going to Bridlington, Hornsea and Withernsea, all of which had opened in the early thirties. Dorothy Scholefield, who between 1936 and her retirement in 1982 worked in no fewer than twenty-three different branches, remembers going to Withernsea as a junior, tenpence on the 'bus in company time. She took great delight in standing at the stop watching everyone else go by on their way to work at eight o'clock.

Vincent's memories of going to Bridlington are coloured by the extra payments he received: ten shillings on top of his regular wage and a guinea for lodging. Good lodgings were easy to find at fifteen shillings then, so he was making an extra sixteen shillings a week. The work at these seaside places was hard but the experience was invaluable, and staff morale seems to have been

This branch at Anlaby Common, opened in December 1933, was to be a model for many new shops.

consistently high. What is striking about the recollections of just about all the former shop staff is the combination of long hours and hard work with cheerfulness and occasional high spirits. For every complaint about the winter and its chilblains there is a fond memory of the fun that was had, and the pride that people took in their work. Within any shop a spirit of amiable competitiveness seems to have been the rule. Staff were generally encouraged to take pride in their - and their shop's - performance. Frequently they would be asked to take part in competitions. Dorothy Scholefield recalls how keen Miss Jules was on these. Whoever sold most of a given line in a week would receive a prize, maybe a quarter pound box of chocolates. At Severn Street the staff were offered a halfpenny commission for each Turog loaf they could sell. A Turog was a little like a Hovis loaf, being made to a special recipe under licence. Dorothy and a friend decided that they could make a lot of money out of this,

The Turog loaf promotion. Staff got a halfpenny commission on each one sold.

Severn Street assistants: from left, Stella Evans, Muriel Panther (neé Stephenson), Enid Hellings and Elsie Finch.

and went selling door-to-door in the vicinity of the shop. They had no joy, however: this was evidently not a Turog neighbourhood. Dogs went for them, children ran them ragged, and they were shouted at by all and sundry. Undaunted, they sneaked off to one of the nicer neighbourhoods near Dorothy's own home. Their success there was astounding: in no time they had sold a thousand apiece, raking in a pound each, or the equivalent of almost two weeks' wages.

Dorothy was at the Brunswick Avenue shop when the celebrated Heinz Soup Week came around. This was a competition, sponsored by Heinz, offering a prize for whichever shop sold the most tinned soup. The Brunswick Avenue staff could hardly believe their luck when they found that a royal visitor to the city was due

to pass their front door. A large crowd formed on what was a very cold day. Ever the opportunist, Dorothy dashed upstairs to Mrs Ramsden who lived over the store, borrowed a large stew-pan off her, and boiled up cans of soup as fast as her colleagues could open them, selling them in cups to the frozen - and grateful - royal-watchers.

During the war Dorothy recalls all the shops participating in an 'aeroplane race', each one charting the progress of its plane across a map of England as sales reached certain targets. Dorothy's shop won that race. The prize was a dinner at Paragon Street and a theatre trip. There was an air-raid while they were in the theatre, but the show went on and the girls stayed to watch it.

At least until the fifties there was a banner awarded for the shop with the best monthly sales figures. Fred Standing, who joined the firm in the fifties, remembers it as "laughable, really - but we all took it very seriously". Supervisors would submit names of the most deserving shops in their patch and someone like Gordon Russell - "G.R." - would select a winner. The staff got two extra days' holiday and the banner would be displayed in the store. Even the customers seemed to take a kind of pride in it. Margaret Robinson, who worked as a young girl in the Stepney branch, perhaps put her finger on one of the reasons for this high morale among staff before the war: "working was better than not working, for 'out of work' was rearing its ugly head in the thirties, and we were all well aware of it."

While discipline in the shops was strict, there was always someone willing to risk a ticking-off for a bit of fun. When Muriel Panther started at Charles Street in 1930 it was common practice to send a new girl over to Lipton's across the road 'for a long stand'. When the people over there thought she had 'stood' for long enough they'd send her back, older and wiser. One of the young lads she worked with thought it great fun to wrap an iron weight in some brown paper and place it on the pavement outside. Some passer-by might stoop to pick it up out of curiosity, but the best fun was when someone took a kick at it and stubbed a toe. Brenda Dyke at Hessle Road remembers the time she and her manageress Dorothy Tucker put on their roller-skates and skated the length of the counter as they served the customers in double-quick time. "You can't sack me now for telling you this," she says. Besides, the customers - back in the late forties - were "highly amused".

Vincent Pearson suffered sheer physical torture at the hands of one youth while on relief at Bridlington. G.R. was at the counter asking him how he was getting on in Brid, what did he think of the staff and so on. Vincent, standing behind the provisions counter, saw Pat Gray - "a lovely girl but full of mischief" - creep up beside him on her hands and knees. As he attempted to answer his boss's questions she rolled up his trouser leg and proceeded to pull the hairs from his leg one at a time. Finally G.R, said, "Mr. Pearson, will you kindly stand still while I'm talking to you?"

On another occasion the staff played a joke on supervisor Mr. Percy Booth. He always carried a rolled umbrella which he would leave behind the counter while he checked the sales ledgers. Miss Bennett - "what possessed her I'll never know" - one day unfolded the brolly, poured a pound of dried peas into it, and fastened it up again. It must have been an extraordinarily fine spell of summer weather because it was not until six or seven weeks later that a heavy storm came on while Mr. Booth was in the store once more. He stepped outside, opened the brolly, and was showered with peas. Re-entering the shop he studied everyone in turn, "but after so long a time," Vincent remembers, "everyone had forgotten about the incident, and no-one revealed so much as a twinge of guilt" - all except Miss Bennett, that is. But she had very wisely locked herself in the staff toilet! Mr. Booth went to catch his bus a very puzzled man indeed.

Along with the hard work and the impromptu bursts of midsummer madness there was a certain innocence. While there are a number of instances of managers being dismissed for financial misdemeanours, staff generally were trusted with

Chanterlands Avenue branch display for the Heinz Soup week, 1935. William Jackson attained the all-England record - selling 28,300 tins!

Withernsea branch, formerly Brown's Stores. Bought by Jackson's and re-opened in July 1931. By this time the firm was expanding well outside Hull.

amounts of cash and in such circumstances as to make a modern security-minded shopkeeper blanch. Brenda Dyke recalls working at Dairycoates branch where, there being no safe, she carried the day's takings home with her every night and brought them back in the morning. Dorothy Scholefield remembers that at the age of fifteen, in 1937, she was from time to time sent debt-collecting. It was not always the poorer clients who got into arrears: as often as not it was the wealthier ones. She recalls going to a large house on Princes Avenue. People there evidently had ideas about their station in life: when Dorothy knocked at the front door the lady of the house told her that the tradesmen's entrance was at the rear. Dorothy dutifully trotted round to the back door and knocked again - to be answered by the same lady. This particular customer had bought a wedding cake on credit and was paying it off at sixpence a week.

Many families, in the harsh economic climate of the inter-war years, qualified for Relief Notes from various sources. These might range in value from five shillings to a pound and more, generally depending on the size of the family, and were exchangeable for groceries and other household goods. They were granted by - and redeemable from - either the local authority or such voluntary organisations as the British Legion or the Mother Humber Fund.

Once in a while a manager of a shop might have to deal with a rather more sophisticated attempt to defraud the company. Ted Hewson recalls having to go to see "a rather charming and well-spoken young lady" who claimed that she had been over-charged in the Spring Bank shop. The manageress there, Miss Bragg, had been unable to resolve the matter so Ted, a supervisor by this time, called at the lady's house one morning. Having heard her version of the affair he left and returned to the shop to check her story. Upon his return - and now assured that she was trying it on - he was greeted with a roaring fire and an inviting easy chair drawn up beside it. The customer, dressed in a loose house-coat, lounged in another chair opposite. As he came into the room she let the housecoat slip open to reveal a perfectly naked body.

When Ted told her that the game was up, the "demure young thing" was transformed into a "raging tigress, spitting out the most foul language". At the same time a threatening-looking man sidled out from a kitchenette and Ted was lucky to make his escape through a neighbouring flat. A fortnight later he read in the Hull Daily Mail that the couple had been pulling such tricks on a number of retailers in the district. The woman, at least, was sent to prison.

Not only were there scarlet ladies around in the good old days but there were shop-lifters too, as Dorothy Scholefield recalls. At the Charles Street shop, off Albion Street near the New Theatre, the provisions window was one which could be raised or lowered from outside to allow for dressing. The staff were under instructions that, should they hear it being tampered with, they were to try to apprehend the culprits. One day they did indeed hear the window rattle - and left their posts to give chase. They caught a woman who unwound a voluminous shawl from around her middle and handed over a whole roast leg of pork, still sitting on its doily - and complete with price ticket and parsley sprig! It was a fair cop, the goods were recovered, and so there was no prosecution: that was the normal practice in such cases.

Vera Owen, who started work on the wholesale side at Paragon Street in 1943, was another employee detailed to collect on overdue accounts. Friday was the day when customers were expected to call in at the shop and settle their bills, and Friday was the day that Vera would go calling - carrying a handbag for the cash. She had to be firm, and this was obviously something of a test of character for a young woman, particularly when confronting someone like the manager of the Tivoli. He was several weeks behind but kept trying to put her off, telling her he was a personal friend of Mr. Soulsby.

There were worse dangers for a woman in Vera's position. Opposite the Paragon Street shop was a horse-meat butcher. It had a sign over the window - "For Human Consumption" - although just about everyone who went in claimed to be buying for the family dog. Others, less brave, would place their grocery order and then ask Vera if she couldn't just send someone across the road for a pound of horse-meat. Often Vera would go herself. The proprietor thus got to see a lot of her - and presumably would have liked to see more: he invited her on a weekend trip to London. Indeed, he pestered her to such an extent that she had to get her father onto him.

But nobody who knew Vera would tangle with her unnecessarily. She even stood up to the redoubtable Miss Gash. When Hilda was on her way to a football game with her friends she would often call in at Paragon Street for coffee. She seemed reluctant to settle the bill, the implication being that this was in the nature of a legitimate perk. Not to Vera, it wasn't: she had her own books to balance, and she posted out bills and reminders until Miss Gash settled with her.

Window dressed for Hull Civic Week, 1933. Branches competed to produce the best display.

A row of lorries line up to deliver Heinz soup to Jackson's, September 1954.

Nether Hall, Doncaster: a confectioner's and off-licence opened in May 1950.

"And you know yours. Yours is to run a bakery; mine is to see my shops adequately supplied. I know what they can shift in a day." Vera had her way: the order was met in full - and she sold the lot, all bar six small loaves!

While all Jackson's shops handled the same kinds of goods, each had a character - and a clientele - of its own. The little Hedon Road shop, which consisted of a confectionery counter on one side and a cooked meats counter opposite, had a truly international flavour. Being near the docks it was a handy place for sailors to pop into and stock up in prior to leaving the port. Thus the manager there would look in the Hull Daily Mail to see what ships were in dock or about to sail, and order accordingly. With foreign crews there was a deal of gesticulating, but the staff showed that the language of commerce is truly international.

At Paragon Street, whose customers were altogether more genteel by and large, Ted Hewson had a particularly memorable encounter with some sailors which nearly brought his career to a premature end. He hadn't been there very long when one morning he saw half a dozen stout-looking men, obviously seamen, looking through the window at his sides of bacon. He was outside in a flash to see what he could sell them, but found himself unable to communicate with them other than by signs. They were Russians. In no time Ted had established that they were after some bacon - and had taken an order for something in excess of half a ton of the stuff! The total price - he couldn't just think of the Russian for 'discount' - was over £300, well in excess of a week's takings for many branches at that time.

Vera was not only at odds with reluctant payers and romantically inclined horse-meat butchers; she also took on the bakery. When she became a supervisor she found that they would often query the shops' orders that she submitted. At Christmas one year she did her rounds, went home and sat up all night totting up the figures to come up with a total for the crucial Christmas deliveries. When she presented them to Fred Aitchison at the bakery he challenged them immediately. "You'll never shift this lot," he said. "Oh yes I will," Vera replied. There followed a heated discussion. Richard Hall was called in to referee. "Why," he said, looking at the figures Vera had drawn up, "you could break the company with an order like this." So Vera went home and sat up a second night checking her figures and re-checking them. Unable to find a single error, she re-presented them next morning. "I know my job," she told Fred Aitchison.

The deal was secured, and payment was to be C.O.D. Ted went out with the delivery van to the ship which lay at anchor in Victoria dock. The bacon was hauled aboard and Ted was shown below to await the captain - and the money - in his cabin. After he had been waiting some time he thought he felt the ship move. Hurrying up on deck he saw that it had indeed left the quayside. He created enough fuss for the captain to be summoned, with the money. By now, though, the ship was passing the first set of lock gates and Ted, his mind teeming with visions of exile in the snowbound wastes of Siberia, prepared to jump for it. But there was no way he was going to make it: the gap was too wide. At the second set of gates, with the open sea looming nearer, he took a deep breath, clutched the money to his chest, and leapt, hitting dry land on all fours with inches to spare!

Life for Jackson's shop staff was not always as exciting as this in the years up to the Second World War, but it clearly had its moments. From William Jackson's little shop in Scale Lane the firm had expanded to embrace somewhere in the region of eighty-five outlets by 1939. Some had been built specially, some were bought as going concerns, some converted, others rented - and a few were closed down. In addition to this huge expansion on the retail side which extended the company's reach to York and Leeds, Bridlington, Goole and Doncaster, the company had dipped a toe in other waters. Cafés at Beverley and Bridlington, the restaurant in Paragon Street and another in Prospect Street, Hull - and even a fish and game shop on the Beverley High Road - testified to the management's interest in testing new markets. At the same time the bakery enterprise, a new departure in the early 1890s, had achieved a phenomenal growth.

Special promotional paper bags dating from between the wars.

Chapter Three

THE BAKERY

William Jackson and son George had been operating as grocers in Carr Lane and at 127 Spring Bank for around forty years when they opened a confectioner's next to the Spring Bank shop on the corner of Clarendon Street. An 1891 letter-head describes the company as "Bakers and confectioners" among other things, listing a "bread and confectionery factory" in Clarendon Street. This adjoined the grocery shop on the corner of Spring Bank but later moved further down the street with the stables - the Hull Corporation Rate book reveals that between 1896 and 1898 the company had built a "bake-house and stables" at the bottom end of Clarendon Street.

The confectionery business was started in around 1885 by Mr. W.E. Cooper, a nephew of Jackson who had served an apprenticeship to the founder before going to work for firms in Beverley and Scarborough and eventually returning to the fold. Shortly after this, in the early 1890s, J.J.N. Mackman, chocolatier, joined the company as manager of the new Clarendon Street works. Mackman was to stay with Jackson's for almost forty years and expand this side of the business to a tremendous extent, winning fame for his confectionery products in the shape of some five thousand awards in competitions in Britain and Europe.

Over the decade following Mackman's arrival the shop side expanded, as we have seen. Four of the seven new retail outlets opened in this period were bakers and/or confectioners, suggesting that the Clarendon Street works were thriving. Further evidence that this was indeed a prosperous off-shoot is the opening of a new factory in 1907 on the present site in Victoria Street, off Derringham Street. In June 1906 Jackson's had submitted to the City Architect's department detailed plans drawn up by Hull architects Gelder and Kitchen.

At this time there were between Derringham Street and the railway line that ran into the old Botanic Gardens station three streets of terraced houses, Bank, Victoria and Crystal. Mr. Mackman himself lived at number 16, Bank Street. Remnants of Bank and Victoria are still discernible within the present factory site, and Crystal Street still exists, although none of the houses remain, the last residents having moved out in the 1970s and the houses being demolished as the manufacturing side and the offices expanded.

The precise date on which the new works opened is uncertain, but it will probably have been within twelve months or so of the plans being approved. The 1907 Kelly's Trade Directory lists a factory on the site; and in 1908 the Clarendon Street bakehouse was closed, indicating that Victoria Street was open and supplying the firm's needs.

The company now entered a period of rapid and sustained growth, opening another fifty-odd shops around the city within the next twenty-five years or so. In that the growth was linked to the expansion of the Derringham Street works, and in that Mackman was the driving force behind the bakery and confectionery enterprise, he must be considered, along with 'Bompy' Hall, as another important figure in Jackson's transformation from a small grocery to one of the leading food retailers in Hull.

BREAD AND CAKE AWARDS.

W.E. Cooper, who came to Jackson's as their first confectioner around 1885, and became company secretary in 1904.

John James Nathaniel Mackman, chocolatier, with a few of the 5,000 awards he won for his cakes, pastries, pies - and bread.

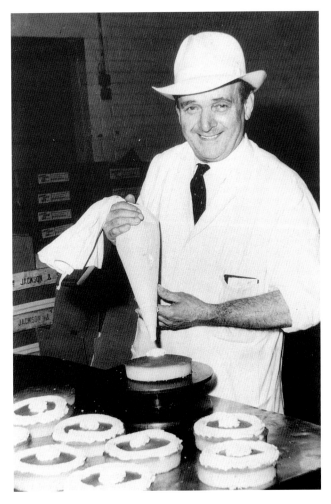

Ernie Smee, who worked for Jackson's for fifty-one years. He and his father put in almost three-quarters of a century between them.

Ernie Smee, who worked for fifty-one years, starting as an apprentice in 1922 and retiring as a new line manager in 1973, clearly remembers how he got started. He left school at the age of fourteen. His father, who had been at Derringham Street since about the time it opened, told him, "Your school days are over. Take a week off and then come to work with me. I've got you fixed up at Jacksons."

Perhaps he had always expected to follow in his father's footsteps. As a ten-year-old boy he had sat with his father on a wagonette as they rode up to Welton Dale for the company's annual Gala Day in 1918. He remembers going to the Green Dragon pub opposite the pond. Above the stables they sat, fifty to a table, to be served with their dinner. The men were given a pint of beer apiece, the ladies having a sherry and the children lemonade. How George Jackson Bentham squared this with his 'no beer, no baccy' policy we can only guess - but the company paid for it. In fact it seems that the policy was of necessity winked at in one or two other areas. Former employees still remember how Mackman listed his purchases of rum for Christmas cakes as "sundries" lest they be queried by the eagle-eyed chairman.

Ernie started at the bottom, earning 5/-, or 25p, for a five-and-a-half day week, finishing at one or two o'clock on a Saturday and often working twelve hours at a stretch for no overtime. His first job was sweeping up, and making tea. "Those old-time bakers loved their tea," he recalls. "They had big mugs and they liked it strong." Seeing that the mugs were thoroughly blackened inside he thought he'd do the men a favour and clean them. He grabbed a handful of salt and scrubbed them out. Far from being pleased with the new lad the men played merry hell with him, complaining that he'd ruin the flavour.

The figure of Mackman looms large in the memories of several retired employees who served in the 1920s and '30s. A number of these men and women, some of whom worked for the company for fifty years and more, were sons and daughters of Jackson's workers.

Ernie worked in a number of departments during his apprenticeship, including sweets. Jackson's were always keen to expand their range: more or less anything they could sell in their shops - from cut flowers to Easter eggs to potato crisps - they would at one time or another produce. Mints, boiled sweets, chocolates and lettered rock were all made in the confectionery department, in many cases by staff enticed away from Needler's, now Hull's major sweet manufacturer. Once qualified, Ernie went into cakes and pastries rather than bread. Like every bakery employee of the period he has an opinion on Mackman. He recalls the time when, as an eighteen-year-old keen to make an impression, he saw the boss coming around and tried to hurry his work. He got a clip around the ear for his trouble.

"What was that for?" he asked, rubbing the side of his head.

"Slow down," was the answer. "I want quality, not quantity."

That single remark aptly sums up Mackman's guiding philosophy, and suggests one of the main reasons why he parted company with the firm later on.

Another employee with memories going back to the very early days at Derringham Street is Joan Hutchinson, whose father William Oswald Richardson - "Ossie" - was transport manager after the First World War, having previously been chauffeur to Mr. Bentham. In 1922, when Joan was three, the family moved into number 11, Bank Street, later moving to number 5, and finally leaving the area when her father

The S.S. Queen Adelaide, one of cake decorator Jenny Tinker's creations - this being to celebrate the 'launch' of a film in Hull.

left the company after Mackman moved on. As well as running the transport side, Ossie was responsible for maintaining and repairing the bread machinery. Mechanisation was proceeding apace between the wars with the purchase of a semi-automatic bread plant in 1928 and a state-of-the-art Baker Perkins travelling oven in 1934 - for £4,500! At the A.G.M. in 1928 Bentham had spoken of plans to extend the factory due to the increase in trade. Ossie would now be called out at all hours of day and night to attend to breakdowns. Frequently he had to fabricate new parts.

While many Jackson's people who remember him - and even some who don't - speak of Mackman with less than undying affection (he was, to say the least, a controversial character who certainly had a fondness for the ladies) Joan remembers a kindly, caring and very proud man. He was proud, she says, of his craft, totally committed to quality, and very concerned that Jackson's, as a back-street outfit in a provincial town, should establish a name for itself. His much-criticised - and admittedly expensive - jaunts to Brussels, for example, where he won a number of his cups and medals, were part of his concerted campaign to put the company on the map.

Mackman brought in the best craftsmen he could find. Many old-timers will recall the temperamental French-Swiss André Boillard. Joan vividly recalls looking out of her bedroom window into the confectionery department where, through the half-frosted window, she could see - not André himself but his hands, busily creating exquisite roses one petal at a time, and each one "so perfect that you believed they were real".

To talk with people who lived within the factory area is to realise how intimately connected with the community William Jackson's was, then as now. Joan Hutchinson's uncle, George Thompson, who lived at number 10 Bank Street, was for a time Mackman's secretary. Previous to him Vernon Bourne, who once lived at number 5, held that job. He would leave the company in the late twenties to become a manager with the Co-op, returning to manage the bakery after Mackman's departure.

At the end of the Richardsons' garden was the butchery department, established around the beginning of the First World War. Jack Canty the butcher would often pop in for a cup of tea. He would later open up his own shop on Newland Avenue.

The neighbourhood was, obviously, a bustling spot. Not only horse-drawn carts but also motor-vans and lorries came and went, loading up at the end of Victoria Street. In order to turn into the bakery yard they would have to mount the pavements, and in doing so cracked the slabs and created hollows. In wet weather these filled with muddy rain-water which would be splashed onto the freshly-scrubbed front steps. Joan remembers Mrs Armstrong at number 19 having particularly heated rows with Mr. Mackman on this score.

Mackman was generous to people close to him. At Christmas Joan's family received mince pies, a cake, a pudding, a pork pie, a piece of roasting pork - and a goose as well! "Yes," Joan recalls, "he had a lot of lady friends. We all knew that. But he never spoke a word out of place to my mother."

Another resident in Victoria Street whom many would remember was Mrs Holmes who, incidentally, would be the last private resident to move out of the area in the 1970s. Mrs Holmes was one of a number of women living in the vicinity who was in the habit of cooking her Sunday roast in the bread ovens. The ovens were as a rule closed down late on Saturday until Sunday afternoon but would remain warm throughout. One week the watchman, who for some reason had fallen out with Mrs Holmes, told her to put her Sunday roast in a particular oven knowing full well that it was much hotter than usual. He got his revenge all right: the joint was burned to a crisp! Mrs Holmes is also remembered with wry affection by the present chairman. He and his father used to call on her every Christmas Eve and could never escape without the statutory glass of her potent cowslip wine.

Jack Mainprize, who lived at number 10 Victoria Street, also had long established conections with the bakery. His father, prior to the Great War, had been a tinsmith there. Injured in France - shell-shocked and with parts of several fingers missing - he returned in 1919 unable to take up his trade. Mr. Mackman gave him a job as a time-keeper, clocking men in and out, checking goods as they came and went. When Mackman asked him, "What about that son of yours, doesn't he want a job?" Jack's fate was sealed. He started work on the ovens, then went into the bakehouse itself and the mixing and fancy rooms.

The woman who was to be his wife, and who sixty-five years later supplied this information, was a music student looking to a career as a teacher, 'Pat' Lowes. Her ambitions sadly came to nothing, through an accident of fate. Her sister's husband was a painter. One day when working on the dome of the Grand Arcade in Leeds he fell to his death. His widow came to Hull to be near her family, and when she died of cancer Miss Lowes found herself looking for work locally in order to help support the two orphaned girls who now moved in with her and her family at 17 Victoria Street.

She got a job labelling fruit wines, later moved to the chocolate room, and finally to the fancy room. She vividly remembers the chocolate, which the company used to buy in from elsewhere, being melted in large bowls for the decorators to dip biscuits into prior to decorating them. She too remembers André - the man whom Jenny Tinker would later describe as "erratic and erotic". When he made a grab for her she slapped his wrist and told him in no uncertain terms to keep his hands to himself. Mr. Mackman, who happened to be standing nearby, roared with laughter and said, "Oh, we've got a right Irish Pat here!" And from that moment she was known throughout the department as Pat.

It was in the fancy room that Pat met Jack Mainprize, whose service stretched from 1924 to 1975 when he retired as bulk stores buyer. One of his early jobs had been to make fresh cream for use in the fancy room. When number 4 Victoria Street became vacant he was moved in there with a couple of assistants. This was the creamery which would be destroyed by enemy bombs in the Second World War.

In 1928 one of the bakery's best-known staff, a true 'star', joined the company. Jenny Tinker's father Charles had been with Jackson's since 1918, and she herself claimed that the craft was truly in her blood - for she was born in a bakery! Her father, prior to his time at Derringham Street, had a small bakehouse on the corner of Sculcoates Lane and Folkestone Street.

A brace of pheasants (top) to celebrate Peter Oughtred's 50th birthday. For Gordon Russell's 50th Jenny produced this gorgeous salmon (above). The staff at the Royal Station Hotel were convinced: they put it in the fridge and surrounded it with ice!

Brian Oughtred's 50th birthday cake.

Charles Tinker had a number of different jobs at Jackson's, and the list gives a further indication of the variety of lines produced there at that time. He made custard powder; he was involved with bread-baking; he made chocolates and cakes, fish-cakes and ice-cream. He even made up the seasonings for the butchery department, frequently coming home with a running nose and having sneezing fits from breathing in the pepper and other spices. Then too there was the pickling plant and the jam - as far as possible the firm tried to manufacture every food item its shops might stock.

Mr. Mackman got Jenny a job in the piping room. It has been said of the manager that he was particularly anxious to employ the close family of his confectionery staff in order to protect the secrets of his recipes. Much of the best work was actually carried out behind locked doors, and every effort was made to maintain security.

So Jenny Tinker started in the piping-room. She had always been interested in cake decorating - indeed, in any artistic activity. She had known Mr. Mackman as a young girl when she used to take her father's tea across to him at his watchman's post. Of her former boss she says, "He was big in girth and height and ambition. He wanted to win those competitions at any cost. He took on the very best craftsmen he could find from all over the country." She remembers Harry Price-Fox, a pork pie and savouries specialist, André Boillard, of course - she suspects he had come to England to avoid going into the trenches in France; and then there was Robert Birch who came in with his three sons for the Christmas cake season and to help prepare for the Brussels exhibitions. They were from Tottenham,

north London, where Birch ran some sort of craft workshop or teaching establishment. He used to refer to "my academy", although what it was is anybody's guess.

But mostly Jenny remembers Mackman for his forays into international competition. There is no doubt in her mind that these cost the firm dear and were a factor in his untimely departure.

As the time for the Brussels exhibition drew near excitement mounted. The specially baked breads, cakes and pork pies were packed into boxes to go off by 'plane. Then the staff would wait for Mackman and his right-hand man 'Cocky' Gardham to return with the results. By 1926 he had won over 2,000 awards in total, by 1933 over 5,000. These would range from such prizes as a championship cup for wheatmeal bread which he won in Manchester in 1910 and 1913, to the National Association of Master Bakers' Gold Cup (1925) to the Minster Den Cup of the Institut de la Boulangerie, Brussels, which he carried off in 1932. In its Review, the National Association spoke in glowing terms of the Wizard Baker, as he was known: "We must take this opportunity of congratulating Mr. J.J.N. Mackman, the managing director, on securing the Gold Cup for his firm, Messrs W. Jackson & Son, Ltd., of Hull. Mr. Mackman fairly swept the board and has achieved one of the ambitions of his life as a confectioner."

Jenny Tinker was a mere beginner when most of this was happening. Her first job had been covering cake boards with silver paper. Later she learned to make such intricate items as marzipan flowers. As she recalls, she learned very much on the job, copying André and the other craftsmen. She was, in effect,

Making sausage rolls in the Derringham Street bakery. Producing savouries was very labour-intensive, a factor in their being abandoned in the 1980s.

A group of Derringham Street staff, including Harold Cross (fancy room), Cec Thurlow (driver), George Spence and Molly Masters (Miss Twinkletoes).

self-taught. There was no day-release in those days. After Mackman's time, yes, there was a bakery school in town, on Hessle Road. But her education was practical, and very much biassed towards the decorating aspects of the craft. She had as little as possible to do with baking the cakes she would finish so artistically. "I was useless at baking," she admits. "Still àm!" Not that that mattered: the pictures of her creations reveal a true artist.

Bob Tyson, who started at Derringham Street in 1924, was yet another whose family connections brought him into the company, his father having been night foreman for eighteen years. Bob himself started in the bakery at twelve shilling and sixpence a week, which was something of a step up from his previous job, that of part-time delivery boy for Wilson's on Spring Bank. They had paid him half a crown: "Threepence for myself, the rest for the housekeeping," he recalls.

As the newest employee he was assigned the duties of grease-boy, lubricating loaf-tins and trays with a brush or a rag. After a year he moved up to a job on pastries, thumbing the crust into tins for Mackman's celebrated cheese-cakes and curd-cakes. A great deal of the work was still manual at this time, of course, and in one sense the history of the Derringham Street bakery is the history of gradual mechanisation.

Whether it is from loyalty to the firm or from a residual fear of retribution, few employees admit to having helped themselves to a free snack on the job - even though it may have been fifty or sixty years ago. Maybe it was indeed something of a rarity for such a thing to happen. But Bob remembers snaffling a custard tart and being spotted by an eagle-eyed overseer - a relative of Mackman's. He was fined a penny. "But I made a profit on that," he recalls. "They retailed at a penny halfpenny!" Another former bakery man remembers that the worst offenders were generally the directors themselves when they were showing visitors around the plant. His policy, as foreman, was to make sure that these dignitaries got their freebies off the production line, not off the trays where each item was carefully accounted for. One former overseer has said, "I always told my men that if you worked in a food factory and went home hungry it was your own stupid fault." Cyril Marshall, who started at the bakery in 1943, remembers perfecting the art of whipping a cream cake off a tray as they were carried past on their way to the creamery. His wife Kathleen was once reprimanded by her foreman: "You're not allowed to eat the products." "But I'm pregnant," she told him - she was at the time expecting twins, and this was in the midst of food rationing. "Aye, okay - we'll make a special case, then," she was told.

Bob Tyson remembers Mackman as an imposing, rather intimidating, figure. One Friday, he recalls, he was caught pinching a handful of sweets to slip to the girls in the pastry room. Mackman was incensed. "Go home!" he roared. Bob slunk away, fearing he had been sacked. Just in case, however, he showed up on the Monday - and the incident was never referred to again.

Justice seems to have been summary, occasionally severe. Certainly there was no union in those days, and for many years what there was would be weak. Tyson remembers an incident over lunch. Meal breaks were taken in the changing-room, and staff would often buy a Jackson's fourpenny meat pie. Just remembering

Bread and confectionery window. Displaying a selection of the bakery's wide range of products.

Vans await their loads outside the old Victoria Street factory, Derringham Street.

them brought a sigh to Bob's lips. "What I wouldn't give for one now," he said. "They used to put Bovril in them." One day the lads were having their lunch and making a bit of a row, banging their cutlery on the table. The engineers next door complained about it and the outcome was a fine for all of them: a two shilling rise they had been awaiting was held back for a week.

Tyson also remembers how basic some of the amenities were when he started. The company was expanding rapidly, trying out new ventures, and the buildings and plant were not always up to scratch. He particularly remembers the machine for washing currants which stood out in the yard with no protection from the weather. "If it rained, you got wet: as simple as that."

Just before the departure of Mackman another 'star' began her working life with Jackson's: Molly Masters, later Molly Baker, started in 1933 at the age of seventeen in the stock-room. She hadn't really wanted to go to work, but her father had only a labourer's wage and there were four children at home, so her wages were needed. Her first wages were 4/6 a week, of which she was allowed to keep 2/-, or ten pence.

In all probability she too came as a result of a family connection. Her uncle was 'Cocky' Gardham, a bakery foreman, and her brother Herbert was forty-four years at Derringham Street and the Dudley bakery. Although she rose to be a forewoman she never really liked the factory, and just before the war managed to get a move across to the offices. In this, she admits, the fact that she was going out with the brother of Mr. T.F. Dodsworth, the bakery manager, cannot have done her any harm. "He must have thought it would look better if his brother was going out with an office girl," she recalls.

Molly's forte was sports, particularly athletics. She won numerous prizes at the annual sports days up at Inglemire Lane, was a champion swimmer, an expert dancer, a fencer, and she coached and played for the firm's netball team well into the 1960s. One member of that team married the legendary football star Raich Carter. To him, Molly was always known affectionately as "Miss Twinkletoes". Her swimming exploits included entering a championship one year - probably 1935 or '36 - and having to swim in Scarborough harbour!

Esther Baker is one of several former Jackson's staff who would say they could write a book. Unlike most of them, however, she has - a volume about her experiences with the fire service during the war entitled *A City in Flames*.

Esther started her working life in a bakery in the old town, Winns, Close and Winsells in Dagger Lane. They had a shop in Prospect Street and a number of other outlets. But being a traditional bakery, reluctant to move out of the horse-drawn age, it folded. It was losing custom to modern, more aggressive and adaptable companies like Jackson's. When the axe fell - Esther, aged fifteen, had only been there eighteen months or so - a Jackson's foreman visited the place, saying that he could take on maybe half a dozen of their staff. The employees suffered an anxious few days, and then Esther heard that she had been offered a place at Derringham Street.

A travelling oven, brought in 1946 for £20,695. Bread or confectionery would be fed continually, the speed of the conveyor being variable.

She was thrilled. "We all thought Jackson's was really rather posh," she recalls. During her time there her three sisters, Anne, Mabel and Irene worked with her. Of the four all except Irene married Jackson's men - and left. "In those days you had to. They wouldn't have married women on the staff."

Naturally she remembers Mackman. And she has good reason to remember his son Eric, who worked with him: it was she who taught him to ice buns. This wasn't simply a matter of slapping the icing on: the finish had to be up to scratch. "Woe betide you if they didn't dry shiny!"

Mackman knew everything that went on, and he knew every facet of the job. He had a very able foreman in Joe Williamson, a man who would put in fifty years' service in Hull and at Scunthorpe. Esther remembers the staff as "a friendly lot who got on well together: Molly Masters, Madge Marshall, who later became welfare officer; Molly Morrell and Milly Grabine. There was Phyllis Cowham, Carrie Ling - whose sister Edith worked in the offices; Eileen Bolland who moved to New Zealand, Ada and Gertie Starkins and their father Jim. He made the jam and was known throughout the factory as 'Jammy Jim'.

It was during Esther's time that the slicing and wrapping machine came, in November 1934, not long after Mackman had left and about the time John Flew took charge of the machinery. Mackman's views on machinery were well-known: "It'll be the ruination of good bread," was his verdict.

Mackman's departure was to be a shock, leaving a lot of the staff completely baffled. There followed a brief period under Vernon Bourne's management, then under a Mr. Winship, before Mr. T.F.Dodsworth took over in February 1935. The staff were equally bemused when he assembled them all in the bottom bakehouse, stood on a table, and began his address by saying, "I've heard that you're rather a rough lot, but with a bit of give and take I'm sure we'll get along."

There is no doubt in Esther's mind - and this is something others have corroborated, both shops and bakery people - that quality suffered after Mackman left. The new management, it is routinely assumed, were more interested in profits than in cups and medals. Fancy items, of course, cost money, being labour-intensive, and become a luxury in a competitive world, more especially for a large company with massive overheads. Others, closer to the boardroom, reflect on the "very definite upward surge" in the manufacturing side's performance under Mr. Dodsworth's management, for it was he who brought in the wholesale side.

Mechanisation, as has been noted, was proceeding throughout this period. Prior to such innovations as the slicing machine the process of mixing the dough and dividing it into loaf-sized portions had long ceased to be done manually. Travelling ovens - that is, ovens into which risen dough passed on a continuous conveyor belt, emerging as finished loaves at the other end - were taking over from the old Peel and draw-plate ovens into which batches of loaves were slid on long-handled beechwood peels or metal sheets.

Sid Charlton, who joined the company in 1934 as plant maintenance engineer, saw a lot of changes in the next four decades. He had been an apprentice-trained engineer with Rose, Downs and Thompson in Cannon street. Mackman had several times asked Sid to come and work for him, but he only made the move when Mackman left and Ossie Richardson followed, leaving the firm in urgent need of an engineer.

What happened to Ossie was that he expressed his disapproval of the new bakery management, and Mackman arranged finance to set him up in his own garage and petrol station - the present-day Canal Head service station at Leven, on the Bridlington to Hull road.

Sid Charlton's connections with Jackson's in fact went back to the very early days. His father, a butcher by trade, raised him on the land off Inglemire Lane, Cottingham, which was soon to be sold to the company by Harry Crawford for its new meat department.

Charlton, then, saw many of the changes from manual operation to automation in such operations as dividing the dough, de-panning and slicing. He himself supervised the construction of the new conveyors which shifted the rows of tinned loaves from prover to ovens to cooler. He designed and built the cooler.

By the time war was approaching in the late 1930s, the Derringham Street bakery was modernising and expanding to meet the needs of an expanding shops division. A fairly stable and long-serving staff were loyal and close-knit, reflecting the family firm which employed them. However, great changes had been taking place within the upper echelons of the company.

Chapter Four

A TIME OF CHANGE

The death of George Jackson Bentham in October 1929, barely three weeks after the opening of the prestigious Paragon Street Branch, brought about a critical phase in the company's history. His will appointed three executors and trustees who were appointed as directors for a period of five years. One was his second wife Ada, still a young woman with two sons of her own by her first marriage. The others were insurance broker Frederick Atkinson and Eric Wilberforce Soulsby, the latter being the only one to continue in office after that period.

They had a delicate task ahead of them. The Oughtred brothers who had married Bentham's daughters had, as has been already suggested, opposed Bentham's autocratic style, Norman largely distancing himself from the company, Jack resigning his position and therefore having to surrender his 2000 shares. Both too were cool, if not hostile, to the widowed Ada. Norman had, however, spoken up at the Annual General Meeting in April 1929, supposedly on behalf of Miss Annie Jackson for whom he held proxy, questioning the chairman about directors' remuneration, complaining about a low dividend - he, unlike Jack, was still a shareholder - and querying Bentham's bonus payment to himself.

At this time Mackman, 'Bompy' Hall and Soulsby were all directors. The trustees now brought Harry Crawford onto the board along with Edward Kenneth Locking as Company secretary, and Atkinson himself as Chairman. Atkinson's appointment was only temporary. In March 1930, when Jack and Norman were made directors, Atkinson would be replaced by J.W. Carmichael of the well-known Hull jewellery firm. As an outsider he would maintain the peace between the 'new boys' and the old guard. In fact, it seems as though the tensions were to some extent defused by the fact that Hall, now very much a senior director, had the absolute confidence of Doris and Phyllis, the late chairman's daughters.

Bentham had been an autocrat. Not long before his death he had produced a document which extended his powers as chairman to those of a dictator, more or less. Legal opinion had been sought and it seemed that there was no restraint which could be applied to the man: it was his company and he could do more or less what he wanted.

But now he was gone and a wind of change swept through the company. On the shops front the stage was set for a further vigorous expansion into a far wider territory. Throughout 1930 there was a proliferation of sub-committees discussing the future. In 1931 the firm bought a business at Welton, Francis Myers Ltd, for £5500 and set up a board of three - Jack Oughtred, Eric Soulsby and 'Bompy' Hall -to administer it. From there the first off-licence would be opened, and a fleet of travelling shops operated.

On the bakery side Mackman still reigned supreme. In May of 1930 the factory's telegraphic address became WIZARD, an acknowledgement of his achievements. Through 1932 and '33 he was winning ever more awards for the company - or, some might suggest, for himself. September 1932 saw him in Brussels carrying off the Minster Den Cup, gaining more points in total than any other single entrant. Early in 1933 he was awarded the Cross of the Chevalier of the Order of the

Doris, elder daughter of George Jackson Bentham, married Norman Oughtred in 1917.

Phyllis, Bentham's younger daughter, married Jack Oughtred in 1919. His letters to her from France vividly describe the horrors of trench warfare.

Phoenix by the President of the Hellenic Republic. And in June, on what was probably his last visit abroad as a Jackson's man, he won three major prizes at the Brussels Exhibition: first prize for bread, first for confectionery, and the Sir Charles Batho Cup for best British exhibit. Two months later he would part company with his employers of almost forty years.

There is little doubt that the company was in some turmoil at this time. Despite the new blood on the board and the expansion into a wider territory, there were financial difficulties all around. This was at the height of the Depression. People had little money to spend, and those who had money tended to hoard it. The shops - in particular the grocery side - were not performing well: and there were problems in the bakery. One shop manager had even had the temerity to complain about the quality of bread received, and had been "severely dealt with" by Mr. Mackman.

These troubles followed not only the death of Bentham but also complaints from the auditors, Messrs Buckley, Hall and Devin, that the company's books were not being kept properly. While the company as a whole continued to show a profit, successive years in the early thirties brought losses in the grocery and fruit warehouses, at the Cottingham slaughterhouse, in the cafés, on sales vans, and in the fruit shops. The auditors found that the books contained a large number of errors, that the purchases section was in chaos, the departmental accounts inaccurate, the wages system out-dated and that individual shop managers had far too much scope regarding takings, wages and stock-taking. The system, they reported, was rife with faults which laid the company open to wastage and "leakage" which would be undetected and uncontrollable.

In 1932 Locking resigned as secretary, his place being taken by Mr. A.W. Cruickshank, a member of the audit team who had unearthed this web of mismanagement. However, Cruickshank had learned perhaps too well the company's weaknesses - and revealed some of his own. When, a few years later, a team of electricians was sent up to Cruickshank's house - the one in Davenport Avenue formerly belonging to Phyllis and Jack Oughtred - to install some wiring connected with his new indoor swimming pool, Jack Oughtred reflected, "He's not doing badly for a new bloke". He got the firm's auditor Donald Jones to go through the man's books immediately. In 1937 Cruickshank was sent to prison for six months for defrauding the company, falsifying accounts, and for a number of "defalcations admitted and proved". In his place the company appointed Mr W.R. Russell an accountant who had been with the firm since 1935. He would continue to serve the company in this capacity until 1970.

In the bakery Mackman, as can be imagined, had long resisted any form of mechanisation. On the shops side, however, the young modern-minded Gordon Russell was pushing for higher sales while at the same time struggling to meet the demands of the expanded network of retail outlets. He wanted mass production and modern mechanical methods to be introduced. It is probable that this friction, between the traditional and the modern, between craftsmanship and the needs of the market, lay at the root of the company's dissatisfaction with the Wizard of Derringham Street.

In July and August of 1933 a series of four special board meetings took place at the offices at 129 Spring Bank. These meetings bore more than a passing resemblance to judicial procedure. Mackman was, in effect, on trial. He absented himself from the first one, at which "evidence" was produced to suggest that the bakery manager was "working against the best interests of the company". At this first meeting it was resolved that Mackman be suspended on full pay *sine die*. Only Mr. Atkinson voted against this motion. Mr. Jack Oughtred was appointed factory manager in Mackman's place.

At a second meeting four days later the board - once more in the absence of the 'accused' - heard that Mackman was issuing writs against Jack Oughtred and 'Bompy' Hall for slander, against the company for wrongful dismissal, and against Cruickshank.

Mackman did attend the third meeting on July 26th, and here the chairman, Carmichael, set out the charges. These were in the main that he had spread amongst factory staff rumours of financial instability, causing general unrest; that he had passed on confidential information to the staff; that he had given false information to those staff, and that he had

Jack Oughtred in uniform visiting Phyllis. He was awarded the Military Cross in France.

generally "suborned the whole discipline of the factory and the employees of the company".

The indiscretions Mackman had committed included letting it be known that the company had an overdraft of some £40,000 and had not fully paid for the businesses bought at Welton (Francis Myers) and Withernsea (Brown's). He had also told some of his staff that their loyalty to Jackson's was foolhardy: the ship was sinking. And he had asked one employee if he would go with Mackman "should anything happen" and he set up elsewhere. He had further told numerous people that they had better join a union because the new board proposed to close certain departments and in any case cut wages.

At a fourth and final meeting, on 2 August 1933, the Chairman moved that Mackman be dismissed, Mr. Norman Oughtred seconding the motion. Mr. Atkinson again opposed this step, speaking of Mackman's admitted weaknesses but pointing to his "very valuable services".

Mackman was contrite, explaining that he felt "very keenly his great indiscretions" but pointing to his poor state of health at the time and adding that his doctor had advised him to take a long vacation, which he had declined to do out of concern for the work to hand.

Mackman was given three months' pay in lieu of notice, amounting to £335, compensation of £1365, and legal costs totalling £300: a package of £2000. He was also given an unqualified letter of testimonial from the board.

So Mackman had gone, and with him an era came to a close. In March 1934 came the first Baker Perkins travelling oven, and later that year the thing Mackman had dreaded - a bread slicer and wrapper - was installed for a three-month experimental period. In the first week of its operation the company sold 3000 sliced loaves: the experiment was a success, and in January 1935 the company bought a fully automated bread wrapper and slicer from Rose Bros of Gainsborough for £925.

Mackman went into business with a Mr. George Reed as Reed and Mackman, allegedly threatening to open up opposite every Jackson's bakery shop in Hull. A rather sad footnote to this affair is a brief note in the directors' minute book of April 1937: a number of his gold medals were sold off for the sum of £642 13s 2d

John Alwyn (Jack) Oughtred, director from 1930, Managing Director from 1942 until his death in 1958.

Norman Oughtred, a director of Jackson's from 1930 to 1960. His interests were more in his own shipping and insurance business.

Chapter Five

WARTIME

While the 1939-45 war is remembered by many as a time of danger, dislocation and even excitement, for those Jackson's staff who did not get into the fighting forces it seems to have been memorable mainly for the efforts they had to put in to maintain normal service against a tide of bureaucratic controls, disruption of supplies and their customers' inability to buy more than their most basic requirements.

Many of Jackson's men and women were either drafted into the armed services or else volunteered to join. A shortage of manpower thus brought a newer, younger and more predominantly female workforce. Married women were retained for the first time in the company's history. The working day was reduced, partly to conserve fuel and light, partly to conform with blackout regulations, but also because there were simply less goods for sale.

What most shop staff seem to remember of their wartime experiences is fire-watching. As air-raids became almost routine staff volunteered to stay behind after work on a rota basis, camping in the shop or perhaps above it and, in the event of a raid, keep watch for fires - either those resulting from bomb damage or those ignited by the many incendiary devices dropped by the Luftwaffe. After a night on watch staff would take a day off. Some remember having been paid - as little as two and six for a junior hand, but up to ten shillings for senior employees.

While many went into the services or volunteered for civilian duties - as Esther Baker did in the Fire Service - others undertook more prosaic duties. Ted Hewson, for example, ran a First Aid class one night a week after hours. But in 1941 he himself was called up into the RAF.

Alf Turner, a joiner with the firm, kept a complete record of all the work he had to do to protect various premises, and of material damage which was suffered throughout the hostilities. As early as September 1938 the board had had an emergency meeting regarding possible air raids in case of war. They bought twelve electric torches and several loads of sand. But with the passing of the Munich crisis they parted with the torches, keeping the sand. Alf began work in late August 1939 blacking out the factory's roof-lights and covering flour stocks against possible gas attacks. The first shelter that was built was made of sacks of flour. Through the lengthy 'phoney war' period various orders came through as to what steps might be taken in the event of an invasion. All machinery was to be smashed for a start. As a precautionary measure, the office staff were transferred to Elloughton Dale for the duration of the war, and installed in a large country house there. Some commuted, but about 50 - particularly some of the young clerks and secretaries - were at various times boarded there through the week in small makeshift dormitories.

The first premises to suffer damage, according to Alf's record, was not in Hull, strangely, but in Bridlington on August 22 1940. Within a matter of days, however, Hull received its first raids, shops at Fountain Road and Severn Street being damaged. Then it was back to making preparations. Jack Oughtred, Colonel in charge of an East Riding battalion of Home Guard, had the firm's joiners make up some targets for his men - in the event of their ever

These shots of staff outside Preston Road and East Park branches show how windows and doors had to be boarded up during the Blitz. Inside, the shops were very gloomy indeed.

having any live ammunition to practise with! In the autumn a team was sent to Rotherham, to make blackouts for the factory and shops there. Early in 1941 a roof-top observation post was built for the Derringham Street bakery.

The spring of 1941 brought a relentless succession of raids with shops damaged throughout the city. Mostly this was repairable, but Bright Street was wrecked, according to Alf Turner's diary - although later records have it re-opening in the summer. Porter Street suffered serious damage. Early in May Paragon Street had its window blown in and set ablaze. In that same raid the Wellington Street warehouse was consigned to oblivion. In 1942 the factory received a fire-bomb on the roof, but this apparently did little damage. In July a bomb missed the factory by a mere ten feet, and in August Alf noted that "three of us practised disabling machinery, taking thirty minutes".

May 1942 saw the offices in Bank street and the creamery bombed. Fortunately the men were able to salvage the machinery from the creamery, and it was taken to Holme-on-Spalding Moor, half-way to York, and installed there.

Typical of the kind of scene that would await staff when they arrived for work at the end of a raid would be a shop window blown out and all the contents of the shelves and fixtures sucked off onto the floor. Even getting to the site of a raid was fraught with danger, the streets a litter of broken tiles and glass, with piles of soot and huge puddles dotted between mounds of rubble and fractured water and gas mains. One severe attack cut off the mains water supply to the Derringham Street works, and water had to be brought in from Cottingham in milk churns, a relay of vans

On May 1st 1942 a direct hit flattened the dairy in Victoria Street.

keeping the plant and boiler going until the damage could be repaired.

In the shops rationing meant less goods for sale, but it also meant an increase in the amount of paperwork. Customers registered with a particular grocer or butcher and their papers were sent to the Food Office. The Food Office then sent the shopkeeper a permit for each customer. Customers could - and did - occasionally change their registration to another shop, but by and large a shopkeeper could expect to retain the same list throughout the war.

One Jackson's manager who did account for a number of 'desertions' was Herbert Cockerill at Withernsea. He had worked under Mr. Lundy in that branch until going to war in 1941. After VE day Herbert came home and opened his own shop. He needed fifty ration books to get himself started - and obtained them by signing up all his friends and family as well as a number of customers who remembered him from his Jackson's days.

Due to motor vehicles being requisitioned by the Government, the familiar horse-drawn rully made a reappearance during the second world war.

A familiar sight - right up to the mid '50s

Different sources offer differing opinions as to how strictly rationing was adhered to. Many who worked in the shops through the war will state categorically that there was no opportunity at all for favouritism, let alone black marketeering. The paper-work would reveal any attempts at fiddling. Others, however, speak of wangling special treatment for favoured clients, or of prized goods being kept out of sight for friends or relatives. One former assistant remembers a jar of sweets being shared out among the staff - in exchange for coupons, of course - with the customers never getting so much as a smell of them.

C.R. Taylor remembers the time he got into hot water through taking pity on a customer who claimed to have lost her ration books. This woman came into his shop and said she had moved to Hull from Beverley and mistakenly left the books with a grocer there, so would C.R. please let her have a few items to tide her over. He obliged, but it transpired that she had been playing this game elsewhere, that her books had in fact been kept by the Beverley grocer against a bad debt. She ended up in court and C.R. ended up in the newspaper. But there was no scandal to face up to: under the headline HULL FIRM FINED FOR DOING A GOOD TURN he was cited as a gallant gentleman cruelly punished by uncaring bureaucrats!

Dorothy Scholefield offers another reminder that not everyone put self-interest aside in deference to the war effort. She was at East Park, under Miss Evans' management, during the war. For fire-watching they took turns with a number of other shops along Holderness Road. She remembers one night as she stood her turn seeing a man rush out into the street and gather up armfuls of canned goods which had been blown out of a bombed shop-window.

The poor quality of much of the bakery produce during the war caused grief to the shops staff. Vera Owen recalls the sad state of the goods she had to sell - rock buns that bore an unfortunate resemblance to rocks, and jam sponges with barely a hint of fat in them. And then there was all that paperwork. She had two girls working full-time doing little else but handle food coupons and fill in the various forms for the Ministry. And not only were the goods sub-standard, but the shops themselves were robbed of much of their charm by the blackout. As windows were blown out they were replaced with boards rather than fresh glass. The insides were rendered dark and gloomy, and from the outside customers had to peer through a little square opening into a thinly-stocked window.

While employees were being called out at all hours to shore up shattered windows Sid Charlton was turning out night and day to maintain machinery - not only in Jackson's own factory but in their competitors' bakeries! While Sid was deemed to be on work vital to the war effort, engineers at other plants were called up willy-nilly, or so it seemed to him. Admittedly, bread 'zoning' in the war eliminated direct competition amongst manufacturers, but it must have seemed strange to him to be repairing plant for Ostlers, Hicks, Skeltons and Fields.

Later he would have to tend to breakdowns at Jackson's new outposts in Wakefield, Rotherham, Scunthorpe or Dudley, generally on his reliable Norton motor-bike. To say it was a busy time would be to damn Sid with faint praise. He was effectively on call twenty-four hours a day, and as soon as the war was over he collapsed, suffering a minor nervous breakdown.

Frequently during the war he worked alone. He was never backward about clambering into hot ovens, taking all kinds of risks to get things moving. However, he has good reason to remember one assistant he was assigned, Bill Shepherd. In addition to Sid's roving commission he had, like so many others, to put in extra hours fire-watching. His particular job was to go up to the roof-top observation post during raids and alert the men in the factory when a direct hit seemed likely. He went to night school to learn to identify the various enemy and friendly aircraft, and during raids to assess the likelihood of a bomb landing on the works: how high were the aircraft? Were they heading for the docks or the power station, or were they targeting the railway that ran alongside the factory site towards Botanic crossing? Hull was a prime target for the Luftwaffe, suffering devastating structural damage in over eighty major air raids.

If there was a real likelihood of a hit the observer was to press a buzzer which sounded in the works and alerted the staff to head for the shelters. But the one time the factory itself was hit, in July 1943, Sid and Bill Shepherd were inside attending to a mixing machine. They had just got done and, hearing aircraft overhead, went out to see what was happening. They heard a bomb apparently heading straight for them and both dived for cover, in opposite directions. Sid was blown off his feet by the blast, back into the factory. When he emerged to look for his mate he found him dead, the top of his head blown off.

Apart from the temporary flour-sack shelter built in 1939 there were two other shelters at Derringham Street. The first, built in 1939 just after the war started, at a cost of £1,029 12s 10d was an underground affair at number 27 Victoria Street. "It was never used," Sid recalls. "It was always full of water. We used to have to pump it out night and morning. Some of us reckoned that was what caused the Hymers College lake to dry up!" In any case, it was destroyed along with the dairy in the May 1942 raid. As to the other shelter, above ground at number 6 Victoria Street, that served, when peace finally came, to house the steamed pudding plant!

Apart from all these familiar aspects of the war - the rationing, the bombing raids, the occasional chaos - there were other, longer lasting effects both for Jackson's itself and the food industry in general. The restrictions on international trade brought a dependency on domestic flour, but bread rationing did not begin until the war was actually over. Even then it only lasted a year or so, and was largely the result of Britain's foreign exchange difficulties and the devaluation of the pound. A more immediate worry during the war concerned the supply of fresh yeast, a substantial proportion of which came from Holland. When the Dutch were invaded by the Germans in May 1940 the British government became worried lest domestic supplies, which came from a mere handful of factories, be interrupted.

The government therefore considered such steps as the introduction of potato barm in place of live yeast and went so far as to issue leaflets on the use of sour doughs. Potatoes were also put forward as a possible additive, to make the flour go further, but this was never necessary on any great scale. Indeed, where it was tried the public resisted it fiercely. The one area of the country where the yeast supply was interrupted briefly was Coventry, following the infamous raid of November 1940. Here a number of bakeries, including Jackson's were able to step up production to make up the shortfall. Later, when the city of Sheffield was blitzed, Jackson's were able to augment local supplies.

When war came Jackson's bakery division covered an area as wide as, if not wider than, the retail side. Following the rapid expansion of the retail arm in the 1930s the Hull bakery and its transport fleet had been stretched to the limit. While Beverley, Hornsea and Withernsea were all within easy reach, the new shops at York, Doncaster, Scunthorpe, Leeds and Harrogate required better service than could be provided from headquarters.

An early attempt to attract - and keep - customers in far-flung places was the mail order department run from Paragon Street which sent out specialities to the country at large and in some cases abroad. One former manageress recalls sending Jackson's Christmas cakes to India, another packaging consignments of Mackman's celebrated cheese-cakes for a director's children at boarding-school. But this venture only lasted a matter of months. Despite advertisements being placed in a dozen different newspapers, there simply was not enough response to make it worthwhile.

In April 1935 a wholesale department had been set up for bread and confectionery products, and in the following two or three years a number of regional depots were opened to serve the widening market. The Doncaster depot seems to have been the first, opened in January 1936. By March 1939 it had been moved to larger premises, leaving Athron Street and moving to Carr Grange. Leeds depot had opened at Millwright Street in 1938, and York - a little place off the Hull Road - in 1939. That year the wholesale department made a total profit of £18,000, although the greater part of that sum was generated from the Hull depot.

The depots were in some cases the advanced guard of further expansion. Business was attracted as more reliable deliveries were offered, and before long Jackson's began to look for bakeries within their new territory. In February 1940 the bakery and shops of H. Adams and Son of Rotherham were acquired. And then in 1944, with peace on the horizon and the board looking very much to the future, four important acquisitions were made. In Wakefield Swale's bakery and shop were bought; in Scunthorpe Mitchell's grocery and confectionery; in Dudley in the West Midlands Woodhouse's two bakehouses and five shops; and in Mirfield near Leeds the Golden Grain Bakery.

Jackson's had suffered no great permanent structural damage in the war and it had held onto its trade. The company's employees had served in the fighting forces abroad, at home, and put in sterling efforts to maintain production and ensure distribution. Gordon Russell was awarded an O.B.E. for his services in this field. These had been very difficult years and it was thanks to the unstinting efforts of Jack and Norman Oughtred, Eric Soulsby and chairman Jim Carmichael that the company had not only survived but managed to make significant plans for the future.

Chapter Six

MEAT

Jackson's had started, as we have seen, as a tea-dealer. By outbreak of the First World War the shops now included confectioners, bakers, grocery and greengrocery departments. In 1915, about the time the "pork department" was built in Victoria Street, the first pork butcher's shop was opened at what was known as the East Park branch, on 618 Holderness Road. A second such shop opened at 278 Hessle Road in 1919, others in the succeeding few years at 59 Charles Street, at Porter Street, at Severn Street on the corner of 299 Holderness Road, and in 1936 at Hornsea and Withernsea. At least a dozen butchers seem to have been opened around this time, but that represented only a small fraction of the eighty-odd shops Jackson's had opened up to 1939.

From the minutes of board meetings we see that in 1922 a Mr. Harry Crawford had written to Mr. Bentham offering his services as cattle-rearer, along with certain land and buildings. The offer was accepted. Barely ten weeks later there is a record of one thousand £1 shares being transferred to him from Bentham's personal holding, along with fourteen one hundred pound debentures. In 1929 Crawford would join the new board brought together under Ada Bentham's temporary governance.

The land which the company acquired was the fields and buildings in Inglemire Lane, Cottingham, which was to become the site of the Cottingham Meat division and, later, the Tryton Foods plant. In December 1933 the firm would acquire a further seven acres of land across the road. This would be the site of the company's playing fields and sports grounds.

Inglemire Lane was not the first farm land owned by Jackson's. For some time - at least since 1916 - they had land at Preston and, since 1919, at Bilton, to the east of the city. These farms appear not to have yielded much in the way of a financial return. The Manor House Farm at Preston was sold in 1925, and the Red House Farm at Bilton went to Trinity House in 1927. Whether this sale had any connection with a flock of geese, reared for the Christmas market, which took flight before the big day and were never seen again, we can only guess! A third deal in September 1927 saw the sale of the Tower Grange Nursery to Hull Corporation. This Holderness Road site, a source of cut flowers and other nursery produce, had made a loss for three consecutive years.

The Inglemire Lane land, however, was to be a success, first as a slaughtering and meat preparation centre, later as a butchery department. One former employee with memories of the site even before Jackson's took Mr. Crawford up on his offer is Sid Charlton. His father had worked for Crawford as a butcher and Sid was raised in one of a pair of cottages which stood by the roadside where the offices would later stand. The site had once been a brickyard. There was a pond at the bottom of the paddock, now filled in, which Sid remembers skating on in wintertime. The old cottages were demolished between the wars and replaced by a pair of semi-detached houses which are there to this day.

Like any establishment where livestock was housed and slaughtered, the farm attracted vermin. Sid has vivid memories of a large old farm wagon in which offal was collected: it seemed to draw the rats from miles around. So at the tender age of five Sid picked up a Daisy air rifle and tried his hand at shooting.

Harry Crawford, cattle-man. Not your average director!

Slaughterers and butchers at Inglemire Lane, about 1949. The dilapidated caravan housed the chicken-pluckers.

His first instructor was the local bobby, a sergeant Piercey who used to call by and sit in the saddle-room for a chat, taking occasional pot-shots as he drew on his pipe. Sid would sit there watching, dying to have a go. One day Piercey asked him, "D'you want a shot, son?" "I'd love to," the boy replied. The bobby told him to aim at an old china basin lying on the floor. His father used to feed his ferrets in it. He hit it first time, breaking it in two, and was rewarded with a shilling. Piercey told him there was another shilling for him if he could hit one of the halves, which he did first time.

Soon Sid was given a shot-gun of his own - perhaps the bobby complained to his father that he was running short of shilling pieces - and each evening he would go out to shoot rats. His father kept a strict eye on him, keeping the cartridges and allowing him just one at a time. This, Sid says, made him both a careful and an accurate shot. He was never allowed to point the gun at anything until he was well away from the house. But he was soon free of the one-cartridge-at-a-time restriction: collecting a penny from the Council offices for each tail he produced, he was soon making enough pocket-money to ensure that he never wanted for ammunition.

He never ran short of targets, either. There were always rats about, and he particularly remembers the time he and his father broke up and lifted some old concrete in the stables and killed close to sixty.

Sid would become an excellent shot, representing Hull in small-bore rifle competitions. Later, he claims, he had a hand in teaching Norman and Jack Oughtred to shoot. As ex-Army men they had naturally handled rifles and small arms, but neither of them had much experience with a shot-gun. Sid remembers John Flew, who had a farm out at Elloughton, inviting him to take part in a shoot with the brothers, from this time Sid got to go on a number of shoots each year. Later the odd brace of pheasants or a hare or two he was allowed to keep helped him and his family through some thin times in the Second World War.

Jim Bark started work at Jackson's before he left school, as a part-time errand lad at 278-282 Hessle Road, or Eton Street as it was better known. This was in 1927. The following year, upon leaving school, he went to East Park, 614-620 Holderness Road, as an errand-lad to the butchery department. He soon ended up at Inglemire Lane, then a comparatively small-scale set-up. His duties included driving cattle the firm had bought at the livestock market up to Cottingham for slaughtering. Persuading the beasts out of town and along unmade roads was not easy; and there were plenty of mishaps for four young lads with a small herd of cattle and three or four country miles to travel.

Jim remembers at least one occasion when a recalcitrant beast not only got loose and entered a house, but actually climbed the stairs and entered a bedroom while the occupant, an elderly lady, threw a fit downstairs. Another beast got into a barber's shop, and a third - Jim has sworn this is the truth! - got into a china shop, and out again, without a single breakage. The company, of course, were insured against such incidents. They needed to be. A householder in Cottingham claimed damages after a cow had entered through the French windows and, in Jim's own words, "liberally re-decorated the place".

The animals in these situations tended to panic. They were in any case liable to become excited, making it all the harder to re-capture them. One old sow ended up on a dining-room table - prior to being butchered - on its back and spinning round and round as the lads tried to persuade it back out of the door.

And when the boys had got the animals to Cottingham there was Harry Crawford to confront. Where all the other directors of Jackson's look, from their photographs, like rather austere members of the Establishment, true English gentlemen, Crawford looks like nothing more nor less than a broad, rough-and-ready pig farmer in his round-necked sweater and flat hat. But perhaps he was off guard when this picture was taken. As often as not he was to be seen wearing a stetson and driving around in a six-cylinder V8 Ford. Generally speaking, people appear to have been in awe of him, if not frightened. He was a large man with a very loud voice, and his vocabulary was, according to Peter Oughtred, "extensive".

Jim Bark and his brother Bill recall a young lad they worked with who had expressed dissatisfaction with his wages. They told him he should go and ask Mr. Crawford for a rise. The lad set off and found him.

"W-would it be po-possible," he began.
"WHAT? SPEAK UP, LAD!" the boss shouted.

"W-would it b-be possible..?"
"SPEAK UP, I CAN'T HEAR YOU!"

"I s-said, w-would it b-be..."

"LOUDER!!"

The boy took a deep breath, plucked up his courage and shouted with all his might, "WOULD IT BE POSSIBLE..."

But that was as far as he got, as Crawford bellowed back at him, "DON'T BE BLOODY SHOUTING AT ME, LAD! I'M NOT DEAF, Y'KNOW!"

Different from the other directors Crawford might have been, but he had at least one thing in common with Jack Oughtred, a liking for whisky. Jack, like a lot of soldiers, had acquired a taste for whisky in the hell of the trenches during the First World War. But he only drank after sundown. Harry appears to have shown less restraint. On one occasion when he was making his way across the fields at Inglemire he fell into a ditch. Three of his men together couldn't pull him out. Worried for his safety, and unsure what was expected from them in such circumstances - he was, after all, the boss - they hurried back to his house to tell his wife what had happened. It was evidently no surprise to her. Pulling out a couple of blankets from a cupboard, she handed them over to the men. "Here," she said, "take these and throw them over him. He'll come home when he gets cold enough."

Like many such characters, however, Crawford's bark was worse than his bite. He was known to lay on hot soup at the slaughterhouse in wintertime, feeding a number of poor people from the neighbourhood. And he would hand out to the impoverished farm-hand a shin of beef or maybe a cow-heel to make soup with.

Jim Bark's brother Bill, two years his junior, started at the slaughter house about the time that Jim went there full-time. There were no more than half a dozen men there at that time, he remembers. Sheep, pigs and cattle were shipped in, killed, dressed, and the carcases taken to Victoria Street. It was not until 1938 that the butchery department would be moved from there to Inglemire Lane. Even when the animals were safely in their pens the men's troubles were not always over. The beasts - particularly the pigs - would escape, and a gang of men armed with staves or boards would be seen chasing an errant sow over the fields or down the road, hoping it wouldn't emulate the mad cow which one time crashed through the garden of the Sacred Heart church and demolished the greenhouse there.

Occasionally an animal in the pens would become over-excited, causing damage and panicking the other beasts. In these cases the men would send for John Bone who would fetch his gun and put the animal out of its misery. Bone ran a market garden just down the road, adjoining what is now the Endyke Tyre Mart.

The Bark brothers had a tough trade to learn, but they were not apprenticed. They acquired the skills much as Jenny Tinker learned the more delicate art of cake-decorating at Derringham Street, by practical experience. They worked from six in the morning until six at night, and it was not unheard of for them to be sent down to Victoria Street on a Friday to work the eleven o'clock night shift in the butchery.

The worst aspect of the slaughtering business, Bill recalls, was the smell - of blood and excrement. The first job a young lad would be given was sweeping up - blood, viscera, lungs and the rest of it. Perhaps it was better that way: he would very soon find out whether he was going to be able to stand the job. Many left within minutes rather than hours. But those who stayed and learned the

Inside the slaughterhouse. Not a pretty sight - although it was the smell that made most people leave the job after five minutes.

trade came to take great pride in what was, after all, another craft.

When the Barks started, livestock was still killed by the crude, but effective, method known as pole-axing. Tremendous skill and not a little nerve was required. A bullock, to take one example, would first be lassoed, then led to the killing-pen and fastened in place. Its head had to be secured, immobilised, in the angle between two stout rails. The slaughterer would then mark a spot on its forehead, and take a free swing with his pole-axe, a hollowed spike which would penetrate some considerable distance. At this the animal would drop, quite stiff, and the four-foot long pithing cane would be inserted into the hole and forced the length of the vertebrae, thus relaxing the central nervous system and rendering the carcase limp. Finally, the jugular vein would be cut and the animal bled. Gutting, skinning and quartering the carcase completed the process.

In the early days at Inglemire Lane the blood was of little value. It was allowed to set in pans. The clear serum would then be run off to be used for medical purposes. The Barks remember a doctor from Castle Hill who came to collect it. Later on, they recall, a theatre technician used to call for the sow's hearts, the valves being used as replacements for faulty valves in human hearts. The coagulated blood at this time went off to John Bone to feed his fruit and vegetable crops.

After the animals had been gutted, the liver, kidney and such parts separated and the remaining parts dumped in a large concrete pit, the carcases were hung some seven to ten days before going to the butchery.

The work was heavy. The men would have to handle a forty- or fifty-stone pig into a scalding-tub, wrap a metal chain about it and scrape it clean of hair and bristles, using a stout wooden jemmy to roll it over as they worked. The methods in those days were evidently basic, the very nature of the work repellent to many people. However, slaughtering and dressing a carcase is an art, perhaps more so if one considers the circumstances under which it is performed. The Bark brothers speak with pride of producing the best dressed meat in Hull. Their products would be on display to the buying public in the shops, often adorning the window. It had to appear attractive and appetising, and that was their job - to see that it was.

Harry Lyons was one of a number of true craftsmen employed at Inglemire Lane in those early days. He came to work in a waistcoat. And like many a master butcher he would leave his personal trade-mark on each carcase he handled, cutting a daisy or a Christmas tree motif. Thelma Freeman, who worked in the Bean Street and later the Spring Bank branches as a butcher, remembers that she could often identify a side of beef, for example, as having been killed by a particular slaughterer, just by the look of it and the finish.

As any number of former employees have remarked, and the Bark brothers have re-iterated, "you had characters then, and they made the long hard days enjoyable." There was the young woman who, when told to stir a pan of blood to stop it from setting - this was before the days of anti-coagulants - rolled up her sleeve and used her forearm. There were the one or two slaughtermen who would actually drink the blood with their morning snack, or dip a sandwich in it to get the salty flavour. And there was Ken Edwards, the man who was so good at First Aid, always willing to attend to the many cuts and abrasions that were part and parcel of the trade. However, the time he cut his own finger the sight of the blood made him keel over in a dead faint. And to add insult to injury he gashed his head as he fell and needed seven stitches when he came to.

The rather primitive conditions and practices continued until well after the war. For many years there was no electric lighting, at least outside, and men had to venture out into the yards with hurricane lamps. With as many as a thousand pigs to feed twice daily there was a lot of outside work, and in the poor light of winter it is not surprising that accidents happened. But this is not necessarily an indictment of management, more a reflection of the general state of the meat industry at that time.

Harry Crawford died during the war and for a period from early 1943 T.F. Dodsworth took charge at Inglemire Lane. The government requisitioned the slaughtering facility and it seems that things improved little during the emergency. Thus Ray Critchley, who was recruited to the firm in 1951 and retired as general manager of 'Cott Meat' in 1987, has confessed to being almost embarrassed to recall the state of affairs when he arrived. Like a lot of Britain's workplaces, the place was in a mess. However, he spoke in glowing terms of the efforts of Mr. Ron Mountifield, the director in charge of meat, particularly in respect of hygiene and working conditions. Ron Mountifield, an east Yorkshire farmer, who married Norman Oughtred's daughter Jean had joined the company in 1951, became a director in 1960 and vice-chairman in 1984.

Ray had been working in Blackpool as a meat inspector for a Lancashire chain, Carter & Co. He was a very highly qualified butcher, being a member of the Institute and one of the very first to gain their Higher Certificate. He had attended night school for three years, studying such subjects as meat production, anatomy and physiology, meat inspection, microbiology and hygiene, food chemistry, nutrition and the principles of refrigeration and cold storage.

He had first been approached by Mr. Dodsworth - "a grand chap" who still, in the early 1950s, wore a top-hat and carried a cane. Here is a prime example of Jackson's propensity for finding, and obtaining the services of, the most able staff, what the Oughtred family like to refer to as 'talent-spotting'.

However, much as Ray had been sought out and courted, he was hardly treated as royalty when he came to Hull. He travelled across the Pennines in February 1951, leaving his wife in Blackpool while he got himself settled. He arrived at night and found his new home, a large unfurnished flat, one of four above the shop at 540 Beverley Road, on the corner of Clough Road. It had previously been occupied by a number of RAF personnel. Not only had it no furniture but it had no heating either. Late on that first evening, frozen stiff, Ray was reduced to taking out his pen-knife and prising the tacks from the twelve-inch squares of linoleum with which the floor was covered. These he burned in the open hearth, trying to warm the place up before he wrapped himself in his great-coat and went to sleep on the floor.

In the morning he managed to wash himself at one of two fire-buckets full of icy water. No sooner had he finished this than there was a knock at the door. There stood a council employee demanding immediate payment of some outstanding bill on the property of four

Herefords in layerage at Ron Mountifield's farm at South Wold in the East Riding.

pounds. However, Ray soon got sorted out. At least he and his wife would have no rent to pay: the flat came with the job, and their furniture was soon on its way to Hull.

Cottingham Meat was, in Ray's apt phrase, "a bloody shambles" when he got there, a cold, raw spot surrounded by bleak open fields and very much on the outskirts of Cottingham village. The bakery might have been a million miles away. "Those people hardly knew we existed," was his first impression.

The staff at that time numbered about eighty or ninety, over half of them women. In the early fifties, as meat rationing gradually ended, the cold storage capacity of the place was increased and output just about trebled. To Ray the men and women he worked with were "a first-class team", albeit one surrounded by muddy footpaths and unmade yards. While they worked generally from eight in the morning to five at night, Ray would often be on the job until eight, sometimes as late as eleven. As well as having fond memories of the team, Ray also thought well of the board. "They were a grand lot - but they simply wouldn't spend money on the place, not until the late seventies or so."

The factory was not only primitive. It was also a very cold place to work in. The Factory Act stated that such premises had to have an ambient temperature of sixty degrees Fahrenheit when work started. It generally took two hours to achieve that, Ray noticed, the place being heated by an old coke-fired boiler which cranked out steam heat. One additional source of warmth, however, near the boiler, was the plant where beef dripping was heated up for the manufacture of potato crisps. From the late forties up to about 1963 Jackson's produced, packaged and sold their own brand of crisps. Mr. Peter Oughtred was very much in favour of this enterprise and wanted to expand it, but the board as a whole considered it something of a nuisance and voted him down. The crisps were sent out in bulk to the shops where staff would weigh them out in one-and-a-quarter ounce portions and put them into bags. Thelma Freeman at Spring Street remembers adding salt on her own initiative - and occasionally vinegar!

Ron Boult who, after spells as a delivery driver, became slaughterhouse manager under Ray Critchley, confirms the generally dilapidated state of the Inglemire Lane site. "They ran the place on a shoe-string," he says. He offers as an example the old barrow used for years and years to cart various items around the yard. When it fell to pieces he naturally asked for a new one. "Where did you get the old one?" he was asked. "Why, I got it myself. Pinched it from one of the shops on my round." "Well, there you are," came the answer. "Go and pinch yourself another one!"

But all of this, shocking as it may seem today, has to be set against the standards of the day. The Meat and Livestock Commission did their rounds, grading carcases, and the Environmental Health people made regular inspections. Like any company, Jackson's would steer as close as it could to the required standards. Thus in July 1954, in response to a warning by Haltemprice Council's health department, certain improvements in the slaughterhouse were carried out "as a matter of urgency".

Mr. Mountifield's role vis-a-vis the meat department was to liaise with the shops, promoting new lines at the retail level. The range of products was constantly being renewed and updated. It included all the various types of domestic ham; pressed beef; savoury rolls; polony and haslet; several sizes of pork pie; numerous kinds of beef and pork sausage; saveloys, black puddings and pressed tongue; meat paste; brawn, and a whole range of prepared pie fillings to be sent to Derringham Street for steak and kidney pies, veal and ham, and the various meat puddings and pasties produced there. At one time they were sending out as much as 800lbs of pasty meat alone in a single day.

During the period of the Grandways expansion, production would grow at an astonishing rate. Where in the 1950s they were killing some fifty animals a week they would now be handling close to a thousand, and keeping nine large refrigerated trucks and three Transit vans fully occupied with deliveries.

Ron Boult started with Jackson's in 1956. He had been with Reckitts since 1942, apart from a spell in the Army, then in the Fire Brigade. When he came to Cottingham Meat as the division's sole driver he was shown "a clapped-out 1938 Dennis with solid tyres and a hand-cranked starter." When Ron Mountifield later went with him to Market Weighton to pick up the first new lorry it felt like going to see the eighth wonder of the world. Instead of a crude wooden shell in which to transport the sides of meat this one had a metal body equipped with proper racks. It was convenient and hygienic, easy to clean out at the end of the day.

In Ron Boult's day vermin were still a problem. Poison was not used, and guns were the favoured method. Alternatively Harry Lyons would set his ferrets after the vermin and leave the rats to the tender mercies of his dogs Jip and Nell. In times when the infestation reached critical proportions the men had a particular method of dealing with it: they filled a sixty-gallon tub with scalding water and tipped that over the huge midden-heap where the rats lurked. For Ray Critchley, however, cats were every bit as much a problem as rats. They waxed fat and multiplied in this happy hunting ground, breeding around the yard and buildings or in the hedge bottoms. Where the young Sid Charlton had gone across the fields at night with his shotgun to pepper the rodent population, Ray went out with his .22 rifle to keep the cats in order.

Interestingly, Ray found when he retired that he could no longer countenance the idea of being a slaughterman, nor even work in such a place. "You get soft when you're away from it," he said. "Back then you had to be hard: killing was your livelihood, but now I'd no sooner kill a pig, or a cat for that matter, than fly to the moon." The bulk of the output from Cottingham was, of course, processed in some way or other. There were, until Grandways came along, never more than a dozen or so Jackson's butchers open. At Christmas there would be thousands of turkeys, geese, ducks and chickens to prepare - a fantastically busy period for all the staff. Ron Boult would be at it until the last minute, setting out for his last delivery to the shops as late as five o'clock on Christmas Eve. If he was lucky he would get done in time for a drink at about nine.

The shops stayed open late on the 24th. At Charles Street they would auction off their left-over meat and poultry last thing, around ten o'clock, from their open shop window. Shops such as Severn Street and Bright Street, Greenwood Avenue too, would send their unsold stock across, and men would emerge from the pubs, full of Christmas spirit, to put in their bid and hope to go home with a turkey under their arm. Sometimes these revellers got carried away with themselves. Ron remembers his own brother-in-law making a successful bid for a brace of pheasants - and then 'phoning him late at night in a panic. "What'll I do with them, Ron?" "Are they alive?" Ron asked him. "No," the lad replied, sounding a little puzzled. "That's a pity, isn't it? Otherwise you could have set them loose over the golf-course." In the end, of course, Ron had to turn out and dress the birds.

Jim Bark had started work as an errand lad to a butcher. Ron Boult, as a delivery man, was well acquainted with shop staff: if things weren't right he would probably be the first to hear about it. Harry Lyons, the foreman up at Inglemire, had a brother managing the Spring Bank shop. But in this man's world there was one remarkable character with a treasure trove of memories - for years Jackson's one and only lady butcher, Thelma Freeman.

Thelma Freeman left school in the summer of 1937 and got a job in Hammonds in Hull city centre. She ran cash for the counter-hands, firstly in the toy department and then in knitting wool. She was the lowest of the low, an assistant's assistant. She was not happy, for she nurtured an ambition. Her ambition, much to her mother's disgust, was to work for Jackson's. She had grown up, and still lived, on Hessle High Road opposite the Gipsyville shop. Her mother shopped there, and Thelma was enchanted by the place. She admired the girls who worked there and was captivated by the special atmosphere, particularly the gorgeous smells of the provisions, the aroma of fresh ground coffee, the displays of cakes and pastries.

Inside the butchery. You could write your own caption for this.

A splendid display of meat. Windows such as this one could be opened from outside, and occasionally attracted thieves.

After six months at Hammonds she managed to get an interview with Jackson's. She cycled to Clarendon Street and was seen by Miss Barker who gave her the usual assurance that should anything suitable arise she would be considered. That very lunchtime Thelma's front door-bell rang. It was a girl from across the road with a message from her boss. Would Thelma start at Bean Street that afternoon? Her mother, knowing nothing of the interview, said, "Well, you've done it. You've made your bed. Now go and lie in it."

She started at the grocery under Mr. Arthur Lunn at nine shillings a week. One shilling was deducted for her uniforms and six shillings went to her mother for board. As part of her training she spent six weeks at Paragon Street under the watchful eye of Mr. Laurie Howiantz, another first-class man who would later rise to shops supervisor.

Thelma's experiences differ notably from those of people ten years her senior. Things in the shops were beginning to change. With the outbreak of war eighteen months or so after she started there were a number of breaks with tradition. Firstly, with the black-out, working hours were cut; secondly, married women were kept on. Wages began to rise as bargaining power shifted. As an example of the pressure that might be exerted on a company like Jackson's, anxious to hang on to its trained staff, Thelma cites the time she was told she would have to go and work at the Beverley Road branch. She didn't want to go; she was very happy at Bean Street. So she went and fixed herself up with the Co-op who offered her seven and six a week more than she had been making. When she gave her notice her supervisor called by to ask why she was going. She told her she was going for better pay. "And how much are the Co-op going to pay you?" Miss Barker asked. "An extra ten shillings," Thelma told

her, without so much as a blush. Miss Barker thereupon offered her a rise of twelve and six and told her she might stay at Bean Street.

How delighted Arthur Lunn was at this news is a moot point. Thelma, by her own admission, was a living breathing disaster area. Before she had even served her first customer she had been told one day to empty a window which, as usual, displayed a beautiful arrangement of goods. In this case the centre-piece was a large pyramid of canned or bottle produce set on a circular plate-glass table which in turn stood on a wooden support.

Not thinking to dismantle the thing systematically, Thelma tore into one side of the stack with gusto, packing the tins away in a box as she worked. When the inevitable disaster struck, it was truly spectacular. Not only did the pyramid collapse, but the plate-glass stand went too - and the entire assemblage crashed straight through the shop window onto the pavement. Yet Mr. Lunn, Thelma recalls, was very patient and understanding with her. "We should have shown you how to go about it," he said, reproaching himself. "It's our own fault, really".

He was not quite such a model of forbearance, however, when the grand day came when Thelma was to serve her first customer. Her first customer was a little boy carrying an empty glass jar and clutching four pennies. He wanted a pound of golden syrup. Thelma took the jar, went out to the store-room, filled it from the puncheon, and then went proudly back into the shop to ring up her first takings. Some considerable time later there was an enraged bellow from the back of the shop. Mr. Lunn had been to the back room and found himself ankle deep in syrup.

Thelma had not, it appeared, shut the outlet properly. "What'll I do?" she wailed. "You've done it; you clear it up," was the answer. So Thelma smothered the sticky mess with sawdust and reached for a shovel.

She was sent to the provisions side. "She can't do any damage there," her manager said. Her new manager was Mr. Tom Priestley, the head girl Miss Kathleen Self. The two were courting, although that was a well-kept secret among the staff: Jackson's made it a policy never to allow a couple to work together. On the day the pair were to go and buy their engagement ring they wanted very much to take their lunch-break together. This was against the rules since it would leave a junior hand - Thelma - in charge alone, although Mr. Lunn in groceries would be in charge of the entire premises.

During the break Mr. Lunn came through and told Thelma to take a stack of eggs out of the window and set them on the counter. He enquired as to the whereabouts of Miss Self and Thelma told him she'd just popped out for a moment. She then picked up four of the trays - ten dozen eggs in total - and started for the counter. On the way her foot landed on a piece of bacon-rind that someone had carelessly left on the polished parquet floor. She skidded - and dropped her load.

"Well," Mr. Lunn said with a sigh, "I don't suppose we can blame you for someone else leaving bacon on the floor. Go on, clear it up." It was back to the sawdust and the shovel. When Thelma had done she stood back and admired her work. The floor fairly gleamed. "By heck," she said, "that's put a right good sheen on that floor."

At that precise moment the door opened and the courting couple entered, gazing rapturously into each other's eyes. One after the other they skidded, on their backs, the entire length of the shop, crashing into the cash desk at the far end. Their injuries weren't serious, and they were both back at work within a day or two.

Three days later Thelma was sent to Severn Street - and was halfway there, head down and dragging her heels, when they chased after her and confessed it was only a joke.

However, Thelma's days as a re-arranger of shop fittings were numbered. She was about to find her true vocation - in her own words "her destiny". The butcher at Bean Street had been called up into the armed forces; and the man who had replaced him was fired for short-changing the customers. His trick was to 'palm' a coin - maybe a shilling or a half-crown - and as he swabbed the counter to let it drop through the drain-hole into the drip-tray. In desperation, the company had Mr. Lunn take over temporarily while they sought a replacement. Then they had the bright idea of asking Thelma to go on the counter. She shuddered at the thought of it. Just for a month, they pleaded; to help us out of a jam.

Thelma relented. Just so long as it was only for a month, and so long as she didn't have to do anything horrid like cut up pieces of meat. On her first morning she had a customer who insisted on having some meat cut specially. Mr. Lunn was tied up elsewhere, so Thelma had a go with the knives. She loved it, and her fate was sealed.

Her responsibilities soon mounted. Mr. Lunn was transferred to Driffield, and although Dick Lyons came in from Spring Bank each day to cut meat for her she was often alone. It was to be from Dick Lyons that she would learn the trade. He was, she remembers, a hard task-master but a fantastic teacher.

Her mother was outraged. The idea of a young lady cutting up meat shocked her. But as Thelma pointed out to her, butchering wasn't such a bad job as all that. It was cleaner than a lot of people realised: if she followed Dick's guidance she stayed pretty clean, and there was always hot water available, which was more than could be said about the provision hands - always covered in bacon-grease and butter.

Thelma soon learned that this was a highly skilled craft. The Lyons brothers, she recalls, were turning out work as close to perfection as was possible in terms of preparation and presentation. She also learned how jealous a butcher - like any craftsman - was of his tools. Let anyone even touch one of Dick's knives, let alone use it, and there would be hell to pay. He maintained that the different weight of a person's hand, the way in which they wielded the blade, could dull an edge that he had perfected over weeks of careful honing.

Naturally, Thelma attracted comment, being a woman in what was supposed to be a man's world. She found she had to gain the respect of her fellows by proving herself their equal. This even carried on into her days as a supervisor - the only woman doing that job at the time. She even remembers a light-hearted bet she once had with a delivery driver that she couldn't shoulder a side of beef and take it through into the shop. She won half a crown off him, and several more the same week as she enticed other people into a little gamble. At the end of the week she gave all her winnings back: 2/6 was still a fortune then. But she had proved her point. "I was as strong as a little bull in those days," she says.

During the war Bean Street was particularly busy. It was a dropping-off point for all the meat which was allocated to the half-dozen Jackson's butchers on the west side of the city, Bright Street being the corresponding depot for the east side.

Having found her metier, and being given considerable responsibility at Bean Street didn't mean that Thelma's penchant for calamity had deserted her. For it was here that one of her most spectacular escapades took place. Thelma fondly recalls the wartime days when Jackson's had to resort to horse-and-cart deliveries. She adored the horse that called at the shop and would find a carrot for him every day, or perhaps a sugar-lump, then go and spend a minute or two fondling him. The driver, Little Harry, she remembers, "got nothing but a cup of tea and a lot of lip".

One particularly busy morning when the shop was full of customers, the deliveryman came and Thelma forgot all about the treat for the horse. Unfortunately the horse, a creature of habit, did not. After stamping his feet a time or two he grew impatient. He mounted the kerb, approached the doorway and tried to enter the shop. While the customers stood and gaped the horse made a beeline for Thelma, a hurt look on his face - and promptly wedged himself in the doorway.

With Little Harry inside pushing, and the manager outside pulling on the cart, and Thelma shoving sugar lumps into the horse's mouth as fast as she could find enough coupons, they finally got the beast free. Miraculously there was no real damage - "and the customers loved every minute of it"!

After the war as men returned from the armed

forces and a number of married women left work, things returned to normal. Thelma was exhausted: she had run this busy shop more or less single-handed, never losing any money and managing to win more customers. She had desperately wanted to go into the forces herself, for the experience, and had been shocked to find that Gordon Russell, the shops supervisor, had been getting her deferred on the grounds that she was engaged in work vital to the war effort. Ironically, when she did manage to get as far as

a medical, she failed it, and that was the end of that ambition.

By way of a rest-cure after the war, she was sent to Spring Bank to learn the book-keeping side of things for twelve weeks under Mabel Pulford. When that was over with she started work in the butchery under her old mentor Dick Lyons, remaining there until 1964 when she was made a supervisor.

Meat produce on display. At one time there were thirty-five varieties of sausage alone.

Chapter Seven

ANCILLARY SERVICES

As the retail side of the business grew, and with it the bakery and meat divisions which served the shops, so a whole range of ancillary services were developed. These encompassed a wide variety of activities, but essentially revolved around transportation and the fitting out and general repair of the company's properties - mainly the factory sites and the shops.

For many years the services and transport divisions were to be closely linked. Tensions, or conflicts of interest, which ultimately led to the two areas separating, came about as the result of a number of factors. Firstly, there was the transport division's diversification into servicing and selling vehicles to customers outside the company, to the motoring public at large through autonomous agencies. And secondly there was the retail expansion - although this would come some time later - into the Grandways enterprise, which utilized the services division. Thirdly, the two sides grew apart as they moved in different directions at different speeds.

A fourth major factor was that these divisions were encouraged by the board to seek contracts outside of Jackson's ambit. This says a lot about the company's general business philosophy and its view of its employees. It also reflects one of the dynamics of a family business with members of a new generation occasionally coming into an established organisation: these younger members feel the need to have their own individual spheres of activity, somewhere to channel their own fresh energies. What better, then, than businesses within businesses?

It was further considered that having engaged - or in some instances "poached" - the very best craftsmen in the area, the company could not hope to hold onto them if it did not offer some challenge, variety or interest. Good men - and many of these had indeed been hand-picked - would either become stale, complacent, or would take themselves off to rival firms. Additionally, since one division would charge another for work done in-house, there needed to be some confidence in each division's ability to offer both fair and competitive prices. Being able to win outside contracts on the basis of prices arrived at within the company provided sound assurances that the shop-fitters or joiners or motor mechanics were indeed worth what they were charging. That is not to say that sections within the firm didn't from time to time complain that they were being 'milked': to this day some former executives maintain - or admit - that

John Holmes, driver, with horse-drawn van, 1912. Some of these horses got their noses in where they weren't wanted.

A row of hand-carts for door-to-door confectionery sales. These 1938 models cost £16 apiece.

Jackson's Humber van, number 14. This was one of the firm's very first motor vehicles, bought in 1908.

this occurred. But in theory the outside work did safeguard certain standards. Just as importantly, of course, it provided continuity of work and employment, as well as allowing for accelerated growth and expansion.

Jackson's began, naturally, using horse-drawn transport to haul goods from their warehouses and factories to the shops, and from the shops to customers' doors. Hand-carts too were in use and as late as July 1938 the company invested in sixteen smart new carts with rigid lids to keep the rain off the goods, mostly bread and confectionery sold door-to-door.

With the horse-drawn and hand-pulled carts and wagons, then, joiners and painters would be hired, along with motor mechanics and electricians, to maintain this varied fleet. These tradesmen, of course, with the exception of the motor mechanics, would also be engaged in shop-fitting and property repairs. The first record of a motor vehicle being bought by Jackson's is for October 23 1908, but it was not until August 1931 that the company bought a garage in Blundell Street for £1800, creating a new transport department under Jack Oughtred and leaving the Victoria Street site where wagons and vans had previously been garaged. By 1933 there was a fleet of some thirty motor vehicles.

Through the 1930s the company bought and sold, or rented, a succession of premises to accommodate this division. In 1935, for example, they rented a garage in Lister Street from East Yorkshire Motor Services. In July 1937 they sold most of the Blundell Street premises, keeping two smaller properties in Norfolk Terrace, and in the same year renting number 3, Clarendon Street. Here they housed the garage's office staff and its electricians. Then in September of 1938 they rented 23 Mytongate to house their joiners, electricians and painters as well as a portion of the publicity staff. The publicity staff were responsible for anything from price tickets to notices of special offers, to displays announcing events at Paragon Street ballroom, even to devising and fabricating floats for the Lord Mayor's parade.

In 1936 Jackson's rented a garage at Doncaster, presumably to house and maintain their vehicles working out of the depot there, and another similar site in York, within the city walls along Skeldergate. They also bought for good measure a garage with petrol pumps out at Withernsea.

Tommy Jackson, who started work at the Derringham Street factory as a dough mixer in 1937, remembers that although there were a number of motor lorries delivering bread at that time, the flour still arrived at the bakery in one-hundredweight hessian sacks on flat horse-drawn wagons. The 1935 film about Jackson's, "Food For Thought", made and distributed by Temple Films to advertise the company and its products, shows just such a wagon, drawn by two heavy horses, leaving Rank's mill and entering Derringham Street.

When Tommy got out of the factory, however, and went delivering bread it was with one of the hand-pulled barrows. It held a hundred loaves, unwrapped, which he would frequently have to deposit on his customers' door-steps.

Allan Jewsbury was a shops delivery driver but towards the end of his career spent more of his time running errands for various directors and their families. He had started work in 1936 as an errand-boy in Dairycoates branch just off Hessle Road. He earned seven shillings and six pence a week, of which he handed over five shillings to his mother. His first job in the morning would be to cycle in to the offices, then in Spring Bank, and hand over the shops' orders for the day.

Although horse-drawn vehicles were just about phased out by this time they were re-introduced at the outbreak of war in 1939 as one of a number of economy measures, only being dispensed with in the late forties. It must have been with an acute sense of irony that the Jackson's board in October 1939, having seen thirteen of their motor vans commandeered by H.M. Government, went out and bought twenty-five horses, a number of carts and harnesses, along with a house, stables and a yard in Trinity Street, opposite the factory site on the other side of Derringham Street.

A month later they were to buy four steam wagons as a hedge against the rationing of petroleum which had come into effect in September 1939. Memories of those steam-wagons are still fresh in the mind of Sid Charlton. He recalls John Flew, who had joined the company as transport manager in 1932, travelling to Cardiff to buy one second-hand. He describes it as "part-way between a lorry and a railway carriage". It was in fact their first Sentinel. It had pneumatic tyres and was capable of speeds of up to fifty miles an hour. It ran on coal. Jackson's used these vehicles for delivering bread to Lincoln and to Fulford barracks in York, as well as to a number of other Army sites where they had secured contracts which lasted for the duration of the war.

The only trouble with the wagon, Sid recalls, with a typical engineer's mistrust of the operator, was that no-one really knew how to drive the thing. The regular drivers were scared witless of the steam, which was continually blasting out through the escape or safety valve; and, hardly surprisingly, they couldn't get the hang of having to press the accelerator down in order to stop the machine!

Another considerable difficulty was the provision of water along the route - these were, like railway engines, thirsty beasts. When it was decided to use the lorry on the Lincoln run Sid had to set out on his faithful Norton to plan a route and locate a few convenient watering-holes. He found some, but apparently not enough. When the run started he was always getting calls to go and help drivers who had run into difficulties, more often than not a shortage of water. He recalls the time when the lorry was stopped out in the country. Seeing a cottage nearby, Sid peered over the fence that surrounded the garden and was delighted to spot a large butt full to the brim with rain-water. Not troubling to ask the inhabitants, he slung the inlet hose over the fence, sucked the barrel dry, and made tracks!

Sometimes it was naked fear rather than ignorance which stalled the steam-lorry. Sid was once called out to a laden wagon part way up the long incline on the A15 going into Lincoln. "Why, there's nothing wrong with this," he told the crew when he arrived on the scene. "She just wants opening up to maximum power." Sid proceeded to stoke it up to 250 lbs per square inch at which point, naturally, the safety valve blew. The driver and his mate bolted "like a couple of frightened horses" and Sid was left to drive the machine majestically up the hill with the crew panting and gasping in its wake.

An early motorised van sporting Jackson's name and 'phone number. All the shops had 'phones by 1933.

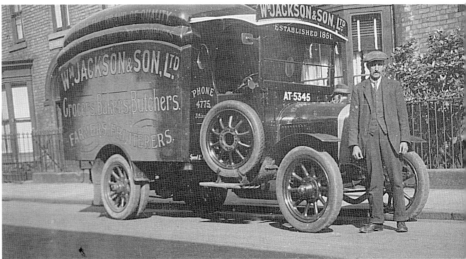

This 'cottage loaf' was one of a number of novelty vans. Another was done up as a pork pie.

Jackson's transport outside Brown's Central Stores, Withernsea. From the left: a Model 1924 T Ford (driver Bob Morrill); a Model A Ford (driver E. Moisley of Cottingham Meat); a two-ton Morris (Tommy Chapman); a Morris van.

A further reminder of the steam wagon's idiosyncrasies comes from a story Sid tells of the time he had to bring one back from York. He left the city in thick fog, but around Wilberfoss it lifted. As he trundled along he remarked on how little traffic there was: normally there would have been a succession of cars overtaking him, lorries at that time being restricted to twenty miles an hour. When he pulled over some miles further along the road, an oncoming lorry having signalled to him, an endless stream of vehicles sped past him, all covered with black smuts. They'd crawled all the way thinking they were still in the fog, Sid realised. "In fact, it was nothing but the trail of black smoke pouring out of my exhaust!"

While people like Sid were the pioneers of Jackson's motorised transport fleet, Walter Varney was a pioneer on the shop-fitting side. He joined Jackson's in 1934 at the age of fourteen as an apprentice joiner. His father already worked for the firm as a delivery cart driver working between the huge warehouse in Wellington Street and the various shops. He had attended the lad's interview with Bompy Hall in the Spring Bank offices. The joiners' shop at this time was in Norfolk Terrace adjoining the Blundell Street properties. "In this shop," he recalls, "we made absolutely everything for the company." The ground floor housed the motor transport department and fitters' shops. The paint shop, polishers' and joiners' shops being on the first floor.

A Jackson's van, with slogan. For a long time Jack Oughtred had insisted on having nothing but the firm's name on the side. "If they want to know what we do, they can ask," he said.

A van still proudly proclaims Mackman's achievements, long after he had gone.

Jackson's fitters re-furbish a shop-front.

Here we see how intimately linked the various departments were. Walt's foreman was Dick Lockwood, the site general manager John Flew. Walt's first job was to keep two glue kettles full and hot, and to make absolutely sure that they never burned. "The smell of burning fish glue," he reflects, "is never to be forgotten." As well as that he would be detailed to collect items from the various timber companies the firm dealt with, and this he would do using a hand-cart - "not a very pleasant job on a wet day."

After a year Walt progressed to learning the rudiments of carpentry, then moved on to making simple items such as three-, four- or eight-tread steps for the shops. The variety of work that Walt and the other tradesmen undertook once more illustrates the scope of the firm's activities. It all added up to a wonderful proving-ground for a young joiner. One week he might be fabricating a shop counter according to the standard design - a one-and-a-half inch mahogany top with a facade decorated with copper strips. The next he might be working on the solid teak tubs in which a fresh-killed pig would be turned and scraped clean. Or he might be repairing the stout posts of the corrals where the animals awaited slaughter, or for the killing-pens themselves. Alternatively he might be assigned to repairing and creosoting the fences or fixing the pavilion up at the Inglemire Lane sports ground. Along the way he could observe - and learn from - what he believed to be "the finest craftsmen in Hull" as they applied the seven coats of paint to the company's vans, then the name in gold leaf followed by two coats of protective varnish.

An apprenticeship in those days might last seven years, which included three nights a week attendance at the Technical College in Park Street, seven o'clock to nine-thirty with one night set aside for homework. "And," Walt remembers, "you went to bed tired."

Jack Gallant came to Jackson's in May 1933 as an electrician. He had served most of his time as an apprentice with another local firm but, due to the Depression, he found he was working some weeks and not others. When the chance came to go to Jackson's, whose reputation for craftsmanship and security was held in high esteem throughout his trade, he jumped at it. He knew, for example, that the money wouldn't be that great, but he also knew that he would be treated well if he was sick. In addition, they were offering him two weeks' paid holiday which was, as far as he knew, unheard of at the time.

Jack never did get to complete his apprenticeship, but that didn't stand in the way of his rising to a directorship of Jackson's Services before he retired in

Salesmen with vehicles at Doncaster depot.

This retail vehicle, seen on a Doncaster estate, won a competition for cleanest van in 1948.

An early 'artic' with detailed inventory of its load.

1979. He began work at Blundell Street where there were a manager, four office girls, five fitters, four painters and a French polisher - one of the Quine brothers. Stan Tillotson, later another director of the company, was senior electrician, and there was a scale mechanic who doubled as van driver. Here once more we see Jackson's preferring to secure the skills they required in-house rather than having to depend on outside agencies.

As an electrician Jack worked on the factory lights and equipment, in the shops, and on the transport fleet. He was, in his own words, "something of a jack of all trades". It was while working around the factory that he got to know Jack Oughtred whom he remembers as being very sociable over a glass of whisky. Later he would be asked to go and work on Jack's farm in upper Teesdale, Wodencroft, which he had bought in 1945. Wodencroft was a country house with one hundred upland acres not far from Barnard Castle, once an old boarding-school and the model for Charles Dickens' Dotheboys Hall.

Another long-serving Jackson's craftsman, Alf Turner, spent several months at Wodencroft, first surveying the building, then designing and supervising the fabrication of a whole range of new fitments to be made up at Mytongate. Alf was another traditional joiner, although he remembers quite vividly the changes after the war to a more modern style of shop-fitting. "I've handled acres, never mind feet, of formica," he recalls. "And making the sheets match was the devil's own job: you'd be surprised how many shades of white you can find!" This was a far cry from the oak shop-

The Travelling Shop

Will be at Your Door On:—

	Monday	Wednesday	Friday
Appleton Road	12.45	9.15	9.15
Thorgel Close	1.00	9.30	9.30
Salton Close	1.15	9.45	9.45
Ebberston Grove	1.30	10.00	10.00
Castleton Avenue	1.45	10.15	10.15
Slingby Close	2.00	10.30	10.30
Cropton Road	2.15	10.45	10.45
Appleton Road	3.45	12.30	12.30
Knapton Avenue	4.30	2.30	2.30
Grammar School Road	4.45	2.45	2.45
Skelton Avenue	5.00	3.00	3.00
Hartoft Road	5.15	3.15	3.15
Cloughton Close	5.30	3.30	3.30
Hutton Close	5.45	3.45	3.45
Hartoft Road	6.00	4.15	4.15
Cropton Road	6.15	4.30	4.30

	Tuesday	Thursday	Saturday
Northolme Crescent	9.15	9.15	9.15
Northo'm~ Road	9.30	9.30	9.30
Gisburn Road	9.40	9.40	10.00
Sandingdale Road	9.45	9.45	10.30
Glam's Road	10.00	10.00	10.45
Belvedere Road	10.15	10.15	11.00
Fishmor Avenue	11.00	11.00	12.00
Springville Avenue	11.15	11.15	12.30

Castleway	12.00	12.00	Half Day
Beacon Close	12.15	12.15	Half Day
All Saints Close	12.30	12.30	Half Day
Danes Drive	12.45	12.45	Half Day
Bannister Close	1.00	1.00	Half Day
Station Road	1.10	1.10	Half Day
Champney Close	1.15	1.15	Half Day
Rokeby Avenue	2.30	2.30	Half Day
Rokeby Park	3.00	3.00	Half Day
Spring Gardens	3.30	3.30	Half Day

If you require a special call——Please ring Tel. 35394.

When arrangements will be made to call on you as requested.

Travelling Shop on its round. Note the poster regarding rationing, still in force for some goods ten years after the war.

Timetable for the travelling shop taken from Jackson's own "Travelling Shop Times".

fittings he made up at Blundell Street under Dick Lockwood's supervision when he first started with the firm in 1934, before being moved into the factory.

Gallant, like Turner, was quite close to the Oughtred family. He particularly remembers Jack's wife Phyllis - in his words "a marvellous woman" who, although she had the use of a Bentley, would be quite content, if need be, to take a ride to the shops sitting next to Jack in his dirty old electrician's van. Of Doris, her sister, he has one particular memory: it was she who reminded him - as if he needed it - to use the back stairs when he came to work at her house.

The tradesmen's move to Mytongate came in the late thirties. When war broke out Jack found himself roped in with the joiners and painters, boarding up shop windows and slapping black paint on everything. With the black-out there was less electrical installation work and it was all hands to the pump. In 1941 he joined the Army, spending the next six years in service, much of the time in North and East Africa. When he came out in 1947 some considerable changes were, or were about to be, effected.

What happened was that the motor transport side and the shop-fitting side were brought together formally in one company, an arrangement which was to last through to the early 1970s. Through the war the maintenance of motor vehicles had been undertaken on a site at the back of Paragon Motors on Boothferry Road. In 1946 this depot was servicing some hundred vehicles, Mr. T.C. Waite taking charge in April 1946. In August of that year a new company was incorporated, the Crystal Motor, General and Electrical Engineering Company Limited, with a board consisting of Eric Soulsby (chairman), Jack

Oughtred, T.F. Dodsworth, Gordon Russell and John Flew. All of these were, of course, Jackson's men, yet the new company had, in legal terms, nothing to do with the parent company. It was, in theory, independent. At about the same time, in the summer of 1947, a number of houses were cleared from Bank Street and the new outfit, describing itself as "motor vehicle repairers and specialist joiners and electricians" moved in. A fourth important division of the company had now taken shape.

Damaged vehicles await repair in the Bank Street garage.

Chapter Eight

A NEW STYLE OF SHOPPING

During the war, as we have seen, Jackson's had been planning ahead. Not only had a number of bakeries been acquired in the wider region, but several new retail outlets had been bought.

In 1930 the company had owned a total of sixty-two separate units, more or less exclusively in Hull. By 1939 this total had risen to eighty and included shops as far out as York, Withernsea, Doncaster, Leeds and Harrogate. The bakery acquisitions at Wakefield, Scunthorpe, Harrogate and Dudley all included retail outlets too, no less than five at Dudley. In 1944 the country grocery Wilson's of Weaverthorpe had been added.

A more ambitious acquisition was the firm of Barkers Ltd, a south Yorkshire company comprising nine shops in Castleford, Wakefield, Normanton and a number of others in the Leeds area. Later that year, 1948, a Featherstone branch was added. Finally, one more purchase - the York firm of John Cross - brought another seven shops into the fold. The total number of units was now in the region of one hundred and fifteen.

Changes were in the wind, however. Not all the shops were doing as well as previously, and a good many were in any case very small, back-street establishments. Several still bore the scars of war; and the population was shifting as damaged or sub-standard housing was cleared after the war. Many shops too were parts of a group of four or five which effectively comprised one large shop. There was certainly scope for rationalisation.

The Jackson's board was not unaware of the need to move forward. Gordon Russell, promoted to director in charge of shops in 1945, had been to the United States and seen the future of retailing there. And the future was in self-service. In May 1945, barely a week after VE Day, members of the board along with thirty or forty shop managers and manageresses were apparently very impressed by a 'lantern show' sponsored by National Cash Registers which illustrated the American self-service store concept.

Wilson's (Weaverthorpe) Ltd., a country grocer bought by Jackson's towards the end of the war.

On November 27th 1948 the rented premises at 336-338 Priory Road was opened as the company's first self-service store. It was in fact the first of its kind in the Hull area, beating William Cusson's by a mere ten days. With the exception of ice-cream and certain rationed goods customers were invited to serve themselves with

The new 'Jackson's of ...' concept, with its now familiar turquoise livery, sits comfortably with the old inner city store fronts.

Jackson's have owned two racehorses, Tryton Lines and Friendly Baker (seen here with top northern jockey Mark Birch sporting the Grandways silks). Since 1969 the company has sponsored a number of race meetings, notably at Beverley, Thirsk, Ripon and Market Rasen.

These faded mosaics were a feature of a number of classic Jackson's facades designed by Hull architects Gelder & Kitchen. Grafton Street, Newland Avenue, opened in 1913 (right), Chanterlands Avenue, Marlborough Avenue, opened in 1928. (left)

groceries, provisions, bread and confectionery, fresh fruit and vegetables, even hardware. During the first week of the experiment the public were reported to be reacting well, and cash takings were appreciably increased despite the adverse weather conditions. Over the longer term, however, the increase was not enough to warrant the additional cost of extending the experiment. It was noted that the wrapping of goods displayed was costly. And, far from saving on staff costs, one extra employee had been taken on. Within a year Priory Street reverted to a normal department-store format. As Richard Hall, the grand-son of 'Bompy', noted in his diary, "It would appear that the public of Hull are not yet sufficiently food conscious to appreciate this hygienic form of service. But," he added, "the time will assuredly come!"

Hall was right in his prophesy. By 1950 there were some five hundred such shops operating in Britain, and by 1957 somewhere in the region of three and a half thousand.

Meanwhile Jackson's continued to make every effort to move with the times. In 1953 refrigerated counters were introduced for the display of cooked meats. In February 1955 the first pre-packaged cheese and bacon, prepared at the central warehouse, made their appearance. And in that same year as many as a dozen shops were closed down as the board sought to cut overheads and weed out unproductive units. These included three adjacent departments at 249-251 Anlaby Road, three more at 130-132 Hessle Road, and the confectionery at 309 Hedon Road.

Quite when Jackson's first successful supermarket was opened is subject to hot debate. This may be because such terms as 'supermarket', 'self-service grocery' and 'convenience store' become confused in people's memories. Suffice it to say that a number of further attempts were planned - and effected - to promote the self-service idea.

In 1954 plans were under way to convert Eton Street to "the Woolworth semi-self-service principle". Prototype fixtures and fittings were made, but it was later decided to switch to Newington branch at 485a Anlaby Road. Eton Street was not forgotten, however. In the following year plans were afoot to convert it to a "quick-sale super store", and it opened as such in July of 1955.

In July 1960 Gordon Russell again visited the United States on a fact-finding tour, and in November the Toll Gavel, Beverley, branch opened after extensive alterations as "our first self-service food market". The following month a new supermarket was opened at Boothferry Road, Goole, once more a conversion of a traditional shop. "Customers poured into the shops at such a rate that they had to be kept waiting to allow those who had made their purchases to get out."

The conversion which most people seem to remember, however, is that of Grafton Street at 118-120 Newland Avenue. This was the first successful conversion of a traditional Jackson's grocery within the city. It had originally opened in 1913 as a provisions merchants'. At some stage a confectioner's adjoined the premises, but in the 1950s this was leased out to Sewell's the fruiterer. The changeover to self-service was quite abrupt. Dorothy Scholefield, who was assistant manager at the time, remembers the shop-fitters coming in on the Saturday afternoon while customers were still being served, and starting to haul the counters out.

Rear entrance of Grandways. On the first day the shelves were re- stocked three times.

The replacement fixtures were installed rapidly - facilitated by the fact that they were merely temporary: no-one was sure that this experiment would succeed. According to Dorothy they had been brought in from another shop where the change had been tried but not been a success. At closing time that Saturday the staff all set to, piling the stock onto bread trays and loading it into vans which had backed up to the rear entrance. These were then locked up while the fitters set to work. They were at it all through the night and the rest of the weekend, the staff coming in on Sunday to learn the new tills in time for re-stocking on Monday and opening on the Tuesday.

Grafton Street was not yet a supermarket as we know the term today. In some areas of the shop customers did help themselves from the shelves, but bread and cakes, for example, had to be bagged and price-marked by the staff before being taken to the check-out and paid for. Bacon and cheese, too, were still served in the traditional way, except that no money changed hands at the counter.

In the first few days Dorothy recalls having to go outside and persuade the customers through the door. It was all a little weird and wonderful for many of them. "Come on, in," she coaxed them. "You don't

The first Grandways in New York Road, Leeds, opened March 9, 1961. It was demolished in January 1968 to make way for road improvements.

This pre-1914 calculator, made in Leipzig, was put out to grass at Rotherham but reclaimed by headquarters in 1994 as a valuable historical artifact.

This classic delivery bicycle now stands in the foyer of Jacksons Derringham Street offices.

have to buy anything. Just take a basket and have a look around." But this was not the way people had learned to shop, and it took a while for them to get accustomed to it. And despite encouraging her clientele to feel at ease, Dorothy herself was far from relaxed. Seeing people pick up the neatly arranged goods and put them back -often in the wrong place - irritated her. She admits, "I felt like tapping the back of their hands for being so forward!" She found herself also regretting the passing of the personal service she had been used to.

Grafton Street, "a fully-fledged superette", was a success. In the first week the takings were three times what they had been the week before. Before long the company was waiting for Sewell's lease to expire, anxious to get on with knocking through into next door. Later, after they had effected that change they would buy up Mallory's hardware and knock into that too. With enlarged shop premises the warehouse at the back became inadequate, and a new storage facility had to be made on the first floor.

It was around this time that Fred Standing joined the company. He had learned the grocery trade down south, at Ramsgate, then worked for some years for Guildford's Stores in Surrey. He had contacted the Institute of Grocers to ask whether they knew of any opportunities for someone in his position to spread his wings: he could see little scope for advancement where he was, albeit in a shop with over fifty staff.

He was eventually contacted by Gordon Russell, and admits to coming north half hoping for a slightly easier life and the chance to spend more time with his family. He didn't get it, being thrust into what was a retailing revolution alongside G.R. and Alf Stubbins,

the chief shops' supervisor. He was thrown in at the deep end, being made a supervisor with ten stores to look after. His fellow supervisors at this time included Ted Hewson, Roy Taylor, Con Navier on the butchery side, Vince Pearson on fruit, and Vera Owen in bread and confectionery.

Fred was involved in the conversions at Beverley and Goole which pre-dated the Grafton Street alterations by a year or so. Goole he remembers as 'Sleepy Hollow' - until it was converted and its takings doubled overnight. He remembers considerable public resistance to the self-service idea. He was not alone in having to stand at the shop entrance to hand out baskets to people and encourage them to try out the new way. Everything that the modern shopper now takes for granted had to be conceived, experimented with and painstakingly planned. Initially no-one was sure what goods should be placed where. Should the popular items and necessities be easy to reach, or should the more exotic - and profitable - items take precedence? And how might managers find out how their customers were shopping? At the beginning, as an example, Fred cites the case of tea and coffee, which was placed nearest the entrance. He soon realised that greengrocery was preferable for its attractive colours. It was also seen that the more common everyday items - bacon and cheese, for example - were best placed at the far end of the shop in order that customers would pass by all the other attractively displayed goods on their way through. As an experiment some managers were even asked to dust the floor near the entrance with fine chalk dust and then note which route most footprints followed. "I suppose you'd call it basic market research," one former manager remarked.

A typical scene inside Grandways. On the first day police had to be brought in to control the crowd of bargain-hunters.

The shape of things to come. Lorry in Grandways colours outside the Balderton (Newark) store, mid-'80s.

Check-out staff now had most contact with the public - and therefore bore the brunt of any complaints. They had to learn patience and charm, as well as an encyclopaedic knowledge of every item in the shop, its price, and its whereabouts. But in keeping the customers sweet they were helped - it is claimed - by the introduction of piped music designed to soothe the nerves.

The single most significant development for Jackson's retail side, however, came about in March of 1961. In that year the Conservative government of Harold Macmillan was facing a growing public and commercial discontent with the policy of Resale Price Maintenance - that is, laws which permitted manufacturers to recommend and insist upon a certain base price being attached to their goods as part of a contract whereby they supplied those goods to the retailers. As a small but growing number of shops challenged this agreement and threatened to cut prices regardless, a number of legal injunctions from the manufacturing side forced the withdrawal of discounts and bargain price offers.

There was no doubt, however, that British shopping habits were changing and the customer adopting a more flexible approach: they were learning to go where the price was best. There were now some six thousand supermarkets nationwide; and then discount stores made their appearance - for example, Tesco's, with twenty-four branches open by early 1962.

A significant factor in the growth of the cut-price supermarkets was that of size. Supermarkets aimed to cut labour costs - the customer helping herself - and thus reduce prices. Cutting prices reduced the profit margin and thus required a larger sales volume. So "pile it high and sell it cheap" became the axiom for the new entrepreneurs. In order to maximise profits, therefore, supermarkets had to think big. They also found it desirable to stock not only a full range of fresh and packaged foods, but also an increasing number of non-food items, on which the profit margin was traditionally much higher. Non-foods, in addition, offered more potential for long-term growth: in essence the food market is limited, since people can only eat a certain amount per week. But the non-food market, the consumer goods which were coming onto the market in this period, could in theory expand indefinitely, Who, in the late fifties, would have imagined the three and four-television household so commonplace today?

The war that was looming between a retail sector anxious to break into the large-scale, cut-price sphere and the manufacturers, along with the traditional specialist stockists of electrical goods, for example, was noted by the Financial Times amongst others. "The spread of car ownership in the U.K.," it warned in February 1961, "combined with the strong price-consciousness of the middle-class consumer, has undoubtedly created a large market for the stripped-down methods of the new retailers."

Another factor in the equation was the slump in demand in the early sixties, particularly in such previously healthy sectors as electrical goods. Economists at the time felt that the price range of goods, from cars to confectionery, might be reduced by as much as 5% if R.P.M. was abolished. It is against this background, and the Board of Trade Inquiry into the practice of R.P.M., that the next phase of the Jackson's story needs to be seen.

MOPPED UP!

By MICHAEL KEMP

JEFFREY ROSE laughed off a £200 bill after being washed out of the mop trade yesterday.

"The court says we can't sell Prestige mops at 18s. 11d. instead of 30s.—so we just won't sell these mops," he said.

He had just heard Mr. Justice Cross in the High Court grant Prestige Ltd., of

BUT CUT-PRICE JEFF ISN'T WASHED OUT

Holborn, London, an injunction stopping him selling their goods at cut prices.

Mr. Rose, 29-year-old ex-law student, now managing director of Grandways cut price store, Leeds, said afterwards: "We were bound to

lose the case. We wanted the public to see what fantastic profits are being made."

Before opening Grandways—where TV sets are £23 below list price, fridges £16 and electric irons £1—he spent three months in the U.S. studying methods.

If business keeps up the way it is going now he plans a chain of cut price shops in the North.

Taxi! And 29-year-old Jeffrey Rose, Britain's newest cut-price king, hails it with a mop. He is fighting for the right to slash prices ... and that goes for mops, too. Sketchpic by Don Price.

The retail revolution of the early 1960s attracted national press coverage. Grandways co-founder Jeff Rose steals the limelight.

Entrance to Grandways food hall, Vicar Lane, Leeds. Formerly the site of Willis Ludlow's department store.

Jackson's, as we have seen, always kept an eye on developments in the U.S.A. An F.T. report early in 1961 caught the eye of at least one board member who filed it away. This report showed how discount stores for card-carrying members - civil servants or armed forces veterans, for example - had bucked the recessionary trend in California and grown dramatically. Around the same time a report in the *Yorkshire Evening Post* spoke of an "American-style discount store" about to open in New York Road, Leeds.

The first Grandways opened on Thursday March 9th 1961 at ten in the morning. Full-page advertisements in the Post had trumpeted its imminent arrival:

> AT TEN O'CLOCK NEXT THURSDAY
> THE COST OF LIVING WILL
> DROP IN LEEDS.
> - GRANDWAYS -
> SERVE YOURSELF AND SAVE!!

The ad went on to say that at the new store customers could buy anything from a TV set to a tin of beans. This was to be, it went on, "the best news for shoppers since rationing ended". The ad listed the variety of goods on sale, and they did indeed include beans, and tea, sugar, toilet rolls, as well as TV sets. Radiograms (stereo) were reduced from a recommended price of £72 9s 0d to £63 8s 0d; gents' Italian-style suits were down from £6 5s 0d to a flat fiver; ladies' box-pleated skirts down from 37/6 to 22/10; Prestige MINIT mops from 30/- to 19/11; and Nylon Baby Doll Pyjamas, lace-trimmed in pink, lilac or gold - down from 22/6 to fourteen shillings and fourpence.

The opening was a spectacular success. Police had to be called in to control the crowds. As an advertisement in the Post exclaimed a week later, "Sorry about the queues! The crowds of delighted shoppers at Grandways have exceeded our wildest hopes. As you will see, we are now experimenting with an improved check-out system to speed things on."

The national press was also taking note, the F.T. calling Grandways "the first fully-fledged discount store to open in this country". As it reported, Grandways was new for two reasons: firstly for the comprehensive range of goods it stocked, and secondly for its site - outside the main shopping area in a street of garages and car dealers. In fact, although it was off the main streets it was just around the corner from Vicar Lane and the bus station, and advertised itself as "a minute from Briggate". The shop's premises themselves were a converted warehouse rented for a mere £4,000 a year as against the £50,000 that a more centrally sited and purpose-built store might have attracted. By May sales had reached a rate equivalent to £1 million a year.

The two men behind Grandways were, initially, unknown - and happy to remain that way. But twenty-eight-year-old William Bartfield and his partner thirty-year-old Jeffrey Rose, would soon achieve celebrity as they took to the courts to defend their right to pass on to the public the savings they were able to make.

The Daily Sketch (May 3 1961) featured a full-length picture of a suited and bespectacled Rose holding aloft a Prestige mop outside the High Court where he had been told to sell it at thirty shillings or not at all. Of course the public were behind him - and they voted with their feet. It would not be long before President of the Board of Trade Edward Heath would bring the unpopular R.P.M. to an end, but not before Jackson's, who were soon to acquire Grandways, faced up to a hundred separate writs against them from various manufacturers.

Jackson's part in all this was for the moment very discreet. Indeed, a directors' minute book note in February states the firm's policy of remaining anonymous and avoiding all publicity. Their name appears nowhere in the file of press cuttings. Yet they were there, running the food hall and making a mint. One third of the shop's entire floor-space was for food, "sold at cut-price in the conventional supermarket manner," as the F.T. had it.

The man behind Jackson's liaison with an outfit branded as 'cowboys' by the traditionalists was the dynamic Gordon Russell, on the main Jackson's board and also on the board of the company set up to run the Grandways enterprise which itself would be bought up by Jackson's in November 1961. G.R. had for some time envisioned a move into food - as well as general

Grandways in Dewsbury Road, Leeds, opened 1967. These stores were right at the heart of the community.

- discounting, and had been assembling around him the people he felt could help him carry out his plans, among them Fred Standing, who was to be the link man between the new chain and the parent company, and Peter Farley, a Leeds man who was taken on as Accountant.

Beverley, and particularly Goole, had been great successes, and G.R. was anxious for a move into Leeds, feeling that the city was ready for a discount store. While Russell had spent thirty years in food retailing, Rose and Bartfield were newcomers. They were much more 'ideas' men with a mission, or a point to prove. They sought to break into large-scale retailing. Moreover, they badly needed someone with Russell's expertise, particularly in food, which would be the bedrock of the new store. G.R.'s commitment to the Grandways idea was total, and the measure of it was his willingness to sink a sizeable amount of his own money into the enterprise and enter into a partnership with Rose and Bartfield acting as a private individual. He then leased the food concession to Jackson's, who paid rent to Associated Independent Merchandisers.

The Jackson's board were certainly keen to go in, and appear to have been quite happy to give their man a free hand. As G.R. said to Standing more than once, "If anyone queries anything we're doing, just refer them to me. I'm in charge of this operation." As well as being in charge, though, he also stood to carry the can if things went wrong. He told Standing quite bluntly before they opened, "If this thing doesn't work it's my job - and yours too - on the line." But G.R. never feared to take a chance if he felt it was worth it.

G.R. in fact played a central role in setting up this first Grandways operation. Yet throughout this time he kept the name of Jackson's well out of the limelight. Officially they were running the food hall, and that was all.

At the same time as Grandways' name was dominating the headlines Jackson's were preparing to move into another central site in the city. For some time they had been negotiating with Willis Ludlow to become concessionaires for their new foodhall, this time under their own name. The opening date for this venture fell a mere seven days after the Grandways opening - and was to be staffed mainly by employees now sweating blood in New York Road and trying to cope with the flood of customers.

Not only was Grandways' food hall overwhelmed by the demand, but it was evidently far too small for the volume of trade. On the very first day the shelves had to be re-stocked three times. It needed to double in size, at least. And the general running of the place was at times chaotic: while several individual concessionaires ran food, clothing, electrical, hardware and toy departments, for example, the check-outs were all run by A.I.M.'s own staff. While each item from a customer's basket was supposed to be logged against the individual concessionaire, this was not easily achieved: in the mad rush figures were entered incorrectly and there ensued heated debates amongst the various department heads at the end of the day's trading as to who was entitled to what share of the very considerable takings.

It was to be no more than a matter of a few months before Jackson's bought out Rose and Bartfield and took over the entire store. A.I.M. now became Grandways, William Jackson and Son the parent company. G.R. remained as managing director under

A typical Grandways store at Driffield, later sold to Iceland.

the chairmanship of Peter Oughtred and vice-chairmanship of Brian. Ron Mountifield, Richard Hall and R.A. McLaren formed the rest of the board. McLaren's was an important appointment. An ex-Harrods man who had come to Jackson's after the war, he had experience of, and interests in, areas other than food. His buying skills would be vital to the growth and success of the chain. G.R., known as an autocratic figure possessed of a dynamic personality, ran the show. He brooked no interference whatsoever from the rest of the Jackson's board - on which he still served as shops director. Indeed, it has been said that although the Oughtred cousins headed the Grandways board they kept a very low profile. Yet what the new board signally lacked was an expert in running a department store: these people were still for the most part food retailers, and the largest part of Grandways

was non-foods. So in May 1962 a general manager was hired, Fred Smith, a man still remembered in the West Riding as 'Mister Grandways'.

While the press ran stories about Rose and Bartfield's trips to the High Court, and the trade magazines ran features on the novel concept of the discount store - as well as enraged letters from small specialist traders threatened by them - the larger retailers were beating a path to Grandways' door. Mr. Jack Cohen himself, the founder of Tesco, paid at least one visit, as did representatives from Sainsbury's.

Grandways in New York Road was a phenomenon, making huge profits and genuinely rocking the retail world, yet it was to be two years before a second store opened in Goole, and a further year before Albion Street, Castleford, opened. Not until 1966-67 did Rothwell, Horsforth, York and Anlaby - Hull's first branch - make their appearance.

This is not to say that G.R. and his team were idle: far from it. The years from 1961 to mid-1966, when the Grandways expansion took off quite dramatically, saw no fewer than thirty-five Jackson's stores in the region undergo conversion to the supermarket format or, in the case of the smaller branches, to 'superette'. At the same time around twenty stores were closed. But if the closure of some smaller shops reflected the public's drift to larger self-service stores, William Jackson and Son were in fact merely re-adjusting, for in many cases it was the success of their own modern and convenient stores in a neighbourhood that rendered nearby units redundant or unprofitable. What they lost on the swings they gained on the roundabouts.

Two purpose-built Grandways stores: Riverside, Brigg opened in 1981 and Martongate, Bridlington opened in 1982 (Below).

It was in fact the impending closure of New York Road that spurred the Grandways expansion. More or less since its opening the site had been under threat of compulsory purchase. By the late sixties the ambitious road improvement schemes which were to re-shape Leeds were becoming a reality. New York Road was to close early in 1968. So by 1966 the Grandways people were actively looking around for other stores. Bartfield himself was able to offer three sites - those at Horsforth, Dewsbury Road and Rothwell - and these, as they opened, effectively replaced the New York Road turnover.

During the time of the Grandways expansion there appears to have been something of a gulf, both in geographical and in cultural terms, between the Leeds-based operation - it had its own admin staff at Wortley - and Hull. Grandways people were seen as outsiders, yet they saw themselves as a hugely successful team generating the profits which were in fact keeping Jackson's afloat. The threatened loss of New York Road had indeed caused some concern: the shop was taking up to £80,000 a *week* in 1967.

With its closure the management team there became, in effect, the administrative staff of the Grandways chain as it grew. By 1970 there were seventeen stores in the group. There was now a plan afoot to bring together Grandways and Jackson's own stores. G.R., not unnaturally, was vigorously opposed to the idea. But one way and another the original team was being broken up. Peter Farley went to Hull in 1970 as chief accountant - to be made quite well aware that his reputation with the Leeds group counted for nothing at headquarters! Fred Smith came to Hull in 1971 as training supervisor. And in 1972 G.R. died, on the golf course.

With Jackson's joining forces with Grandways the stores were now to be administered as three separate regional groups: Hull, under Terry Shaw; Lincolnshire under Tony Oxley; and Leeds under John Leach. From now on, in the words of one former staff member, it was "the Richard Hall show". McLaren too, on the trading side, was a dominant force in what was to be a period of tremendous success which really drove the company forward. Within the regions shops were divided between those having over 4000 square feet of floor-space and those below that capacity. The larger ones were to operate under the Grandways banner and would incorporate a non-foods side, the smaller ones remaining mostly food stores with a token amount of hardware, for example. It was perhaps this division, along with the uneasy amalgamation of the two very different chains, which led to the crisis of identity within the shops division which characterised the eighties. Pictures of the various shops in that period reveal a wide variety of sizes and styles under a confused array of names.

The expansion - and the conversions of some stores to the Grandways format - was to a considerable extent funded by Grandways' profits, and by the substantial sum received for the doomed New York Road site. Among the more successful conversions in the early seventies were those at Hessle and Cottingham. By 1980 the profits emanating from the united shops division under Richard Hall were very substantial, even though Jackson's as a whole was not now doing very well, the bakery, for example, facing severe difficulties.

In the early eighties, however, problems began to arise. Where the Leeds stores had had to face, in the seventies, fierce competition from new out-of-town superstores, it was now Hull's turn. Asda, opening in Bilton, had an immediate impact on the takings at

Holderness Road, until then the group's third most profitable store, and even on the Hornsea and Withernsea branches. Withernsea, as an example, saw its profits drop like a stone - from £130,000 a year to £20,000.

Grandways had been very much the brainchild of one Jackson's man - Gordon Russell - and had been for a number of years a singular organisation. It had, in a sense, come into the Jackson's fold reluctantly. Now, in 1982, another step linked it to a broader organisation of smaller shops: it joined NISA, the National Independent Supermarkets Association. Where the union with Jackson's would have been very much against the will of G.R., going into NISA would not have met with the whole-hearted enthusiasm of McLaren, the stores buyer. He, like most Grandways people, saw the chain as having some stature: in Yorkshire it accounted for as much as 7% of the retail food market. NISA, in his opinion, was 'small'. But the truth was that by the 1980s the opposition had become huge, and the combined buying power of NISA afforded its members considerably improved discounts.

If the Grandways story was one of spectacular success in the 1960s, and of consolidation in the '70s, it was one of responding to a changing market in the '80s. Joining NISA was one response; going into Central Distribution at Melton was another.

Chapter Nine

EXPANDING THE BAKERY DIVISION

In February of 1940 the bakery and shops of H. Adams & Son of Rotherham were acquired. Miss Agnes Matthewman, who had been working at Adams' Greasborough Street bakery since 1924 - and would continue to work for Jackson's until her retirement in 1969 - recalls that old Mr. Adams had died about this time. Of his three offspring only one had survived, and she was not interested in the business. It was a small company with three delivery vans and, as Agnes recalls, two or three shops.

It was not until late 1943 that Jackson's modernised and expanded the operation, putting in a reel oven for bread baking, but retaining the old draw-plate ovens for confectionery products. The company also acquired property in Hope Street, behind the bakery, where a row of houses would later be demolished to make way for new developments. Mr. Emmett was brought in from Hull as manager. At the same time Sid Slater, later to become Commercial Manager, started as a wages clerk. One of his earliest recollections of the bakery is the bins in which waste bread was collected. The men called it pig-bread - until they saw a gang of Italian POWs from Lodge Moor camp come by to collect it for their own consumption!

1944 also saw the acquisition of a number of other small businesses which would be foundation stones of the company's future expansion. T. Woodhouse of Dudley was bought for £13,000. It consisted of two large bake-houses and five shops, along with some

Mr George Ling, bakery manager at Harpers.

other small properties, five motor vehicles used for door-to-door sales, and a total of thirty-two staff. The business continued to trade as Woodhouse until 1959 when it became William Jackson (Dudley) Ltd. As in the later case of Crystal Motors the company was bought initially, not by Jackson's, but largely by their directors and shareholders - Doris and Phyllis Oughtred, their husbands Jack and Norman, Eric Soulsby, John Flew, Gordon Russell, T.F. Dodsworth and J.W. Carmichael.

The Dudley bakery in fact only operated for about twenty years, up to the early sixties. Even now, though, there are two things which almost everyone in the bakery division seems to remember about it. One is the almost legendary tale about the night shift having to be recruited from the local pub on a regular

Bakehouse and shop belonging to Mitchell (Scunthorpe) Ltd., another acquisition of 1944.

The premises of T. Swale, Ltd., of Wakefield, which Jackson's bought in February 1944.

Harpers of Harrogate - part of the wartime expansion.

basis - although that is one of those tales which is told about just about all the bakeries in turn; the other is about the bread which, due to some unevenness in oven temperature, was invariably scorched down one side. When a representative from Hull pointed out that this reflected badly on the firm he was told, "We've tried to correct it but our customers only complain: they're used to having one side blackened, and they don't want it any other way."

Mitchell's of Scunthorpe consisted of a bakery, a shop, an adjoining house and a garage. It cost £3823, and the 1800 shares were, again, bought by Jackson's directors along with Phyllis and Doris Oughtred. This firm, like its Dudley counterpart, also had a contract to supply bread to the Army. In 1946 some money was spent on extending the bakehouse. The shop was closed in 1950 when Jackson's opened in Frodingham Road, the staff moving across to the new branch. The bakery itself was operated until the early sixties when it was closed, the plant and machinery being transferred to Hull.

Dudley and Scunthorpe, however, remained on the map as depots, handling incoming bread and confectionery from Hull, for example, and delivering it locally to shops and individual customers on retail rounds.

Harper's of Harrogate, which would later form part of the Golden Grain Bakeries group, was bought in July 1945. It consisted of a bakery and a large grocery and confectionery shop. Among its other assets were six motor vehicles servicing a wholesale and retail trade in the area. The value of the trade was reflected in the price Jackson's paid for it: £18,000.

Swale's of Wakefield, the other wartime acquisition, was to have a lengthier and more significant history within the group. Tom Swale had opened for business by 1904 with his bakery and three horse-drawn delivery vans. Within ten years his fleet comprised about a dozen vehicles but, with the Army requisitioning most of his horses in 1914, he was back to three or four.

By 1939 the business had grown considerably but was facing an uncertain future. Tom Swale had passed the business on to his daughter in 1918 on account of his own ill health. In 1939 she passed it on to her niece, a Miss Booker. At this time there was a fleet of seven motor vans, but with the introduction of bread zoning the firm seemed to be having problems. Here was another example of a family business faltering because of a shortage of natural - or willing - heirs, a problem which Jackson's had side-stepped with the marriage of Bentham's daughters to the Oughtred brothers.

William Jackson bought Swale's out in 1944, running it as T. Swale (1944) Ltd. There was a staff of forty, a few wholesale bread contracts, and a number of retail clients served by roundsmen. Jackson's wasted no time in modernising and enlarging, buying three new vans - and a Morris car - and then in 1946 extending the factory to accommodate a travelling bread oven, bought at a cost of £4,500. Business grew rapidly. In 1946 four 30-cwt Morris and three 2-ton Austin vans were added to the fleet and the year-end results were noted as "very satisfactory".

The Wakefield site was, like Derringham Street, surrounded by streets of terraced houses, and problems came up as the business grew. The despatch

The expanded Golden Grain bakery group embraced all Jackson's regional bakeries with the exception of Stockton.

A Swales van. Jackson's didn't change the name until the 1960s.

The Golden Grain Bakery at Mirfield, West Yorks. Bought in 1944.

department was on the opposite side of Alverthorpe Road, and a conveyor had to be built to transfer the freshly baked loaves from the bakehouse to the loading bays. As Mr. Frank Taylor, the former manager of the site, recalls, when the conveyor broke down - which it did quite often - hundreds of loaves might be ruined.

Expansion of this site was not always lateral: sometimes it had to be vertical, as in the case of the confectionery department where a second storey was added to the original bakery in 1949. At Derringham Street residents had complained about the lorries cracking the paving-stones and causing mud to be splashed over the door-steps; here they complained about the noise from the factory itself. In fact in 1949 an injunction was served, as a result of which rubber tyres were fitted to the wheels of the dough-bins to deaden the rumbling as they were moved from mixer to prover. Unfortunately this did not satisfy one particular resident who must have been highly delighted when her solicitor struck a deal with the bakers. Jackson's agreed to buy her Alverthorpe Road house (for £650), also to buy her another house in Morton Parade (at £1375) and finally to pay damages and costs amounting to £205!

An interesting historical sidelight to the story of Wakefield is the discovery, in 1950, of an ancient cannon ball when a garage site was being excavated. The local museum curator identified it as dating from the battle of Wakefield in 1460, scene of the death of Richard of York at the hands of the Lancastrians. This item now resides on the desk of the Chairman at Derringham Street along with a second, smaller ball found on the same site in 1959.

Wakefield, along with Rotherham and, later, Stockton, were to be the company's three main bakeries outside Hull up to the time of the changes which ocurred in the early eighties. From the Hull point of view, Rotherham and Wakefield have tended to be viewed as outposts - important but nonetheless subsidiary to the needs of the main bakery. A trivial - but telling - reflection is seen in a story told by Sid Slater. In 1994 Sid produced from somewhere an antique calculating machine, made in Leipzig, probably before the First World War, and showed how he used to operate it to perform mathematical feats for the accounts books. He recalled it being sent from headquarters, probably back in the early fifties. "Whenever I needed anything new in the way of office equipment," he says, "Hull would send me something of theirs - and then go out and buy a new replacement." The calculator - which still works perfectly - has now been reclaimed by Hull as a valuable historical artefact! (See colour section).

Subsidiary these bakeries may have been, but Rotherham and Wakefield were staffed by men and women who took pride in their work and produced good returns for the company. John Haley, currently Area Depot Manager based at Rotherham, remembers the bakery there producing the best bread and 'ferments' - i.e., tea-cakes, rolls, etc - in the whole company. Rotherham's reputation, however, was built on its confectionery - at least up to the early sixties. Their cream cakes were as well thought of around the town as the Hull bakery's wares used to be in Humberside. Indeed, a friendly rivalry existed between the two. Many remember Mr. Tommy Benyon who was in charge of the decorating and finishing. One young lady who learned the trade under his supervision was Joan Holingworth. She was sent to

Hull to see what she could learn off Jenny Tinker, and later started her own business, three confectionery shops trading as Tanyard Bakeries.

In 1960 Rotherham had around two hundred staff, but its confectionery side was already under pressure from the new supermarkets. The coming of the large self-service stores, along with rising wage levels in what was a very labour-intensive field, severely affected profitability. Production was declining as early as 1958 when the plant was transferred from Greaseborough Street to a new and larger bakehouse in Tenter Street. Supermarkets - and their customers - were now looking for elaborate wrapping and packaging, and new rules affecting hygiene were placing restrictions on traditional methods of production. As unit costs rose, machinery which might have cut out the labour element to some extent was available, but only at a prohibitive cost.

By the late sixties the confectionery department had been closed and the staff - that is, just about all the women on the site - made redundant. Archie Flynn, who started at Rotherham as a motor mechanic in 1960 and later became Transport Manager, worked through many of these and the later changes. An idea of the size of the operation at its peak can be gained by the number of vehicles he had to work on. The fleet at its height comprised twenty-eight wholesale and thirty-seven retail vans.

The retail vans were a part of Jackson's 'Daisy Fresh' door-to-door delivery service which ran until the late 1970s. For a period the company ran between two and three hundred vans and were amongst the major operators. The men and women who worked these rounds, calling at a hundred or two houses a day, some in town, others in remote country districts, provided both a valued service to the community and a sales boost to the company. The majority of the salesmen were honest, diligent and reliable. However, in the words of Frank Taylor, the whole operation was "a bloody nightmare". This was because to him, and to his staff, fell the problem of unravelling the mysteries of a bag of loose change, a handful of crumpled receipts, and a list of exotically imprecise addresses. Not only that, but there was the headache of credit too. For just as in the old days when shopkeepers were plagued by customers taking goods 'on tick' and then forgetting to settle at the end of the week, so the customers on the Daisy Fresh rounds were forever behind with their payments.

This was not always their fault. In the sixties and seventies more and more housewives were at work in the day. They would leave out a note for a couple of loaves, a meat pie and some lemonade, and these would be left on their doorstep. It might be weeks before the driver found his customer at home and able to pay. And when payment was made, the customer was often identified vaguely by the driver as "that ginger-headed woman who lives in the corner house and has one white sliced Mondays and Thursdays."

The nature of the roundsman's job - always on the move, always keen to win new customers, and out in all weathers - meant that keeping orderly records of their transactions was sometimes the last thing on their minds. The job was a low-wage, high commission affair. There were also, naturally, a number of less than saintly characters attracted to a job which allowed its operatives a great deal of freedom. One, according to Mr. Peter Oughtred, had to be discreetly moved on when, one after another, a series of women drivers left work, pregnant - and pointed the finger at him. Others

A shiny new Daisy Fresh van for retail delivery. They didn't stay this smart for long!

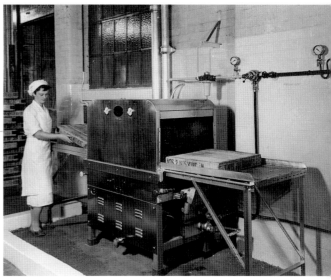

A Hobart tray washer at Wakefield. The humble bread-tray has been found as far afield as the Friesian Islands. A fence built of them once surrounded a north-eastern allotment. In 1952 the company was losing 3,000 a week.

would sell their own wares from the van. Eggs were a particular favourite. Archie Flynn recalls one driver who told a customer that if she insisted on cancelling her weekly dozen she could forget about her bread too!

It was not only the cashiers who suffered the cavalier ways of the roundsmen. The mechanics who maintained the vehicles suffered too. The vans, their clutches generally worn out, their doors sometimes hanging by a thread, would be brought back to Rotherham at night and handed over to Archie Flynn

and his team - total, three men! - to be made right for the next morning. The mechanics worked long hours, officially from seven in the morning to finish. But of course most major problems came to light at the end of the day - drivers reporting in with the van's interior shuttering or racks in pieces. Breakdowns on the road were attended in the depot's spare van - if available. All through the summer the spare would in fact be working full-time at one of the Butlin's camps where Jackson's had contracted to deliver bread - either Pwlhelli or Skegness. The transport men kept a spare engine and a spare gear-box at the depot, and would be

A convoy of fourteen vans leaves the old Seamer depot for the new bakery at Yarm Road, Stockton, 26th June, 1955.

ready at a moment's notice to take these out to a stranded vehicle and replace the faulty part on the roadside. As to the wholesale vans, their drivers would 'phone in the small hours and fetch Archie out of his bed.

To the great relief of the clerks and cashiers trying to make sense out of what often appeared to be organised chaos, the door-to-door van sales were dropped in 1978, largely as a result of changing trends in shopping. People were now using the growing number of supermarkets and filling their fridges and freezers with a week's supply of food. And they were finding the self-service stores markedly cheaper.

Rotherham and Wakefield were thus two important regional bakeries within the Jackson group's 'home' region. Their farthest-flung - and ultimately most important - bakery, the one at Stockton-on-Tees, was in fact built some ten years after the acquisition of these two.

During the war, the Government introduced a system of bread zoning. Bread, as a staple item, was always likely to be controlled in an emergency: the supply could not be left to the laws of the market. This, then, was a system of control through which bakers only sold bread within a designated area. It continued in operation until 1948 whereupon, as Les Bland, former sales manager at Stockton, remembers, there was a kind of phoney war in which bakers kept

Fleet of vans at Jackson's new Stockton bakery, around 1955.

Stockton by night.

more or less to their formerly designated areas but indulged in a little 'pirating'. Jackson's were no exception. They also found that a number of shops in the far north-east of the region they covered were actually coming to them to ask for deliveries because they were not able to obtain reliable supplies from such local producers as Forbes, Savoy and Welfords.

The Jackson's board delegated T.C. Waite, as a Darlington man with contacts in the area, to scout around for a possible depot site on Teesside. He soon came up with what was to become, in November 1951, the Seamer depot - not to be confused with Crystal Motors' Seamer tractor depot near Scarborough which was acquired about the same time.

Keith Paylor, the current Stockton bakery co-ordinator, started work for the company at Seamer in 1952, fresh from his National Service. He started as a night loader, shifting bread from incoming lorries onto the depot's own transport for delivery locally. He remembers that within a year of opening the depot was handling 55,000 loaves a week and the board were confidently expecting this volume to double within the year. There was no door-to-door service then. The main trade was in wholesale bread, although there was one lorry which took out cakes once a week.

Jackson's were in fact the first in this area to operate a wholesale confectionery service. Norman Oughtred, as Bolivian consul in Hull and as a man engaged in shipping, was appointed Port Sugar Officer by the Ministry of Food. Jackson's were thus in the fortuitous position of being able to obtain their sugar rather more easily than their competitors. Thus guaranteed of its supplies, the Seamer confectionery sales thrived. It was on the back of this that the new depot found so many new customers for its bread.

As Seamer trade increased, the need for a bakery in that region became more apparent. In September 1953 the board decided that the volume of business in the north-east was sufficient to warrant a bakery being built, and proposed a nine-sack Uniflow plant. A site was found and more detailed planning began. In July 1955 the Seamer depot was closed, its staff and trade transferred to the new bakery at Yarm Road, Stockton, which came into production at a sackage of five hundred a week.

Sackage in the bakery trade refers to the number of 280lb (or 20-stone) sacks of flour used in a given period. A nine-sack plant, for instance, uses nine sacks an hour. From each sack approximately 225 standard loaves are produced. Traditionally, the number would have been fewer, because until the war the standard loaf was the four-pound (quartern) or the two-pound. In 1943, as an economy measure, the government had reduced the standard weights to three and a half and one and three-quarter pounds in an effort to save wheat and cut shipping costs.

At its peak Stockton would supply bread to over a thousand shops. A number of these were shops in name only, being in fact tiny establishments in little communities up in the hills or in remote pit villages. Some were more or less front-room set-ups serving a few dozen houses and would require perhaps ten dozen loaves at a time. One former Stockton driver remembers being asked to pile an exceptionally large order in front of a customer's front room hearth - only to find out on his next visit that a pile of buns had toppled over into the fire and been ruined.

Les Johnson, who until 1992 was factory manager at Stockton, recalls a particularly far-flung delivery to a hotel, four miles from a little village up a narrow, twisty road. The manager there was in the habit of ordering as little as one loaf - and even from time to time leaving out a note, "NO BREAD TODAY", for the exasperated driver. The deliverymen soon tired of this and went to the management to try to get the hotelier scratched from the roster. But when he organised a slap-up meal for all the salesmen - and wrote a long letter to the Chairman - he secured his deliveries for a long time to come.

Les Johnson was a third generation baker, his grandfather having founded Johnson's of Pontefract. Coming from this traditional craft background and having worked on into the nineties, he saw a great many changes in the baking industry. He insists that bread-making will never be an exact science - "It's an art, a black art!" It is also, in his view, something of an erotic art: "A well prepared dough should feel like the inside of a woman's thigh!" However, some of the mystery has gone out of it through the introduction of mechanised processes.

Yet Les does not subscribe to the view that bread today is inferior to what it used to be. He recalls his grandfather saying fifty years ago that bread wasn't the same as when he was a boy. What is? Yes, it has

Feeling the heat in the bakery - manual de-panning of hot loaves.

changed - the crust has gone, sacrificed to the need to wrap and slice. And with that has gone some of the flavour, produced in the caramelisation that takes place in the formation of the crust, and now lost with the use of lids to protect the tops of standard wrapped loaves. However, in his opinion the baking industry has done a marvellous job in producing a loaf which consistently meets the customer's requirements in texture, feel, and - most importantly - in shelf or pantry life.

When Stockton first opened a lot of the work was still done by hand. The Uniflow travelling oven, for example, still required the dough to be loaded and the finished bread to be de-panned manually. In the mid-sixties the new Turbo oven represented a huge step forward in automation. It was at the time the most modern plant available, and reduced the number of operatives from seven or eight to three or four. One man could now run the mixing, dividing and proving sequence; another could look after the moulding, and a third would place the lids onto the tins; then there would be a supervisor. The operatives would circulate, doing half-hour stints at each post with breaks between.

The men who operated the old Uniflow plant remember it as "a killer". It was hot and heavy work. One man would be de-panning the hot baked loaves from one oven while loading risen dough into another. Standing between the hot ovens, with only a ten-minute break each hour, this man would be provided with damp towels to wipe the sweat off his face and arms. Today, de-panning is done by a series of suction cups, the bread being untouched by hand. Handling hot loaves was hard on the fingers - occasionally wearing away the skin and drawing blood - but it had its advantages. When the local C.I.D. came to the bakery to investigate a wages snatch on the site they were bemused to find that half the staff had no fingerprints!

Jackson's thus had, from the mid-1950s, seven bakeries in production: Hull, Stockton, Rotherham, Wakefield, Scunthorpe, Harrogate and Dudley. Their bread business was expanding, but radical changes were about to affect the industry which would make the company look uneasily to its future.

Chapter Ten

FLOUR AND MILLING

Bread-baking is a relatively simple business which dates back thousands of years. It is said that the ancient Egyptians first made a risen bread by pure accident. Some spare dough, stored in a jar which had previously contained wine, was 'infected' by the residual yeast and fermented, yielding the world's first leavened bread. From that time on bread was made using a natural fermentation process, a portion of each mix being kept to one side to start off the next batch - much as sour-dough is still kept by many a kitchen range to this day. By the Middle Ages, it is believed, brewers' yeast was being used in bread baking, but it is only since then that a separate baker's yeast has been identified and made available.

Although large plant bakers such as Jackson's have invested in modern hi-tech plant to automate the process as much as possible, there has only been one significant change in the way flour, salt, water and yeast are combined to make the standard household loaf. There have traditionally been eight stages in bread-making: mixing the dough, bulk fermentation (up to eight hours but usually two and a half to three), dividing it into loaf-size pieces and moulding into a round ball shape; proving, or rising; moulding the dough back into shape ('knocking back') and allowing a second rising; then baking, and finally cooling. The 1930s, as we have seen, saw the introduction of a ninth stage, that of slicing and wrapping.

The one significant advance, however, came as recently as 1961 when plant bakers, as opposed to the small craftsmen bakers, introduced the Chorleywood Breadmaking Process, or CBP. This was a further step in mechanisation which involved the dough being worked intensively for a short period - five minutes or so - under vacuum conditions, thus obviating the need for the lengthy bulk fermentation (or proving) period. Thus up to two and a half hours were saved in the production process - and time, as in any industry, is money.

In addition to this huge saving, Chorleywood made marginal, but significant, savings elsewhere. In order to achieve the softness of texture which traditional methods would yield, extra water was now added to the flour - as much as a gallon per 280lb sack. At the same time a 'weaker' - and cheaper - flour might be used. Traditionally, U.K. bakers had employed a proportion of 'hard' Canadian flour to strengthen their dough. With this new process a softer flour milled from home-grown wheats could be used. 'Soft' and 'hard' here refer to the amount of protein in the wheat - and it is the protein or gluten which allows the bread not only to rise but also to hold its risen shape: a 'soft' wheat flour would tend to collapse under the old method.

It is important to reiterate, however, that these advances applied only to the larger scale mechanised bakers, not to the craftsmen who baked at the back of their shops. They would not have the technology to employ a Chorleywood Process. For the big bakers, then, this all added up to an increased yield of perhaps 4%, the process also reducing the amount of weight lost through evaporation. The slightly moister product also had the advantage of a slightly longer shelf life.

Bakers had claimed that their customers noticed no difference between the 'soft' wheat bread which was

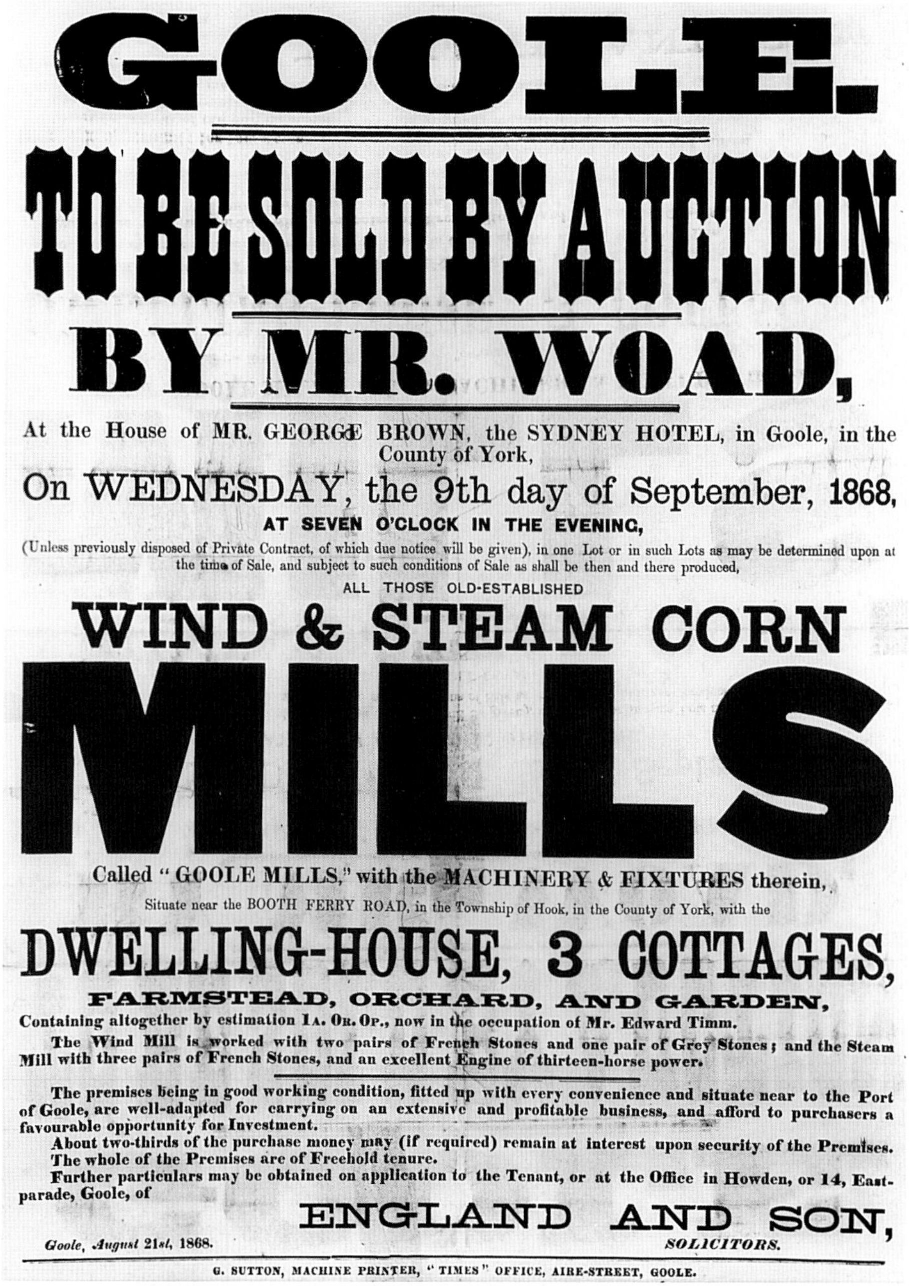

GOOLE.

TO BE SOLD BY AUCTION

BY MR. WOAD,

At the House of MR. GEORGE BROWN, the SYDNEY HOTEL, in Goole, in the County of York,

On WEDNESDAY, the 9th day of September, 1868,

AT SEVEN O'CLOCK IN THE EVENING,

(Unless previously disposed of Private Contract, of which due notice will be given), in one Lot or in such Lots as may be determined upon at the time of Sale, and subject to such conditions of Sale as shall be then and there produced,

ALL THOSE OLD-ESTABLISHED

WIND & STEAM CORN

MILLS

Called " GOOLE MILLS," with the MACHINERY & FIXTURES therein,

Situate near the BOOTH FERRY ROAD, in the Township of Hook, in the County of York, with the

DWELLING-HOUSE, 3 COTTAGES,

FARMSTEAD, ORCHARD, AND GARDEN,

Containing altogether by estimation 1A. 0R. 0P., now in the occupation of Mr. Edward Timm.

The Wind Mill is worked with two pairs of French Stones and one pair of Grey Stones; and the Steam Mill with three pairs of French Stones, and an excellent Engine of thirteen-horse power.

The premises being in good working condition, fitted up with every convenience and situate near to the Port of Goole, are well-adapted for carrying on an extensive and profitable business, and afford to purchasers a favourable opportunity for Investment.

About two-thirds of the purchase money may (if required) remain at interest upon security of the Premises. The whole of the Premises are of Freehold tenure.

Further particulars may be obtained on application to the Tenant, or at the Office in Howden, or 14, East-parade, Goole, of

ENGLAND AND SON,

SOLICITORS.

Goole, August 21st, 1868.

G. SUTTON, MACHINE PRINTER, " TIMES " OFFICE, AIRE-STREET, GOOLE.

Flyer for the sale of the Goole mill, 1868.

The old five-sail windmill, now the site of Timm's modern flour mill.

forced on them during the war and the 'hard' wheat bread to which they had been accustomed. However, after the war there was a perceived demand for a return to flours milled from imported wheats. But this was at odds with the government's policy of reducing imports and actually tightening controls on foreign exchange during what was to become a familiar sterling crisis. It was this crisis which had forced bread rationing on a war-weary public in 1947, although that was only to last for a year or so.

The coming of Chorleywood, then, actually helped ease Britain's balance of trade with North America. The new process produced, from domestic wheat, a bread which, the researchers claimed, was indistinguishable from that made from Canadian grain. British farmers also benefitted, gaining an expanded and secure market for their crops. At the same time plant breeders were coming up with new varieties of wheat which were suited to the British climate and the new baking technology.

For many years Jackson's had bought much of their flour from local millers Timms of Goole. No-one is quite sure how far back the relationship goes, but it had been long established when, in September 1964, the company bought a 40% interest in this family firm. Three years later Jackson's took up the option to buy a further 10% share with equal representation on the board.

It was in 1854 that Edward and his son John Brunyee Timm first rented their Goole windmill, buying it at auction for the sum of £1500 in 1868. Edward's grandson Claude, the latter's son Reg, currently Executive Consultant to the firm, and his son Jeremy, the Managing Director, form a direct line,

father-to-son, which spans the firm's entire history. Jeremy's brother Nigel is currently Operations Director. The firm employs some 120 people on the original site and at the dockside subsidiary Timmgrain.

While the main body of the old mill - minus its sails - remains on its original site, Timm's is a thoroughly up-to-date plant using electrically powered steel roller-mills, the whole process being operated by three men per shift. A reminder of days past is a pair of millstones set into the wall at the front of the office-block.

The town of Goole, incidentally, is something of a historical curiosity in Britain, being a company town built to serve the Aire and Calder Navigation and its docks. This canal, linking the West Riding with the sea, was constructed in the 1820s as an extension of the earlier Selby canal of 1788 to handle coal from the Yorkshire pits and ship it abroad - or around the coast of Britain.

Timms is one of perhaps a dozen independents currently operating in the U.K. There were as many as 2,600 grain millers in the pre-war period - although many of those dealt with grains other than bread flour, such as rye, oats, barley or rice. Even then, though, the three largest firms accounted for something like two-thirds of all flour production. While this concentration eased somewhat during and immediately after the war, by 1968 the five largest accounted for over 80% of all white flour sales.

A character of great significance in the British flour-milling and baking industries has been Mr. Garfield 'Gary' Weston. He had already set up a highly successful bakery business in North America when he came to Britain in 1932. At that time the main 'players' in the U.K. were Rank, Spillers and the Co-op. While the latter were involved in milling and baking, Rank and Spillers were purely millers. Weston started buying up a number of bakery firms, and in 1935 formed the company Allied Bakeries Limited.

Allied bought the bulk of its flour from Canada, but the coming of war in 1939 brought a suspension of these imports, whereupon Allied had to buy its flour from the larger U.K. millers, mainly Rank and Spillers. While rationing of flour was only in operation for one post-war year, government restrictions on imports, and strict foreign exchange controls, lasted to the mid-1950s. Not until these were finally lifted was Allied able to revert to imported hard wheat flour.

Meanwhile Weston continued to expand his operation. Rank and Spillers, seeing the domestic market for its flour shrinking as Weston swallowed up more and more of the baking industry, decided to go into baking for themselves. As a response to this Allied, around the time that the Chorleywood Process was being perfected, started buying up mills. Weston's reasoning was that should Britain enter the Common Market - which seemed probable even then - tariffs on Canadian wheat would follow and he would be forced to buy from millers (Rank and Spillers) who were now his main rivals in the baking business.

It was against this background that Jackson's wisely decided to protect its own source of supply at Timms by buying into the firm, lest one of these giants move in first. The strict fifty-fifty basis on which Jackson's bought into the Goole company is unusual, if not unique: neither partner had absolute control, and the essentially co-operative relationship might not have worked. But, against the prognostications of the lawyers, it did - for close to thirty years.

The company Jackson's bought into has three independent mills at its Boothferry Road site. These enable it to supply a full range of flours, from 100% Canadian through the various blended bread, pastry and biscuit flours, the last being 100% 'soft' wheat. They also make flours for products like chapattis, pizzas and the batter used by fish friers, a total of around thirty distinct types. Their customers cover a similarly wide range, from the out-of-town farmer's wife who might drive in for a single sack for her pantry, to the fish-and-chip-shop proprietor requiring half a dozen bags, to the small baker ordering a tonne a week, and on up to various independent plant bakers with Jackson's themselves taking several hundred tonnes weekly and accounting for a significant proportion of the firm's output.

Bread cooler, holding 12,000 28-ounce loaves. Cooling accounts for almost half the production time.

In addition to the various flours Timms produce are the various co-products - known, prior to EC membership, as by-products: wheat feed for animal food compounders, consisting of 'sharps' or 'middings'; wheatgerm - which is taken from the grain in all but wholemeal flour; and bran. Some twenty years ago Timms acquired the local firm of John H. Heron and moved their plant to the mill site. Here they pack bran and wheat germ into retail packs for various high street clients and numerous health-food outlets. The wheatgerm is also toasted, to stabilise it, and sold as Froment, another health-promoting product which in 1974 helped the Oxford University crew to an impressive Boat Race victory!

Thus it can be seen that the baking industry, just like the retail trade, was constantly developing. Jackson's, like any other firm, had to adapt in order to maintain their position. To stand still might mean being swept away by the tide of change.

A lorry belonging to Timms of Goole, decorated for a local parade.

Chapter Eleven

OUTSIDE CATERING

For many years the outside catering department run by Jackson's was amongst the leaders in the field locally. Indeed, it was for a time Hull's number one caterer. It had its roots in Paragon Street which, unlike just about all the other branches, was built with a dual function in mind, having the restaurant above the shop.

The restaurant, and ball-room which was added in 1950, accommodated any number of special events, generally on Friday and Saturday evenings, throughout the year. Organisations like the Rotary Club and its sister group the Inner Wheel would hire the place for various special occasions, Jackson's providing the catering. Numerous staff events also took place, from informal Christmas Eve parties to New Year celebrations. For children there was a Santa Claus operating the lift: he arrived via a large chimney erected on the roof to cheers from the late evening shoppers.

Cyril Terry, of Publicity, remembers making that chimney - and, when the original volunteer chickened out, having to clamber up on the roof and act the part! He also remembers receiving an order for a huge painting which he was to stretch over a wooden frame. At midnight on New Year's Eve a child was to burst through it and shout "Happy New Year" to the revellers. Mr. Cruickshank - still company secretary then, and the brains behind this stunt - expressed grave concern as to whether the child - his niece - would manage to break through, the paper being rather stiff. He kept pummelling the thing, finally insisting on having a practice, and told the girl to charge it with all her might. She burst clean through, and Cyril had to start all over again.

Paragon Street at the same time furnished the basic raw materials - and some prepared foods - for a number of outside businesses engaged in feeding the public. Bread rolls and sandwiches, for example, would be made up in the shop and taken across to Paragon Station for the Newcastle express and the London Pullman. Hotels such as the Imperial would send across orders for bread and meats. Other

Paragon street restaurant. Customers included H.R.I. doctors, local sporting personalities, and Jackson's directors - who had their own private dining room.

Caterers with van at the Great Yorkshire Show: Allan Jewsbury on left, Sid Maplethorpe (centre), Jack Ford (right).

A stand at the Great Yorkshire Show. Jackson's produced their own brand of potato crisps after the war - but the board saw no great future for them!

customers included pubs such as the White Harte, the Hull Exchange and the Corn Exchange. And then there was the Y.P.I. canteen, the Tivoli Theatre and the Gainsborough fish and chip restaurant.

Vera Owen, who had begun work at Paragon Street during the war, has good reason to remember one early catering job when a huge trifle was required for the annual dinner of Mr. Jack Oughtred's old regiment, the East Yorkshire, which was to be held in the ball-room. The shop had a good relationship with the East Yorks, and the officers there would often 'phone when there was to be a dance, asking whether any of the girls might like to come. The trifle filled a bread tray. It arrived from the bakery on a horse-drawn cart. As the driver went into the shop to announce its arrival, a second cart drew up behind his. It was a dull day, and rain was threatening. The first driver decided he ought to slip into his waterproofs, and began to do so in the doorway. Vera was hopping from foot to foot, anxious to get past him to see what the trifle looked like.

What she saw when she at last got out onto the pavement nearly stopped her heart. The second horse had dragged his load forward and managed to get his nose into the back of the cart in front. He was tucking into the trifle! As Vera let out a yell the miscreant looked up from his snack and turned to face her. She couldn't help but laugh. Festoons of red and green icing hung from his nostrils, and each ear sported a thick blob of whipped cream. "They looked like a couple of ice-cream cones," Vera remembers. Meanwhile a crowd of onlookers had gathered to enjoy the spectacle.

When the bakery took Vera's desperate call some while later they had a job believing her. But they

The Ferguson Fawsitt Arms, Walkington. Did Jack Oughtred buy this as a convenient watering hole after a hard day's shooting?

rallied round and managed, against all odds, to produce a replacement just in time for the night's festivities.

Paragon Street, then, was one source from which the catering enterprise grew. A second source was Jackson's handful of pubs, notably the Ferguson Fawsitt Arms at Walkington, which was purchased for £4,675 in 1943. There are two stories as to why the firm went into pubs. The better of the two is that Jack

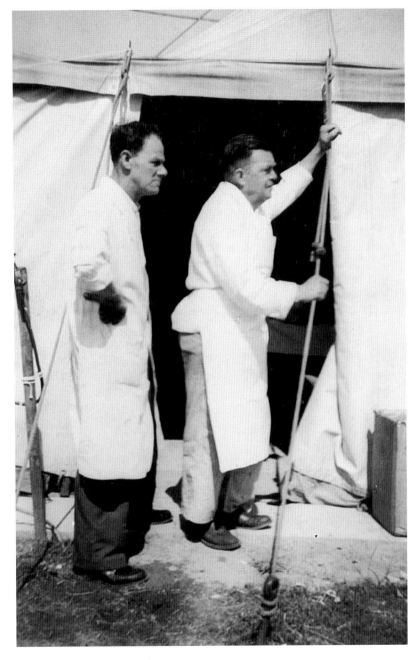

Great Yorkshire Show: Jack Ford (left), who ran the staff canteen, with Jock Wray.

Staff at the Great Yorkshire Show. Jackson's drivers were the backbone of the team. Here they pose with a gang of temporary workers.

and Norman Oughtred wanted to be sure of having somewhere agreeable to have a drink on their way back from a day's shooting. What better way to brush aside such inconveniences as the licensing laws than to buy your own pub?

The second story - and, unfortunately, the true one - is a little more prosaic. It has to do with Jackson's need for a liquor licence. They wished to supply beers, wines and spirits to functions at which they provided the food, rather than rely on someone else - and let them have the profits. Jackson's own shops still had a 'no liquor' covenant attached to them, and until the firm could acquire a shop which had its own off-licence the pub at Walkington was the ideal solution.

Three years after the purchase of the 'Fergie', the Francis Myers shop in South Cave, which Jackson's had acquired in 1931, got a licence. The company now used premises adjoining the shop as its wines and spirits warehouse. But the pub was already a part of the company's furniture. It is still owned by them.

Three other pubs were bought over the years: the Pipe and Glass at South Dalton, the Triton Inn at Brantingham, and the Dacre Arms at Brandesburton. While catering was now undertaken in-house at the Ferguson Fawsitt, a separate outside firm, County Catering, was set up in 1953 in partnership with Moors' and Robson's Breweries Ltd. They operated from Sutton Street, off Spring Bank, in premises which the company had used as a warehouse after the Wellington Street depository had been bombed flat in the war. So now Jackson's had Paragon Street and the Walkington pub as venues, and County Catering able to provide food and refreshment wherever required.

Catering is a business which can idle along for weeks on end and then be required to find enormous resources for huge events lasting no more than a few short days. The Great Yorkshire Show at Harrogate, for which Jackson's provided the catering for many years, is a prime example.

The hard core of perhaps half a dozen full-time staff would, for fourteen hectic days, be joined by as many as four hundred temporary employees to work, in many cases, around the clock in order to meet the needs of tens of thousands attending the three day show.

At the central workshops Jackson's joiners would make up bars and counters for re-assembly on site. The ever-adaptable drivers would step in and haul these and other goods and materials to the showground and then prepare to man the kitchens. Staff would be drafted in from the shops to operate the cash registers. The work would be continuous, and men would sleep on site - some in tents and marquees, some in vehicles, others as security guards in the temporary store-rooms, the luckier ones in the comfort of the cricket pavilion.

The contract for the Great Yorkshire Show included all forms of public catering and some private stands, but excluded the Members' section. The staff thus had to provide anything from snacks and drinks to lunch-boxes, to full sit-down dinners with waitress service. In addition the bars had to be stocked and manned, with anything from a thousand to fifteen hundred tray meals served daily. There was also - an important consideration - a separate canteen for the staff themselves. Here Jack Ford turned out breakfast, lunch and dinner daily over the fortnight.

A show such as the Great Yorkshire is very much that - a show. What is on display belies the frantic activity - and sheer panic - that goes on behind the scenes: the bread lorries arriving after the close each day; the staff then busily making thousands of sandwiches into the small hours; the processing of half a ton of fish for the chippies on the 'popular' side; the chipping of several tons of potatoes in those far-off days before the frozen article was produced; slicing up to two hundred turkeys for the sandwiches and salad dishes; and then getting up at five thirty to clear away all the evidence and set up the displays. Thus the show goes on and the forty thousand daily visitors are spared having to trip over the debris.

How did the staff manage to keep going? They entered into the spirit of the occasion, treating it as a challenge and an adventure. Whatever happened it would all be over in two weeks - and in the meantime they could cheer themselves up looking forward to a couple of fat pay-packets. And when all that wasn't enough to prevent their energies flagging they could send out to the local chemist for some Benzedrine - which quite a few did. It was legal then.

Sometimes, naturally, things went wrong. It might be the weather - always a worry with outside catering. More than once men woke up in their tents to see their socks floating by on a muddy tide. And with so many people under pressure to erect and operate what was in effect a small town in a confined space, disaster was always in the wings, waiting to strike. There was the night a Jackson's driver backed a lorry-load of provisions into a tight narrow space, snagged a power line, and plunged the entire site into darkness. Sometimes the mishaps were more comical than catastrophic - at least for the bystanders. One driver, Jock Wray, was unloading his van one evening, a tray of bread balanced on his head, when he walked straight into a full cess-pit. Jock wasn't a tall man, and he actually disappeared below the surface of the muck and slime. As his mates peered into the murk, speculating as to how deep it might be, Jock resurfaced, his head covered with beetroot skins and tea-leaves, thoroughly chilled, but relieved to see the bread, which he had heroically flung to one side as he fell, safe and dry on the grass.

Jackson's catered at other shows in the north - notably at Driffield and at the Derbyshire show at Bakewell. They were also for several years involved in race course catering - at Wetherby, at Market Rasen, and - right up to 1994 - at Beverley. Indeed, latterly while the food was generally prepared at Melton, the main retail distribution centre, the administrative staff came to be housed at Beverley, under the main grandstand.

Racecourse catering presented similar practical problems to show catering but, being year-round, these were frequently exacerbated by adverse weather conditions. Allan Jewsbury, who worked for the caterers for many years during his spare time, recalls the Boxing Day meetings which, of course, required staff to be available to set things up on Christmas Day. For many years, Allan remembers, he would rise early on the twenty-fifth, open presents with his family, and then set off from home at ten o'clock.

At the warehouse they would load up their wagons. From there the crew would go up the road to the Polar Bear pub on the corner of Derringham Street for a sandwich lunch, and then drive up to the course. There they would work through the rest of the day setting up the bars, tables and counters, finishing as late as two o'clock next morning before bedding down.

On at least two occasions the men woke up to a thick covering of snow - and the glad tidings that the meeting was cancelled! It would then be a matter of loading up and travelling back to town - only to face the vociferous complaints of the neighbours as they unloaded as quietly as possible back at the warehouse.

These large-scale affairs not only placed a strain on the staff directly involved, but also on the bakery and the staff at Cottingham. More than one former caterer has remarked on how much they owed to the tremendous co-operation they received from the meat men and the bakers.

Other major outside contracts included numerous events at Hull's City Hall, which could comfortably hold a thousand guests. There were also formal dinners and other civic events at the Guildhall, rugby club functions, and in the warmer months any number of weddings - some in marquees, some in halls, many at Jackson's staff club on Beverley Road. From October to Christmas Paragon Street would be fully booked for firms' annual dinner-dances.

While Paragon street in its hey-day was considered a classy - even a glamorous - venue, it had by the 1960s begun to lose some of its appeal, and its trade. While its city-centre location had for a long time been one of its attractions it now became something of a handicap. The population was tending to spread towards the city's outlying districts as the old terraced streets made way for new roads and commercial developments. Paragon Street had no car park - and more and more people were using their cars for evening trips out. According to Allan Jewsbury some less than salubrious characters were starting to frequent the place. The decor too was starting to lose

its gloss, and no decision was made regarding a refurbishment.

At around this time, in 1964, County Catering ceased trading, the partnership with the brewery was dissolved, and the Sutton Street premises were abandoned. That operation, now known as Jackson's Catering, moved out to Inglemire Lane as part of the meat division. In December 1967 the Willow Plate café in Carr Lane fell subject to a compulsory purchase order and was later pulled down. It was certainly a time of change.

Various main board members had at times taken a specific interest in the catering division, among them Mr. Peter Oughtred, Gordon Russell, Ron Mountifield, Martin Russell and more recently Michael Oughtred, Brian Oughtred's son. G.R. was responsible for the purchase, in the early seventies, of the Triton Inn and the Dacre Arms. These investments were the beginnings of a plan he was formulating for a series of "Drive-Inn" licenced eateries which would, effectively, encircle Hull. Each approach road would have one. He had picked up this idea on one of his American trips. As Christopher Oughtred has said, it was probably a good idea, one which might well have yielded dividends. The factory could have serviced the restaurants from a central warehouse, offering a good discount and making the most of the comparatively short lines of communication within the business. Unfortunately, however, G.R. was to pass on before he could put this plan into operation, and the idea seems to have died with him.

Several factors have affected the development of the catering trade in recent years and, ultimately, accounted for Jackson's withdrawal. Caterers generally would agree that the quality of food they can

The Willow Plate café, at 13 Carr Lane, 1949-67. Jackson's had a number of other cafés - in Beverley, Bridlington and Withernsea

offer has improved tremendously. New methods of transportation and storage have diminished the reliance on frozen produce, particularly the dreaded frozen vegetable. With the shift to fresh greengrocery has come a return to a more seasonable menu. Instead of having sprouts all year round, for example, customers may expect to be offered whatever is currently available in the market.

Cooking facilities have also improved greatly, enabling a wider range of foods to be offered. Thirty years ago it would have been inconceivable for roast beef and Yorkshire pudding to be cooked in an open field - at, for instance, a Potato Marketing Board promotion. Now, with compact bottled gas available, grills, ovens and ranges may be set up anywhere at any time. Whereas in the old days food might be prepared well in advance and transported to a dining-hall or canteen in insulated containers - much like the school dinners many will remember - fresh-cooked food can now be served piping hot.

However, while these advances have improved standards and made the trade more adaptable, other outside factors have put the squeeze on. Number one, according to a number of sources, is the increasingly stringent application of the drink-driving laws. While adhering to the law should be no problem for a family or a group where one member can be chosen to drive, the psychological effect has been to dissuade people from straying too far from home for their entertainment.

On top of this has come the almost continual recessionary economic climate of the eighties and nineties, with people far less inclined - or able - to splash out thousands of pounds on marquee weddings and extravagant corporate entertainment. Early in 1994 the catering business at Beverley racecourse was sold to Craven Gilpin. The Ferguson Fawsitt remains Jackson's only catering establishment of any size.

Chapter Twelve

TRANSPORT AND SERVICES AFTER THE WAR

Crystal Motors and Jackson's Services are two important companies which grew from Jackson's need to maintain and provide transport for its shops. Both grew to a considerable size during the post-war period and in different ways became independent of the parent company, such was the scope of the work they undertook.

Crystal Motors of Hull, which was to have strong ties with Jackson's right up to the present day was set up in 1946 under Mr. John Flew, who was in charge of transport and engineering. On his death in 1951 Mr. T.C. Waite, formerly of United Automobile Services of Darlington, became Managing Director under the chairmanship of Mr Peter Oughtred.

When he arrived at the Bank Street site he found, in his own words, "a heap of junk". All of the firm's best vehicles had been requisitioned for the war effort, and the company had been left with what the Army didn't want, a random collection of vehicles including the infamous steam wagons, and the horses and carts too. Nevertheless, the "fleet" numbered around a hundred vehicles.

As we have seen, the transport division had moved into the premises at the rear of Paragon Motors on Boothferry Road, but returned to a new garage and workshops in Bank Street in August 1947, sharing premises with the shopfitters. By 1948 the fleet had increased dramatically to number two hundred and sixty. It seemed to acquire some of its many drivers almost by accident. Tommy Jackson started in 1937 pushing hand-carts. He learned to drive cars in his own time, taught by a friend, and soon graduated to shifting trucks from the bakery loading bays out onto the road where the drivers would pick them up. His first run as a driver was to North Cotes aerodrome in Lincolnshire.

Allan Jewsbury was another employee who more or less fell into driving. After beginning as an errand-lad he had progressed by 1939 to a driver's mate on a fruit lorry. Then came the war, and he was off to the South Staffordshire regiment, returning to his old job in 1945. One day Tommy Conyers, the buyer for the greengrocery division, happened to see him moving a van from the street to the warehouse door. "Oh, you can drive, can you?" he remarked. Conyers then got him delivering to customers' doors in a 5-cwt Austin. He worked out of Hessle branch in the mornings and Willerby in the afternoons. He enjoyed the work, but the hours were long and he even found himself turning out on Christmas morning to get finished. After three years of this he went on to the big bread vans, the five and ten-tonners servicing the out-of-town depots, Wakefield, Rotherham and the rest.

Allan didn't in fact stay at this job very long, being singled out for special duties, criss-crossing the area in a Land Rover on various official and unofficial errands for board members and their families. As we have seen elsewhere, he became involved in the catering business.

The company had by this time acquired a Record Tyre distributorship. Another development in that year saw the parent company relinquish its share-holding. Originally Jackson's had held five hundred £1 shares,

A busy scene in Crystal's workshop.

This post-war view of Derringham Street, looking towards Anlaby Road, shows the terraced streets which have since been demolished. The sign Crystal Motors is visible on the corner of Bank Street.

A motor show at Crystal of Scarborough, the firm which was bought from Tommy Wise. A new Zephyr, a Ford Prefect, and a classy-looking convertible are on display.

Transport, like food, continued to be strictly controlled by the government for some years after the war. A Ministry of Transport licence was required for the purchase of any vehicle; diesel and petrol were stringently rationed. Jackson's were thus to some extent stifled and realised the benefits which might be gained by their going into the motor trade as main dealers. Thus at this time the expansion of the motor fleet was matched by an expansion into a number of ancillary businesses.

In 1949 through to 1951 tyre and batteries depots were opened, not only in Hull but also in Scunthorpe and Doncaster. By 1950 they had acquired their first official agencies - for Dagenite batteries, and for three motor vehicle companies: Lea Francis' hand-built cars, Dennis diesel trucks, and Trojan vans. Later they would add one for Bond mini-cars. In 1952 they would take over John Cross's warehouse in Fetter Lane, York, as another tyre and battery depot.

Crystal was, then, an independent company operating within Jackson's ambit and very much on its behalf. In July 1951 Jackson's chairman, J.W. Carmichael, expressed the view that it should be brought more under the control of the parent company. It had been formed with Jackson's money, employed Jackson's staff, and got the bulk of its business through Jackson's. So in December of that year some seventy shares were bought up, from Waite, Tillotson and Jefferson - John Flew had died in the January - and the Oughtreds, leaving Jackson's with a 30% holding. A. Clifford Jefferson had joined the company in 1930. Prior to being made a director of the newly formed Jackson's Services in 1971, he had been group transport manager. Later he would be chairman of Services, combining his role there with his duties as Jackson's estate manager.

but in April these were transferred to Peter and Brian Oughtred, who took two hundred and forty apiece, with a small number going to John Flew and one apiece to Waite and Stan Tillotson.

This was indeed a period of rapid change. No more than two months elapsed before the entire board was reconstituted. John Flew now took the chair, Soulsby, Dodsworth and Russell left the board, and the Oughtred cousins joined, along with Mr. P.G. Martin as company secretary. One of Waite's duties now was to visit the premises of the various outlying companies Jackson's had bought up - John Cross of York, for example, the Rotherham and Wakefield bakeries - and examine their transport assets.

By the following year Crystal were once more independent, and the situation was that while Jackson's Transport had its own vehicles and employed its own drivers, Crystal was to provide those vehicles and undertake the major part of their repair and maintenance.

These moves all took place against the background of Crystal's manoeuvrings in the broader sphere of motor vehicle retailing. Crystal had for some time been looking for a franchise worth the name. Lea Francis and the others were too specialist: they were more interested in something of the size of a Ford or an Austin dealership. Austin proved unattainable: the Hull firm Parrish's had got there first. They were buying some Fords but more Austins, yet were not happy with the fleet discount they were getting. To have their own dealership would give them a much better wholesale price. Ford would never have offered them a dealership while they were part of Jackson's, but now they had gained their independence the situation looked more promising. It had in fact been for this very reason that Jackson's had allowed Crystal to develop as a separate entity.

Ford at that time were repesented in Hull by Harbour Motors as main distributors in Anlaby Road. Crystal had already approached this firm with a view to their having a retail dealership under Harbour Motors' auspices. But Harbour were not interested. Going for a more direct approach, Peter Oughtred, Crystal chairman, took Waite with him to see Ford's General Sales Manager, Mr. Mortimer, and had a lunch at Dagenham with their chairman, Patrick Hennessey. The direct approach paid off, and the retail dealership was theirs. Now they could get better prices on the vehicles they supplied to Jackson's Transport,

and they were in a position to expand their business with the motoring public at large as well as with other businesses in the region. But they were still reliant on Harbour Motors as wholesalers, and the relationship between the two was evidently cool.

Things came to a head the following year when Harbour appeared to be dragging their feet over an allocation of cars. Once more Crystal's representatives headed south, and once more the trip yielded dividends. Crystal secured the disputed allocation direct from headquarters, and the delegation was told, effectively, "Do a decent job and there could be a main dealership in it for you."

Some years later during further meetings with Ford it was suggested that Harbour, by now thought to be rather a poorly administered firm, might be ripe for a take-over. This is in fact what occurred in 1965, Crystal now becoming Ford's sole main dealers in Hull.

In acquiring Harbour Motors Crystal also acquired their showroom at 172 Anlaby Road, and the workshops attached. This now allowed Jackson's Transport to take over some of the Bank Street premises - notably the workshops - and there carry out some of their own routine maintenance, cheek by jowl with the grocery warehouse.

In June 1953 Jackson's lent Crystal the sum of £22,000, and two months later Crystal bought premises at 39 Brunswick Avenue, installing their joiners, painters and electricians. Six months later the specialist engineering department followed. In effect, the shopfitters - or what would ultimately become Jackson's Services - now operated from entirely

Launch of a new model Cortina, October 1967, at Crystal of Scarborough. Shades of Z-Cars!

Methodist chapel, right in the historic centre in Wednesday Market, along with a garden, four houses and a cottage. They planned to demolish all of these buildings, but firstly they had to gain the permission of no less than sixteen trustees, some of whom were scattered throughout the United Kingdom, others of whom resided in South Africa, Australia and Canada. When they finally obtained the signatures they needed they were able to build the House of Ford. Crystal operated out of these premises until 1991 when they sold it to Boyes, the department store firm.

Beverley had opened in 1960. The following year Crystal had made what was a more significant move, buying another main Ford dealership from Wise of Scarborough with branches in Malton and Seamer. This is one of three dealerships still flying the Crystal flag, the others being Ford at Harrogate and Nissan at Grantham.

While these high-level manoeuvres had been taking place, what of life for Jackson's drivers out on the road? While there were always minor mishaps to contend with - like the time Tommy Jackson's mate forgot to close the side door and they lost a load of sausages turning out onto Hessle Road in a hurry - the effects of adverse weather conditions are what seem to stick in the mind more than anything.

Tommy Jackson is one of the few drivers who doesn't have a story to tell about the dreadful winter of 1947. He vividly recalls creeping along roads with drifts piled up higher than the van, but he never actually got stuck. T.C. Waite, however, relates a dramatic incident one Saturday when no fewer than nine of the firm's lorries got stuck in a huge drift on Arras Hill leading into Market Weighton. All of them were fully laden with bread and other goods for the York shops.

separate premises. This made good sense, since the shops side was about to undergo the transformation to self-service and would require the full-time services of a number of such tradesmen for many years to come.

As the business grew, particularly in car sales, Crystal found that they were starting to sell cars further afield - in Beverley, for example. At this time Ford would not countenance one firm having two main dealerships within thirty miles of each other, so the idea of a second outlet in Beverley seemed to be out of the question. However, the firm did find a retail outlet close by, the Halfway Garage at Woodmansey, on the old main road from Hull. A few years later Ford would agree that there was a definite need for another retail dealer in the market town and Crystal set about finding suitable premises. What they finally came up with was a large disused

On the Sunday morning he rounded up some men - among them Tommy Thompson, John Axton the dispatch manager, and Frank Garside the assistant services manager. They set off in three cars, calling at Newington shop to load up with supplies.

They got as far as an isolated cottage a couple of miles short of the stranded convoy but could get no further. So they walked, with their shovels, across the fields. They knew they had arrived when they found themselves treading on the cab roofs of the vehicles!

By nightfall they had dug hollows beneath the radiators and fuel tanks and lit small fires to thaw out the water and fuel. They finally got the engines started before returning to the cottages to sleep. The drivers had the pleasure of remaining with their vehicles to make sure they kept running.

Next morning the team walked back to where the lorries stood, checked on their drivers, and then set off down the hill towards the town. There they found an Army bulldozer clearing a path. They asked the sergeant in charge of the operation whether he might help clear a path through to the stranded lorries. Whatever doubts the sergeant may have had about abandoning his duties evaporated when T.C. pulled out a ten-pound note and a bottle of Scotch. The bread got through that morning. Small wonder that, as one Jackson's driver put it, when the weather closed in you could count on Jackson's men being the first in or the last out.

One of the rare occasions when the bread didn't get through - at least, not on a Jackson's lorry - was at Weaverthorpe in the winter of 1958 when a severe blizzard cut off Driffield and a number of villages to the north and east of Hull. On this occasion the RAF at Leconfield turned out with their helicopters to drop bread to the marooned villagers.

When Bridlington got cut off bread was piled into the guard's van of a passenger train - only for the crew to find that the platform at the resort town was piled so high with snow that the precious supplies could not be put off. Luckily the opposite platform was clear, so the bread was taken up to Scarborough and dropped off on the return run.

Tommy Jackson's worst mishap came in one of his last winters on the road, 1978. An articulated lorry jack-knifed in thick snow at Skirlaugh, near Hornsea, blocking the road completely. In the icy conditions Tommy had little choice but to spend the best part of the day huddled with a group of other men in one of the sheds where road-gangs stored their tools. After a long wait a farmer came by on a tractor. "Are you the bread men?" he wanted to know. Tommy told him he was, and the farmer explained that the shelves at the village shop were empty. In return for a tractor cab full of bread Tommy got a long, slow, and bitterly cold ride to Ganstead, over the fields. From there he was able to get a bus to town, arriving at the depot some thirteen hours after leaving it.

But at least he was safe. In his early days he had on one occasion to fear for his life, finding himself staring down the barrel of a loaded gun! He was on the way out to Hornsea, a run which passed through a number of little villages. At Old Ellerby there was a rather eccentric shop-keeper, an ex-Navy man. One time when Tommy called he had in his hand a sextant. Insisting on showing Tommy and his mate how it worked he took them out into the street to hold it up to the sun. As traffic slowly

The Princesse de Provence, a Rhone cruiser fitted out by Jackson's Services.

Sumptuous interior of the Princesse de Provence. This one was paid for!

built up and horns started to hoot the pair tried their best to look interested while the old salt went through a long and complicated demonstration.

Some weeks later Tommy arived at the same shop to find no-one in attendance. Going through into the living room behind the store he found the proprietor brandishing a revolver and threatening to do away with himself - "And I'll put one through you too if you don't watch out!" Tommy drove on to Skirlaugh and alerted the police. They arrived in time to disarm the poor man, but he was evidently not joking: two days later he jumped to his death from a second-storey window.

Up to 1971 Crystal ran not only the transport side of things but also, through the Specialised Engineering department, Jackson's shopfitting work. In that year, seeing that most of the department's work was now for the expanding retail division, converting shops to supermarkets, fitting out the new Grandways stores and so on, Jackson's Services was incorporated as a wholly owned subsidiary of the parent company and set up in premises in Wiltshire Road. The board comprised A.C Jefferson as chairman, Stan Tillotson, Cyril Terry and Geoff Nurse as Company Secretary.

Services not only carried out this shop-fitting work, but remained responsible for buying, and overseeing routine maintenance on, Jackson's transport - even though much of that transport would be bought from Crystal. The printing and publicity departments were now incorporated.

Now, just as Crystal had spread its wings, obtained its own Ford agency and begun to deal with the general public, so Services started to take on outside work. They started with fitting out the Ristorante Italia in Beverley Road, Hull, and within a very short while were finding work outside the city. Over the next few years contracts were secured with Trust House Forte, with EMI for a Harrow bingo hall, and with Blue Arrow for their offices in London. The most spectacular was for the interior fitting of a series of cruisers including the *Princesse de Provence*, which operated on the Rhone, and the Ra series destined for the Nile. Unfortunately full payment was never received for the last of these luxury liners, a substantial bad debt being incurred. "Christening" the earlier models had proved an interesting experience - a calf was sacrificed on the adjacent quayside before the fitter's very eyes, and the blood smeared all over the hull! Just as the parent company had acquired various subsidiaries over the years so Services too came to incorporate one or two other firms, notably the engravers and sign-makers Northern Engraving and, later, the French polishers Glew & Whittaker.

Another major contract was for fitments to the new Terminal Four at London's Heathrow Airport. Back on home territory the Leeds Playhouse and the Hull New Theatre were renovated. Work was also carried out for Asda supermarkets and extensive work undertaken at the Meadowhall shopping centre in Sheffield.

At its peak Services employed eighty-nine joiners, a dozen refrigeration engineers and sixteen electricians. Roughly half of its work was for Jackson's own shops. The firm trained its own apprentices in refrigeration, joinery, electrical work and painting - even though, as is so often the case, the trainees would move on elsewhere upon graduating. But that was an occupational hazard in any trade. As Brian Robinson, the firm's contracts' director, pointed out, "they went away from us as lads, and in three or four years they'd come back, grown-up." In the mid-eighties the National Association of

Shopfitters placed the firm at number twenty-one in a national league. Men like Walter Varney and Alf Turner, Jack Gallant, Ron Duke and Jack Nurse were the stalwarts of this outfit, working all hours and striving to complete shop renovations to incredibly tight schedules, never knowing when a fridge might fail to turn up or - worse - when Gordon 'half-inch' Russell might show up and insist on a huge display cabinet being moved ever so slightly to satisfy his idiosyncratic interpretation of the plans.

Taking on large contracts was not without its drawbacks. Expansion of the scale of operations meant increased overheads. Pub work, which had been part of the firm's bread and butter for a while, was eventually lost when they found that smaller firms operating out of car-boots were able to undercut them. They had a loyal - but costly - administrative staff of their own to pay.

As the firm grew it became cramped in the Wiltshire Road premises and in the late eighties moved into Concept House on Freightliner Way. There were good years and bad years according to the figures, but there was no pleasing some people. When the firm made money they found that the Grandways people complained they had been overcharging them! Grandways might complain, but having Services available as part of the wider organisation was very convenient for them. Pride and loyalty too came into the equation. Old servants like Alf Turner and Walter Varney worked to a high standard and expected the same of their staff. It was sometimes the high standards they set that pushed the costs up. The shops might have got cheaper quotes elsewhere, but would not have been assured of the same standard of workmanship.

It was the recession of the late eighties which really hurt the shop-fitters. Not only was there less work around, but work on large contracts would even be terminated halfway through as firms hit troubled waters and had to call a halt.

By 1990 the firm, with a staff of 150, had a turnover of £13.5 million, yet within three years it was facing severe financial difficulties. Losses on the third Nile cruiser were undoubtedly a major factor. While some departments were closed down, others were sold as going concerns, printing, for example, being taken over by AIM. The company had been a great asset to Jackson's, one of which they had been justifiably proud. However, the bracing economic climate of the '90s demanded that businesses looked to their core interests. While Jackson's did indeed shed a number of divisions outside that core, it made an exception in the case of Crystal which it bought back early in 1993.

Chapter Thirteen

AIM

We have seen that as Jackson's grew it acquired various ancillary services. Certain of these simply became too large for Jackson's to want to run. Jackson's Services itself, for example, became a wholly owned subsidiary in 1971. The story of their computer subsidiary is another example of the board's ability to spawn successful off-shoots which, finally, have to go their own way.

In the late 1960s the parent company were still using a punch-card system, dating back to the '50s, to handle information passing between its retail and manufacturing divisions. The work was, by its very nature, tedious, labour-intensive and inefficient. And there was a lot of it. So the board went out and hired itself a computing expert.

Brian Oughtred, at this time joint Managing Director with his cousin Peter, hired former computer salesman Clive Telfer. BNO in fact asked him to set up and run the very system which he had just managed to sell to the company - in Telfer's own words "a fiendish thing to do". Shortly after his arrival John Davis also joined the firm as Chief Programme Executive. This pair now established the group's Computer Services. They had to build a team from scratch, write all the programmes, find a place to house the staff and equipment, and train people. Over the succeeding three or four years they got systems up and running for the bakery and the retail arms. A fourth member of the team was Geoff Nurse, formerly Jackson's chief accountant and their Secretary since 1970. Until his retirement in 1982 he held a place on the board of AIM and served as their company secretary.

Computing in those days was fairly basic. Barcoding of goods in the shops had yet to come, and orders were marked on cards in which boxes marked 1,2,4 or 8 were filled in by pencil to indicate amounts required for each line. Nine, for instance, would be coded by filling in the eight and the one. This was the old OMR, or Optical Mark Reading method.

The 'boffins' were viewed by many as outsiders, mavericks, being the one outfit within the company about whom nobody really knew anything. However, in BNO they had a staunch ally. He was a great enthusiast for modernisation, keen to give these technical whizz-kids their heads. He could also be something of an autocrat - a trait he might have inherited from his grandfather, old Mr. Bentham.

By 1970 the system that Telfer and Davis had set up was already running out of processing and storage capacity. The team were often subject to extreme pressure from two sides at once: production managers wanting accurate forecasts of the day's requirements as early as possible in order to plan ahead, and shop managers wanting to delay their orders as long as possible to see what they sold in the day. It was the old retail-manufacturing friction rearing its head again.

When the computer people went to BNO to ask for money to augment their data-holding capacity - and to provide back-up in case of the breakdown which was always at the back of everyone's mind - he came up with a rather far-sighted solution. Knowing that elements on the main board might resent making a huge investment - the sum in question was over £1 million - on what they thought of as a new fangled outfit, he offered them the extra money on the condition that they used some of the surplus capacity to sell their services to other local businesses - that is, to generate a bit of extra income. The increased capacity was required, by and large, for short periods of intense activity - the four o'clock rush as the van drivers returned to the depot, for example - and would otherwise be under-used.

So in the early seventies a twin processor was acquired which placed the company in the fore-front of technological innovation. For a company of Jackson's size, this represented an unprecedented and invaluable acquisition. Computer Services (Hull) Ltd now started seeking outside work. Among its first, and most prestigious, contracts was one for Comet, the electrical goods firm. At the same time as making this extra income the computing arm was evidently saving the parent company money. Around this time Jackson's employed some 200 clerical staff, forty matching shop returns with delivery notes and another 25 in payroll. Within a decade this total would be reduced to sixty.

The massive task of switching to decimal currency in 1971, and the introduction of VAT two years later, plus the gains from the outside work, utterly vindicated BNO's decision to fund the computer division. However, business is never stable. A business that attempts to stand still will fail. Comet, recognising what an invaluable job Jackson's were doing for them, invested in their own computer. The Jackson's team now saw the danger of relying too heavily on any one account and expanded their range, ultimately winning contracts with Safeway, Sainsbury, Tesco, Halfords and W.H. Smith. Their aim now was to reduce their Jackson's work to as little as 20% of their portfolio. So long as Jackson's was their major client, the question might be asked, as at Services,

AIM's state of the art computer hall, 1980. Try fitting one of these on your desk top!

were the outside customers being charged extra in order to subsidise the parent company? Within the parent company, however, the corollary question was being asked: were Jackson's bearing the cost of AIM's competitive quotes to outside customers. The board were well aware of the situation and strove to see that

Jackson's were charged a going rate for its work. Within any large business the transfer price between departments has to be set so that each department's performance can be correctly assessed.

In 1976 AIM was formed. For the record, it now became Automatic Information Management. It was felt that the new name rid the firm of its somewhat parochial image. One of the firm's early achievements, having lost the Comet contract, was to move into the legal business. The company found that a number of Hull solicitors were regularly sending data to London to have it processed. Approaching the firms in question, they offered them a local service, guaranteeing a twenty-four hour turnaround. They then set about developing a whole range of legal systems, selling the hardware and the software to go with them.

Now, perhaps for the first time, the main board were more convinced of AIM's value. BNO had always been proud of his 'baby' - or the company's 'third arm', as he called it. In fact the returns were small compared with the other arms - the bakery and the shops - but here was Jackson's at the leading edge of a new technology, the first name in computing services in Hull.

Christopher Oughtred, talking of AIM, stresses the way it reflected the company's overall policy of giving resident experts their head. They had done a job for the company, but what would they do now? Rather than let them go, the board preferred to give them the freedom to sharpen their competitive edge with outside work. Beyond that was the fact that AIM was now making money.

Up to the time of his death in December 1981 BNO was chairman of AIM. Having him gave the computer people clout with the main board, although it had its drawbacks. Being the kind of forthright, enthusiastic character he was, he could steamroller people. People were inclined to say of a proposal, "Well, BNO's for it, so it'll probably happen." Upon his death, Peter Oughtred, Peter Farley and Christopher Oughtred joined the AIM board, an indication of how seriously the company was now viewed. Meanwhile AIM expanded in the legal software business. For a while it had regional offices in Birmingham, Newcastle and Bradford - and even in central London, which ruffled a few feathers around Derringham Street. Clive Telfer was even envisaging foreign ventures. He sought to open agencies in the Far East, notably in Hong Kong and Singapore. These former outposts of the Empire had adopted the old British legal systems and represented a potential area for growth. Telfer, meanwhile, was coming to see AIM as caught between the bakery and the shops and thus likely to be criticised by either when things went wrong.

In its best years AIM made profits of around £300-400,000 a year. By the mid-eighties, with the rapid advances in computer technology, notably in miniaturisation, there was no longer the need for a centralised bureau based around a mainframe computer: small, portable, user-friendly computers, relatively cheap to install, were now on every desk. The time was ripe, Davis and Telfer felt, for a management buy-out.

From Jackson's point of view too this was attractive. Nobody now really had the enthusiasm and commitment for AIM which BNO had shown. The subsidiary was growing in very diverse directions. The acid test was, supposing AIM came to the main board asking for capital to open a Singapore office. Would it be granted? The answer was that it wouldn't. In 1983-84 the board had been forced to finance a re-structuring of the bakery division and cut costs all around. Now it was turning to the shops. Jackson's still preferred to spend only what it could generate from profits or via its bankers. It could not issue new shares on the stock market like a publicly quoted company. With all this in mind Christopher felt it would be unfair to hold AIM back. Deep down the two were bound to part. As John Davis points out, Jackson's consisted of grocers and bakers: they were there primarily to conserve and expand what they had built up over 135 years. Had they been primarily out to make money and commit themselves to this high-risk hi-tec industry, they might have chanced their arm. But this was not where their sympathies - or their true loyalties - lay.

Even in BNO's days AIM had been pushing for independence. Telfer had felt all along that they were a step ahead of Jackson's, even in their house style. They were the first to produce an advertising video, first to go into marketing; they were even first to lay carpets in their offices - "looks like a bloody Chinese brothel," one main board member was heard to mutter when he first walked in. And at that time computers were very much a specialist 'people business' - computing experts were not as easy to find as shop staff.

As M.D. Christopher Oughtred had a controlling hand in the negotiations. They were not simple. The AIM management were not the only bidders, and at least one outside tender was considered. The talks dragged on through the summer of 1987, and the group Chairman was getting restless. He seemed more anxious than anyone to get the thing over with. Finally he came up with a deadline, a date in the middle of August, after which he would simply be unavailable. It was not until the sale - to the AIM team - was signed, sealed and delivered, that the parties realised that the date was August 12th, the start of the grouse shooting up in Teesdale!

Chapter Fourteen

CRISIS IN THE BAKERY DIVISION

Through the 1960s and '70s the retailing division had increasingly produced the greater proportion of Jackson's profits. The bakery side had been under constant pressure despite the efforts of the managerial team at Hull headed by Fred Aitchison and George Kilburn, who moved to head office from Stockton in 1966, the year of T.F. Dodsworth's retirement. Aitchison had joined the company after the war, become the bakery's production manager in 1951, and a main board director in 1964, retiring in 1979. Kilburn, for whom Stockton staff still have considerable respect and affection, had joined the main board in 1968. Both men were, at various times, on the board of Timms, each serving a spell as chairman.

Government policy in this period had had the effect of keeping bread prices artificially low. A squeeze on prices and profits, with bread a staple item in the inflationary index, rendered bakery products liable to the strictest controls. In many instances the bakers were not even able to pass on compensatory rises as the price of wheat and flour rose. In addition to these difficulties, labour relations within the industry as a whole had soured. Jackson's own staff - to the great regret of many of them - had been involved in two national bread strikes.

The retail side had attracted much of the firm's investment and a great deal of the board's energies, contributing hugely to the firm's overall profits. To some extent this masked the unpleasant reality that the bakery side was making a loss - as much as £1 million a year at one stage. With this in mind, a team was set up to unravel the division's problems and come up with some solutions, Patrick Farnsworth, Allan Wheelwright, Peter Farley, Ron Milligan and the chairman's son Christopher Oughtred forming the core. This was a young team of men - some still in their early thirties - who must have been aware that the retailers, mostly men of an older generation, had a poor opinion of the bakery division after its recent difficulties. In Christopher Oughtred there was a representative of a new generation of the family. He had joined the company in 1975, become personal assistant to Brian Oughtred in 1978, and moved onto the board just prior to the latter's death in 1981. His brother Angus, having joined the company in 1974, had gone into the meat division; Brian's son Michael would join the company in 1982; and Nicholas, Peter's son, would arrive in October 1983 to work in the Crystal Motors group.

One of the first steps this team had to take was the closure of the Rotherham bakery, in April 1982. While this cost the company some business, around eighty to ninety per cent was retained to be shared out amongst the other plants. To counter the loss there were savings in transport costs to take into account. Nevertheless, to the staff at Rotherham, the closure was a bolt from the blue. For manager Frank Taylor it was "a very hard and bitter pill to take". While Rotherham was thus axed it remained quite clear that Stockton, Wakefield and Hull were working below their capacity, even though money had recently been invested in Wakefield. However, the board's rationale was that, having spent money on Wakefield, it could ill afford to shut it down, and closing Rotherham would allow those others to absorb the extra production and thus operate more efficiently. Wakefield would now concentrate on small and speciality loaves, items to which Rotherham could not easily have switched.

All the Rotherham staff were thus made redundant and the plant dismantled, some of it being taken to Hull, and the factory site sold to B & Q for a new store. A couple of the vans were sent to Scunthorpe depot, two more to Wakefield, and the rest remained on site in what was to remain a depot for the time being. A year later this was moved to the present site on Mangam Road, a purpose-built depot.

In September of that year a report the company had commissioned through auditors Hodgson Harris was presented to the main board. Its message was blunt: William Jackson's interests would be served by getting out of baking altogether. To continue to carry losses at the present level - of £2,000 a day! - might threaten the future of the entire company. The bakery must at the very least undergo radical and effective reform, or face closure.

While this report to some extent confirmed what the team looking into the bakery's future suspected, it was felt that a second report would be in order. Early in 1983 a management consultant group was commissioned to look specifically at each individual section of the bakery. They charged a cool £250,000 for their assessment, but offered a guarantee to the company that they would save that amount within a year. Action was certainly needed, for in one quarter Jackson's as a whole actually lost money. These were, of course, tough times for businesses throughout the country, but the results were a shock to a board - and to shareholders - used to seeing profits increase year after year. The exercise was, Christopher Oughtred believes, well worth the outlay: "They educated

us...they suggested ways we might approach the problems we faced."

In this time of crisis - for that is undoubtedly what it was - the team saw a number of possible options, ranging from a complete withdrawal from baking to maintaining three main plants as they were, but investing heavily in Stockton. But that would mean cash - and a lot of it. Rotherham had been sold; Wakefield had the most up-to-date plant but a poor record; Stockton was clearly out of date. It was felt that to get out of baking altogether might genuinely threaten the future of the entire company. In any case it would mean the end of Jackson's as it had been known for almost a century. Nevertheless, the retailers might well have settled for that 'final solution'. But, as Patrick Farnsworth has pointed out, there was still a degree of sentiment in favour of what was, after all, at the very heart of the firm.

Ultimately it was decided to invest heavily in Stockton, to help finance the development by selling Wakefield, and to forge ahead with just the two bakeries. Wakefield thus ceased production. The closure came abruptly, but as no great shock to Frank Taylor - now back at Wakefield and bearing the unenviable reputation of having the kiss of death wherever he went. He was perplexed to find that the workforce there had become, in his opinion, somewhat recalcitrant, occasionally even belligerent, the complete anti-thesis of what they had been during his previous spell there - that is, diligent, friendly and utterly reliable. He lays the blame for this change unequivocally at the door of the management who, he considers, had allowed morale to sink as the plant lost money.

There were other reasons for letting Wakefield go. The bulk of the company's bread business was in the north of the region, supplying chains like Hintons, Laws and Allied Suppliers, so maintaining Stockton made sense on that score. For a while the board had considered hanging onto Wakefield, but when, out of the blue, Laws deserted Jackson's and went to Sunblest, Wakefield was sold, in December 1983, to Warburton's. Warbuton's were in a sense a rival to Jackson's being another large regional independent baker, but there were compelling reasons for making the sale. There were not too many bakers in that region looking to increase their capacity, and the alternative to selling - for a decent price - might have been to dismantle the place. Secondly, whereas Jackson's were still the only major plant baker on Humberside, and prominent on Teesside, they were one of a number battling for custom in the West Riding. The loss of the Laws contract further suggested the way the business was now going, with a new breed of professional buyer taking over from the founders of family firms and having an altogether less sentimental approach to traditional trading relationships.

The money from the sale of Wakefield thus contributed to the new plant at Stockton, a total of over £1.5 million being invested there. A fully-automated fifteen-sack plant capable of producing 3,500 loaves an hour now replaced old plant dating from the original bakery of 1955 which had produced no less than 40 million loaves! The bakery production had now been realigned, the same capacity as before now being located in two rather than four bakeries, and centred very much where the trade was: in Hull for the Humberside region, and in Stockton for the Hintons and Presto contracts. The division's overheads were at the same time halved. The structure of the division was now ripe for the management team, under Patrick Farnsworth, to forge ahead. Their aim now was to concentrate on quality and service and, where possible, to follow the 'own-label' route.

Towards the end of 1984 and into 1985 the tide was thus seen to be turning for the embattled bakery. It was at this time that an important new contract was won, to supply bread to the Hillards chain based at Cleckheaton. This was a psychologically important breakthrough. It had been felt that for too long the bakery had been serving the cheaper end of the market. Now it set out to produce a higher quality own label product - a chance for the bakers to show their mettle. Jackson's had not, of course, been alone in the 1970s in going for mass production at lowest cost and at the expense of quality. All the 'big boys' had done the same. Bread baking had been very much a poor relation of the food industry and it had been left to the smaller independents and the back-street craftsmen to pursue the quality goal.

In May 1985, therefore, the bakery started to supply Hillards' stores with a total of around 200,000 loaves a week under that company's own label. The decision to invest in Stockton had thus been vindicated, and the prodigious energies put in by men like Derek Wheeler and Ken Hawkridge for the bakery had reaped their reward. A new depot was now opened at Morley, near Leeds, to handle the shipments.

The bakery division was now on the road to recovery after a very sticky patch. During the pre-war period it had made a great deal of money for the firm and its shareholders, but changes in the business, the strict controls on pricing, and increased competition had exacted a heavy toll. In 1986 the confectionery and savouries side would be completely abandoned with a number of redundancies. Nevertheless, the bakery is now stronger, more efficient and more focused, with a higher quality operation and a good range of customers in what remains a difficult and price-sensitive market.

Chapter Fifteen

A SECOND RETAIL REVOLUTION

From the latter part of 1966 the original Grandways chain had grown rapidly until, by the early eighties, the number of stores totalled forty, being established in places as far apart as Nottingham, Burton-on-Trent, Skegness and Chapel Allerton. At the same time many of Jackson's original shops had adopted the Grandways name and livery so that the whole chain now comprised seventy shops, the number rising to eighty by June 1988.

As businesses adapt and develop - and even if they do so successfully - fresh problems arise. In the eighties the Jackson's board became aware that on the retail side they were having to gear their operations to the varied needs of a wide range of store types. They faced problems which other retail groups did not encounter to such an extent. Tesco, Sainsbury, Asda, for example, are generally associated with large shops. They may have moved from the High Street to the edge of town, but the public clearly knows what to expect of them: they are not the kind of store you would pop into for a bottle of milk and a packet of cigarettes.

When Jackson's classified those of its shops below the 4,000 square feet mark as 'smaller' and those above that size as 'larger' they still had a problem: the larger variety included such stores as Bottesford at 4,650 square feet, Borrowash at 15,000, and the Boothferry Park store adjoining Hull City football ground at 20,000.

Opened in 1983, and at that time the largest Grandways, Boothferry Park was built on the site of Hull City F.C.'s old North Stand.

The retailers felt that they had been performing reasonably well in what was, after all, a recessionary climate, but reasonably well was not good enough now that the competition was hotting up. The stores were now facing a number of challenges: Sainsbury had been in West Hull since the early eighties, Tesco was in Hall Road, and Asda was well established at Bilton. The retail board, under the chairmanship of Martin Russell, now applied itself to finding a retail formula to meet this threat.

In 1987 experts were engaged from the Manchester Business School to advise them on the way forward. They were to produce two reports over the next three years which would broadly conclude that the retail division was indeed trying to do too many things at once in terms of the variety of its store types.

At the same time, however, the firm was going ahead with plans for one of the most ambitious developments in Jackson's history, the Giant Grandways at Willerby. There had been a feeling for

This picture of Stepney branch which opened in 1914 echoes some of the changes in the shops' division. It became self-service in 1965, later Jackson's discount store, and is here seen sporting the Grandways' insignia. It fell subject to a compulsory purchase order in the 1980s.

162a High Street, Scunthorpe. Not all the shops carried the Grandways banner.

Barkers of Sandal, near Wakefield. Another regional shop bearing the Grandways fascia.

Some of the Jackson's shops continued to trade under their original name - in this case Harpers of Starbeck.

some years that the company should build a superstore. As far back as 1977 a site at Lowfield Road in Anlaby had been acquired, but plans for a superstore there had been rejected by the local authority. Some while later the board had put in a bid for land at the junction of Hall Road and Beverley Road, but lost out to Tesco.

Willerby looked like an ideal site. The board believed that there was room for such a store in that part of Hull, close to the company's heartland and the majority of its existing shops. Work was proceeding on improvements to the A164 road linking West Hull and Beverley with the Humber Bridge and the M62. The site would be served by an excellent communications network. And, these factors aside, there were sound defensive reasons for going into the area: if Jackson's didn't get the site, somebody else would. There was a lot to gain and much to lose in an area where the name of Jackson's had long held sway.

In addition to these propitious factors, and despite the fact that the company had little experience of a project of quite this size, there was a retail board of mainly young men keen to take on the challenge and see what they could make of it, just as previous generations within the company had gone into unknown territory before them.

Early projections, based on careful market research, suggested that there was money to made at Willerby. The main worry, however, was the very size of the site. What would be done with the larger portion of the eleven acres which would surround the new store? Would it be sold off, or would it be included as part of a larger development?

The new Giant Grandways at Willerby and a linked development including a DIY store, a petrol and service station, and eight other shops, was opened by the Mayor of Beverley on December 3, 1990. It represented the largest investment Jackson's had ever made, and was a bold attempt to establish a toehold in the superstore league - that is, in stores of over 25,000 square feet. Boothferry Park, opened in 1983, almost qualified, and as a one-off had been a success. But here was a true Giant, having over 50,000 square feet, of which 35,000 was actual selling space.

The trouble with the big league, however, is that it is full of big teams, public companies with huge financial resources which can raise enough money on the stock market to build up a whole chain of stores and achieve a measure of security. Jackson's has chosen to remain a family firm for almost a hundred and fifty years. It has never been seriously tempted to float itself on the Stock Exchange - and it would have had to bring in outside capital in order to expand to any great degree beyond the Willerby base. In a sense, Christopher Oughtred points out, the firm's heritage - its tradition of only spending what money it has generated as profits - was at odds with this.

Willerby made money. There is no doubting that. The problem was that it struggled to make enough money - and it became, finally, a drain on retail resources. The retail division had its continuing programme of store refurbishment to finance - modern supermarkets ideally need to be re-vamped every five years to keep abreast of structural, technological and design developments. And around the time that work began on Willerby, a large investment had been made in a site at Melton, well situated at the Hull end of the M62, where a new Centralised Distribution depot was established.

An aerial shot of the Giant Grandways development at Willerby.

Cheese counter at Giant Grandways. The Willerby store won the prestigious "retail cheese display award" in a national contest.

The Melton depot represented a huge step forward for a firm of Jackson's size. Central Distribution is a system whereby, as the name implies, stocks of goods are held at a central location for distribution to the stores. The advantage, provided it is linked to an efficient stock-taking and delivery service, is that individual stores no longer need the kind of warehouse capacity they traditionally had. Furthermore suppliers were increasingly loath to deliver to small stores.

With EPOS (Electronic Point Of Sale) monitoring and, latterly, a system of Perpetual Inventory facilitated by the electronic beam at the check-out, stores now have their shelves replenished from Melton, six times a week according to a strictly controlled timetable. As Paul Cross, Logistics Director (Distribution and Information Technology) points out, this to some extent restricts the role of the shop manager. However, it places an additional responsibility on that manager and his or her staff to maintain tight in-store discipline, to keep the brake on leakage of various kinds, be it through theft, spillage or damage to goods. Stock figures *have* to be accurate.

When Jackson's first set up Melton it was run by an outside firm but after a while it was decided that it would be better to exercise closer control, and a team under Paul Cross and Joss Morley, at the time buying director but later to become the Managing Director of the Retail Division, was installed.

Melton, then, was an up-to-date, hi-tech operation where goods could be shifted from the point of production (the factories) to the point of sale (Jackson's shops) with the utmost speed and efficiency. With its advanced information technology, Melton has replaced the army of travelling reps: it can identify a shortfall in any line in any store before the store's own customers have spotted it. Indeed, such is its intelligence network that it often has a better idea than the suppliers how much of a particular item they are shifting.

For Melton, however, Willerby posed one or two problems of its own. Willerby was always a special case. It required a larger volume of goods than any other store and, more significantly, it stocked a far greater range of goods than any other. This many lines had to be acommodated at Melton - and additional space and handling allowed for - just for the one store.

Throughout this time of change, it must be reiterated, the retail division as a whole continued to be in profit. Its problem remained that it wasn't making sufficient profit. Survival is not enough in the modern business world: a company needs to be making enough to fund growth and development as well as keeping the shareholders happy. A modest return on capital might have been enough for retailers in the past but something in the order of twenty per cent was now the order of the day. Furthermore, and even more worryingly, some of the 'big boys' were now starting to cast envious eyes at Jackson's

traditional territory. There could be no hiding away in a clutch of quiet corner stores with the large multinational discounters moving in.

It may well have been that the Willerby adventure came at the wrong moment. But whatever the case, the fact remains that Jackson's was not a purely retail concern. It always had its manufacturing arm to consider. While this may be seen as applying a brake on ambition, it is also possible to conceive it as a safety net - and the same thing applies to retailing *vis-a-vis* the bakery.

In October 1991 Martin Russell retired. The following month Frank Dee joined the company as head of the retail division. Dee's was not a universally popular appointment. While some see him as a brilliant, clear-minded individual, others see his clarity of purpose and single-mindedness as making some of his commercial judgements appear to be somewhat harsh. But, as the M.D. has said, he saw the division through a hard time. And he made important decisions which might have been harder - perhaps impossible - for someone closer to the heart of the company. In terms of the overall history of Jackson's it was perhaps time to bring in another outsider whose opinion would be unclouded by sentiment and tradition. Dee's task was to decide on the future of Willerby and the other large shops, and to point the way forward for the small stores.

On the small stores front progress was already being made. A working group had been set up under Angus Oughtred and James Hall, son of Richard and great-grandson of 'Bompy', along with representatives from accounts, from personnel, and from an outside retail group. One of the first points

Jackson's on Princes Avenue was opened in 1905. Note the circular recess which formerly held the clock. A junior hand would be sent up to wind it on Monday mornings. In the mid-60s most of these clocks were removed.

the new-style Convenient Neighbourhood Supermarket, or C.N.S., a concept which married the traditional strengths of the old shops with the technology and experience gained from the Grandways chain. Customers would now have the convenience of a corner store along with the efficiency of a supermarket.

The return to root values which the new development represented is best reflected in the name chosen for the re-vamped stores. Three separate market research teams worked on the name and the colour scheme, and while such names as Square Deal and Handy Jack were dutifully considered, the clear favourite with the people who knew best - the firm's own customers - was the name for so long associated with their local shop, "Jackson's Of"..Newland Avenue, Malton or Hornsea. The choice of turquoise livery further echoed the past and the beautiful mosaics which still adorn such 'classic' Jackson's shops as Inglemire Lane and Chanterlands Avenue.

The first shop to be up-dated along the new lines was Chanterlands Avenue. It was closed on Saturday 18 July 1991, remodelled, redecorated inside and out and re-opened on Thursday 23rd at eight in the morning as Jacksons Of Chanterlands. This small shop (1800 square feet) saw a dramatic rise in revenue that first week and was voted a success by a consumer panel convened by the small stores working group.

The group had been confident that the new format would succeed. The Chanterlands Avenue site was ideal, being on a busy street which housed a whole range of shops as well as being right in the centre of a densely populated series of streets with a high percentage of single-person households - that is, of

this group noted was the tremendous asset the small stores possessed in terms of location. "Lots of chimney-pots", as they say in the trade. These were some of the firm's oldest shops, close in to the centre of Hull in areas of high population density - in Newland Avenue, Holderness Road, Princes Avenue and so on - the old Jackson's heartland. Yet despite occupying these prime sites their business was being eroded - by a new breed of down-market shops opening seven days a week for extended hours.

What the working group came up with after a period of intensive research and creative thought, was people unlikely to run an estate car up to Tesco's on a Friday night and load up with £100-worth of groceries. The second "Jackson's Of" store to open seemed to be a rather different proposition, being only a quarter of a mile from Giant Grandways at Willerby. Would it succeed as well? The fact was that it was hardly in competition with its neighbour: that was the whole point about the smaller shops, which catered for the more modest shopper.

By the time Frank Dee produced his first report on his findings in the retail division, around Christmastime 1991, two further C.N.S. stores were open, at Spotborough Road, Doncaster, and Hessle Road, Hull. During the period from January to May of 1992 some £1.5 million was spent on refurbishing a total of thirty small stores and converting them to the new concept. The rapidity of the changeover reflected Frank Dee's own enthusiasm for the scheme. This was reflected in his report, which he entitled Project '92. Here he told the board that the small stores scheme was a winner and should be pushed hard. The company should pump whatever resources it had available into a 'fast-track roll-out' programme: the quicker the better, for even in the grocery business the volume of business generally rises in the summer season, and it would be as well to catch some of that seasonal boom.

On the large stores front Dee saw an urgent need for a large injection of capital. He suggested the company come up with a solid five-year plan for each of its divisions and then 'sell' these plans to such financial insitutions as might be in a position to provide funds. However the matter was not this simple. More than mere capital was required in order to establish a successful format for the Grandways stores.

At the same time as producing this report - in itself a prodigious achievement - Dee applied himself to trying out a number of experimental retailing formulae. In the spring of 1992 he opened a discount-format Giant Trading Company in Kirkstall Lane, Leeds, and two more at Skegness and Orchard Park, Hull. He tried re-vamping a number of other stores to appeal to a public in search of high quality fresh produce. But in this latter case he found the cost of re-fitting prohibitive. The Giant Trading Company didn't come to anythng, either. It required a tremendously tight and efficient administration in order to have any hope of realising a reasonable margin.

The failure of these experiments - once more it was the level of profit needed which was the problem - prompted Dee to utter the inevitable, yet sacrilegious, proposition: that Jackson's get out of Grandways and concentrate on the one sure-fire success it had going for it, the Convenient Neighbourhood Stores. The board were by now ready to accept this, but opinion was dead against selling the large stores individually. There was to be no 'pick-and-mix' sale for rival firms to select the choicest shops. The chain should, ideally, be sold intact.

Having made this momentous decision, there came the ticklish business of approaching potential buyers. Frank Dee and Christopher Oughtred together went to the Argyll group and told them that they were thinking of concentrating their energies on convenience stores. Argyll immediately expressed interest. Kwiksave were likewise approached. But in selling the Grandways chain there was more at stake than simply getting the best price: there was the further consideration of ensuring that the valuable - indeed, vital - bread sales to the large supermarket chains were protected, not to mention jobs within the company.

The new Jackson's of Chanterlands combines the clean lines of the modern store with an echo of the classics of the pre-war period.

While Dee and the retail board were applying themselves to this particular problem the main board were taking a broader look at the whole company's future. It was decided that the burgeoning frozen foods division required further investment. They also came to the regrettable conclusion that the company should withdraw from two areas in which it had been involved for almost a hundred years - meat production at Cottingham, and Services, both of which were heavily dependent on their Grandways contracts. Jobs were therefore to be lost, not only at Inglemire Lane and Services, but also at headquarters, where seventy administrative staff were made redundant.

The loss of the large Grandways stores - about twenty split evenly between Kwik Save and the Argyll group - along with the associated closures, were traumatic both for those unfortunate enough to lose their jobs and for long-term or retired employees who felt that much of what they had worked for had gone up in smoke. Fred Standing, retired for fifteen years but still every inch a Jackson's man, felt "crucified" by the changes. Others were shocked at the suddenness with which it all happened. For the press it was the opportunity to write Jackson's off as a failure. "From Corner Shop to Corner Shop in Five Generations" is how one national newspaper rather cruelly summed up what had happened. Yet others prefer to see it as a return to root values. Certainly there have always been people within the company who have felt that, while Grandways certainly made a great deal of money for the parent company, Jackson's should never have got into it. However it cannot be denied that the bakery - and the old meat division - had benefitted considerably from having this secure market for a proportion of their output. The important thing was that Jackson's had once more adapted to shifting economic and commercial trends, had survived, and had found a way forward.

Every man and his dog has an opinion on the Grandways story!

Chapter Sixteen

JACKSON'S PEOPLE

Like a lot of family firms, Jackson's were slow to be persuaded of the benefits of trade unions. With close relationships between staff, management and board in what was for the first half century a very small company, problems could generally be solved at a personal level. The loyalty of long-serving staff bore its rewards - not so much in terms of money on the table, but more importantly, in job security and the knowledge that in times of hardship, sickness or death the company was a friend willing to help.

In a factory or similar workplace where all the staff are under one roof it is perhaps easier to formulate and put into action a coherent policy for dealing with employer-employee relations. But Jackson's employed a large percentage of their people in shops and warehouses or on the road as deliverymen, travellers or errand lads. One way of getting these scattered individuals together was through events like the annual picnic, held for many years at Mr. Bentham's house at Swanland and paid for by the members of the board from their own pockets.

Quite when the picnics started is not certain, but a photograph of one in 1905 has survived. Neither is it known when they ended, although there is evidence of one as late as 1921 - a programme listing the sports and games which followed lunch. Certainly, from the early 1930s sports events up at Cottingham became a regular feature of the social year, with cups for various athletic events as well as for games such as tennis and cricket. In addition to these there were children's outings and Christmas parties, as well as the annual staff dances held at Beverley Road baths.

From very early days the directors' minute-books, and notably the diaries of Richard Hall, reveal numerous references to the broader sphere of employee welfare, a subject that exercised the board's minds continually. Hall, incidentally, kept his diaries scrupulously up to date for forty-one years, noting everything from the price of bacon to events of national significance.

In 1914 a matter of pressing concern - that of staff joining H.M. Forces - arose for the first time. Would their jobs be safe if they went to serve their country? They would: their positions were to be held open for them and, during their absence, between five and ten shillings a week would be paid to their dependants.

At the 1917 A.G.M. it was noted that no fewer than 112 Jackso n's men had joined the services, this from a total workforce, male and female, of under 500. Of these nine had been killed and one died of rheumatism. Notes of condolence had been sent to the parents and next of kin.

By the twenties a number of staff had been with the company a great many years. Mr. Bentham was able to report in 1923 that an increasing number had over twenty-five years' service, and several had taken advantage of the chance to become shareholders. By 1924 all employees were insured under the new Employers' Liability Act, and at that year's A.G.M. Bentham noted the good feeling between the company and its workers and expressed pleasure that more and more were buying shares. This, he considered, was "the best preventive of trade misunderstandings or disputes". In order to induce others to follow suit he now offered £1,000-worth of his own holding at face value to those who had not yet bought into the company.

Staff gather for Jackson's annual picnic, 22nd June, 1905.

By 1928 the numbers employed by the firm had passed the 500 mark for the first time. Wages varied widely according to, status, age, sex and seniority. As we have seen elsewhere, staff coming in from other companies were occasionally able to negotiate their own wages. Cyril Terry, who came into the publicity department from the College of Art, remembers being interviewed by Mr. Cruickshank, the company secretary. He was asked, "Well, young man, and what do you think we should pay you?" "Twelve and six a week," Cyril answered. "Hmm, that's two-and-six more than I was thinking of," came the reply. Cyril was paid ten shillings - and two or three years later when Cruickshank went to prison for embezzlement had cause to wonder about that extra half-crown.

Paid holidays were being granted to all shops' staff at least as early as 1930, for in that year a sub-committee met to draw up the following scale:

Directors...3 weeks

Shop managers...2 weeks

Male assistants with 5 years' service, female assistants with 3 years' service, butchery managers...10 days

Male assistants with under 5 years' service, females under 3 years, boys and warehousemen...1 week

Office staff...14 days

Staff lay down their cricket bats and pose for a group photo.

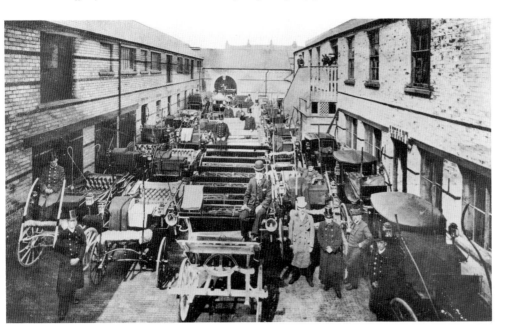

Charabancs prepare for the annual staff outing, some time before the Great War.

Cyclists await the start, annual sports day at Inglemire Lane, Cottingham. Judges include Norman Oughtred, A.W. Cruickshank, Harry Crawford and Chairman J.W. Carmichael.

While the company was thus evidently formalising certain allowances and benefits, numerous emergency situations required more *ad hoc* decisions to be made. When Robert 'Cocky' Gardham, Mackman's right hand man, died in 1933 after 33 years with the firm, an *ex gratia* payment of £20 was granted to his widow. In 1935 a Mr. Powles retired at 75 years of age after 21 years' service. A payment of ten shillings a week was voted for "this old servant of the company".

Workers then had little in the way of a pension and were naturally reluctant to finish work, but in September 1935 it was suggested that pensions be paid to elderly staff "who had ceased to be fully competent". Evidently some were staying on who would be better off out of it. Discussions had been in hand since 1933 for the introduction of a staff pension scheme. Meanwhile payments continued to be made at the discretion of the board. In 1936 a Mr. Smee - presumably Ernie's father - received a pound a week. Others were voted various sums - fifteen or ten shillings generally. But other old retainers worked on. In December 1936 Jack Oughtred brought to the board's attention the case of Mr. Cross, a man of 76 with 40 years' in harness. He was offered £1 10s 0d a week and retired forthwith.

There was also the question of what the company thought it owed - or could do - for widows of long-serving men. In 1937 a Mr. Mosey's widow was granted a weekly five shilling grocery order for one year. In the 1930s, a time of dire economic stress in many homes, union activism was first discussed at boardroom level. The company was quite evidently 'agin it'. When a representative of the Transport Workers' Union succeeded in recruiting a number of Jackson's drivers to its membership John Flew was recorded as having "interviewed" them, as a result of which all but three quit the union. The note in the minute book is revealing: "In some instances it was necessary to give an increase in wages, but this action was approved by the meeting."

In the bakery it seems there was no significant union membership at this time either. Mr. Mackman, prior to his leaving the firm, had actually advised some men to join a union - he foresaw bleak times ahead, and was probably anxious to protect his fellow-craftsmen - but they had been reluctant, and until well after the war such a union as there was remained relatively inactive. Hellick Millson, who joined the firm in the late forties, after a spell down the mines as a Bevan Boy, remembers being surprised by what he found at Jackson's. "It was no more than an under-the-counter union," he says. Nevertheless, Jackson's were

Staff dinner-dance in the 1930s. These were held at Beverley Road Baths, the pool being boarded over.

paying their bakery staff above the agreed national rate which, Hellick recalls, was £4 7s 9d for a basic 52-hour week. It was not until 1965 that, in common with many other bakers, Jackson's were forced to operate the 'closed shop'.

During the 1939-45 war *ex gratia* payments were once more made to the families of men in the services where hardship was evident. These were generally up to 12/6 a week, mostly paid in kind. Again, as in the First World War, it was generally accepted that jobs would be waiting for the men when they returned to civvy street.

We have already seen that a number of married women were retained during the war. When peace came the company faced difficulties in maintaining staff levels. Servicemen were only returning in dribs and drabs - it being government policy to stagger demobilisation and thus avert the sudden flood of manpower onto the labour market which had caused such problems in 1919. And meanwhile women were resigning faster than they could be replaced, some to get married, others to resume an interrupted domestic life. The shops, in 1946, were not actually able to keep open as long as was now permitted due to the shortage of staff.

In addition to difficulties in finding and keeping staff the board now found the attitudes of the workforce changed. It has been pointed out by many commentators that the war had revolutionised social attitudes in Britain. A nation that pulls together through a six-year emergency and puts its young men and women through the great levelling experience so many found in the armed forces will not easily return to the hierarchical relationships that characterised the pre-war retailing world where, as an example, the senior grocery hand would stand nearest the window, the second hand next, and the junior furthest from the public gaze. Thus Gordon Russell had cause to "speak strongly" to the board about staff attitudes and the quality of service in the shops.

This new situation saw hours being reduced - from 48 a week to 44 for the drivers in 1947, for example - and wages increased. This was in part a response to the rising cost of living - as in 1919 inflation was taking hold - and in part "a desire to attract a better type of assistant than those now applying for work". Later that year Richard Hall noted that the applicants were of "a very low standard...totally unsuitable for shop assistants".

Other trends reflected the post-war mood: in 1949 a higher than usual incidence of staff sickness was put down as "possibly due to the ease with which certificates are issued by doctors under the new National Health Service".

Generally, however, employee relations appear to have remained fairly good. In November 1965, while bread workers struck in many parts of Britain and bread actually had to be rationed, Jackson's worked on - despite the presence of pickets at the factory gate. But more troubled times were to come in the 1970s. Although the problems of this period must be seen against a background of general industrial unrest they reflected in some ways the legacy of the baking industry's tradition of a low basic wage enhanced by excessively long hours.

While the employers had been happy to let this situation persist, the union - the Bakers, Food and Allied Workers - also lacked the will to bring about change. It was not until Sam Maddox became General Secretary that a more radical stance was taken on the employees' side.

Allan Wheelwright, currently personnel director, joined the company in November 1977, just after the first of the national bread strikes which shook the industry. He remembers being surprised at the conditions and hours then prevailing in the bakeries, which seemed out of place in a modern automated working environment, perhaps even more surprised at the apparent lack of any organised unionism.

The hours worked, right up to the late seventies, were astonishing. This was especially so in busy seasons - in summertime, for example, when extra orders would come in from Butlin's or from the coastal resort shops. Most employees were working a regular seventy-two hour week over six days. At Derringham Street the norm was six twelve-hour shifts, plus an extra half shift on a Saturday. As one former bakery worker has said, "If you didn't put in the hours you weren't one of the lads." After a week of nights, finishing at six o'clock on a Saturday morning, staff would return at six on the Sunday morning to begin a week of days. A "long weekend" lasted from the noon finish on a Saturday after a week of days until six o'clock Sunday teatime when the night shift began. Basically, staff expected to work enough hours to take home double their basic pay.

Les Johnson, former manager at Stockton bakery, vividly remembers men finishing work after a sixteen-hour turn at Saturday lunchtime. "They'd sit on the wall across the road waiting for the bus home. Many's the time you'd see a man fall asleep and miss it. Or just let it go through sheer fatigue and hope to get on the next one." The low-wage long-hours syndrome was a vicious circle, hard to break in a time of full employment. Men got used to the money and didn't want to lose the overtime. At the same time, up to the seventies, Jackson's had a hard time recruiting staff in places like Stockton where employers like ICI paid high wages and absorbed much of the surplus labour. Stories of slack practices at the bakeries reflect the fact that the company could not afford to be choosy about whom they employed. Not that a little judicious skiving was entirely new - witness the story of a rugby player from the bakery in the thirties who sloped off from work for a big game, scored a memorable try, made the back page - and got the sack!

The national bread strike of September 1977 came after successive years of high inflation when the members of certain weaker unions had fallen far behind in the scramble for compensatory rises in wages. The union's primary aim was a flat £40 a week. Other departments had already had a taste of conflict: in January of that troubled year the TGWU had tried to recruit shop staff, and a number of stores had been blacked by Jackson's own warehouse drivers who refused to deliver to shops employing non-union labour. A note in Richard Hall's diary records a reminder to the union that "the company had been operating for 126 years without their assistance and could probably manage another week or two."

In July the General & Municipal Workers Union was demanding a closed shop at Cottingham Meat. The company reluctantly agreed to "this undemocratic move which is alien to our thinking". In August bakery workers went on a go-slow, unwilling to work the end-of-the-month Bank Holiday. For the earlier Royal Jubilee holiday they had been allowed to take the day off and work Sunday in lieu, and it seemed the union was trying to establish that precedent as a right. In September there were further "rumblings of unrest".

Against such a background came the national strike of September, the staff meeting on a Thursday lunchtime and walking off the job by three o'clock. Interestingly, Fred Aitchison, then the director in charge of the bakery, would have been quite happy to meet the union's demand for a flat £40. However, for the employers' side the Federation of Bakers was calling for a national agreement rather than a series of local ones; and likewise the BFAWU also called for solidarity. When an early offer by the Federation was rejected the strike dragged on and the dispute finally went to arbitration. The outcome was, ironically, a settlement at around £1.50 a week below the previous offer. With the men back at work it now took some time for sales to return to their previous level. Small independent bakers had, of course, worked through the stoppage and cashed in.

Meanwhile, further disruption was threatened. In October the company's drivers and warehousemen came out on strike after some recalcitrant drivers had been threatened with the sack over a dispute concerning a consignment of Christmas crackers after it had been agreed not to handle Christmas goods. And in November, for the first time in the company's

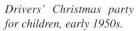

Drivers' Christmas party for children, early 1950s.

The Paragon Street ballroom, opened in 1950. The band is "Alan Bond and His Music" backed by the Mellowmaids.

history, there was a strike in the retail division when staff in the food hall of Willis Ludlow in Leeds walked out over a matter of union recognition. The following month the bakers were working to rule once more when it was found that the recent pay award conflicted with the government's 10% guideline and might therefore be forfeited. In the early weeks of 1978 USDAW, the shop workers' union, wanted to approach retail staff and there were fears at board level that this would invoke a conflict with the Transport & General. That same month, February, the factory electricians were on strike.

November 1978 saw a second national bread strike. To some extent the causes of this dispute lay in developments within the boardroom, far removed from the bakery floor. In April Spillers, one of the big three bread companies, had pulled out of baking in response to the evident over-capacity within the industry. A number of their plants were sold to their major competitors, Allied and Rank, the rest closed. A considerable number of redundancies resulted. The bakers union now agreed to introduce a five-day week in order to absorb some of the job losses, as well as to remedy the anomaly of the seventy-six hour week. It was suggested that members of the Federation take on one additional employee for every six currently on the pay-roll. While many would probably continue to work six days, the rest-day at least would be optional.

Many Jackson's workers were opposed to this second strike, more than in the case of the first one. But it was a national action, and the men and women came out, even picketing the National Avenue warehouse. However, there was general sympathy for the idea of a local agreement being sought. Jackson's own board would have welcomed that, but for a while at least their hands were tied. The Federation felt strongly that since the price of bread was determined by national rather than local factors - not least government tinkering - then wages should be treated likewise.

However, the board could see that they were in no position to withstand a second damaging strike and subsequent loss of business. They met with their workers and came to an agreement. A firm of Jackson's size was in a sense caught in the middle in this dispute. Where smaller companies would work on, taking trade from the majors, the big bakers were supposed to be closed. In fact, in many of these the management pitched in - at Rank and at Allied - to meet some of their urgent needs.

A crucial element in the discussions which led to making an agreement with the bakers was the view put forward by Allan Wheelwright and Christopher Oughtred. They pointed out that the main reason the staff were striking was not for more money but for a principle: they were the only major group within the company who did not have a private agreement. It seemed that to reach a private agreement would allow the company to be free of the restrictions imposed on it by the Federation. Once it was agreed to start negotiations the picketing of the warehouse ceased, an agreement was reached next day, and work resumed the day after that. This strike had lasted only four days.

At a national level the dispute rumbled on, more or less successfully, for close to a month. The big bakeries claimed that they were meeting up to 60% of their needs, but for Jackson's the main aim - that of keeping their shops and wholesale customers supplied - had been achieved.

A Jackson's football team at Inglemire Lane: (back) G. Bell, H. Millson, R. Elsam, J. Caldicot, J. McCann, K. Harrington; (front) J. Kowlanski, D. Lewison, F. Todd, R. Harker, G. Sandilands. Jackson's lost 5-1 to Bridlington Town in the final of the 1949 county league cup at Lund.

Looking back on the agreement the board had negotiated with the shop stewards, Allan Wheelwright says, "Yes, it was a good agreement - for the men! We negotiated rather naively, the talks locally at short notice giving us little time to prepare our case." Certain sundry concessions the union had been pushing for - the consolidation of recent rises into basic pay, double time for Sunday night working - were granted by the management side before the parties set to discussing an increase in basic rate. Normally, the basic rate would be established first, and the sundries used as bargaining chips. At a national level, no other company had yet conceded double time for Sunday nights.

A third major dispute of this period was the national drivers' strike in January 1979, in the thick of the 'winter of discontent' that contributed to the

downfall of the Labour government in May of that year. The bakery itself was not directly involved but, like many other businesses, it got caught in the crossfire between the TGWU and the Road Haulage Association as the union tried - and almost succeeded - in bringing all HGV traffic to a halt. Hull was targeted by the pickets, and very nearly cut off. Jackson's lost a lot of business: the company's shops were poorly and erratically stocked and the Derringham Street bakery had to lay off staff. There were additional lay-offs at National Avenue and at Cottingham Meat. Nevertheless, the staff had to be paid, at least a basic wage.

This strike was run locally by union shop stewards on a very *ad hoc* basis, with a Dispensation Committee sitting. To this body a company had to appeal in order to be permitted to move certain goods,

Exterior of old recreation club in Beverley Road, fitted out by Jackson's Services. This opened in 1949 and closed in 1980.

New recreation club on the corner of Clough Road and Cottingham Road, opened in June 1980. Fittings by Jackson's Services.

and such a request might be granted if the old, the sick or the handicapped were at risk, or if it could be shown that a business might actually go to the wall.

It was precisely this kind of action, Allan Wheelwright believes, which enabled the vigorous anti-union legislation of the eighties to be brought in. While he feels that the pendulum has swung too far the other way just now he is reminded that such arbitrary actions in the recent past are still being paid for by moderates and radicals alike.

The transport strike started to crumble after a while, lasting less than a month. The local branch of the TGWU said that Jackson's men could shift goods if a sum of money was paid into the strike fund for each lorry on the road. The Jackson's board could not agree to this. Nevertheless, as BNO pointed out at the time, the company had a duty to the people of Hull to stock their shops. It was therefore agreed that payments would be made - not to the union, however, but to a charity, the Hesslewood orphanage.

Since these troubled times, relations between management and staff have been remarkably trouble-free. A consultation process, introduced in the late '80s, now sees regular meetings between shop stewards and the bakery board. At these, board members attempt to give an honest picture of the state of current finances before such items as wage-rates are discussed.

The antiquated shift system in the bakeries, which lay at the heart of the disputes of the 1970s, has been dismantled. Staff now work no more than 48 hours a week on average, spread over five working days. The measure of the new system's success is that no-one

On stage at the opening of the new club are Brian Oughtred, Joe Hunt (club chairman for twenty-five years) and Paul Cross (vice-chairman). Later star turns included Ken Dodd, and Brian Clough.

would go back to the old - even if they do occasionally talk with wry amusement about the inefficiencies associated with it.

Improved relations at shop-floor level in part echo the changed times we live in, but also reflect a more stable - and ageing - workforce, rather as in the 1920s and '30s. The rate of staff turnover is really quite low compared with the 1970s.

In the shops, however, staff are still - as in those pre-war years - mostly quite young. Roughly a quarter of the 1,200 or so employees in the retail division have less than one year's service.

Jackson's - unlike the bakers Swales, or Woodhouse, for example - have retained their status as a family-run business. This has been perceived as a drawback by some people, who might have felt that their chances of making it to the very top have been limited. But as Mike Igoe, formerly manager of the Willerby superstore, has said, the advantages are that you know the people who own the company - and you have a continuity of management style. While he has seen some individuals leave the company because of that style, he has been openly envied by people he has met from other large and more impersonal institutions. In the long run, it is probably the family sentiment which has kept alive the firm's core interests in times of severe outside pressure, and thus preserved manufacturing and retail jobs for the region.

Allan Wheelwright sums up his view of the family firm: "Even though business has become infinitely more sophisticated and competitive in the last twenty years, and senior management in industry has become more remote from the workforce at large, here you know that you have access to the people who make the important decisions."

While the Welton Dale outings are now a distant memory, and the Cottingham sports ground is now a housing estate, Jackson's employees continue to enjoy social and sporting occasions through a variety of clubs and societies. Long-serving employees throughout the region get together annually under the banner of the Twenty-Five Year Club, and the Retirement Association meets every summer, as many as 200 pensioners getting together to share news, memories and the occasion itself.

To see former directors, shop assistants, drivers, managers and bakers sharing memories over a drink is to catch the feeling of belonging, the sense of family, which those associated with the company continue to enjoy.

Chapter Seventeen

THE MANUFACTURING DIVISION TODAY

The bakery division currently has a staff of some 600. As well as the two main bread plants there are four depots, at Rotherham, Birtley in County Durham and, of course, at Stockton and Hull. The bakery division keeps a hundred sales routes supplied as well as sending out nine or ten articulated lorry-loads of wholesale produce a day.

What first strikes the visitor to the bakeries is how few staff there appear to be. With as few as six operatives working on one of the computer-controlled bread plants 5,000 loaves per hour are produced. Late in 1993 an ultra modern, multi-purpose plant was installed to manufacture both bread and morning goods. Previously this would have involved two separate plants. From producing 18-20,000 buns per hour it can switch over to 400 gr speciality loaves at an hourly rate of 4,000.

The bread making process, however, still takes about three and three-quarter hours, a large slice of that time being required for cooling. Mixing is now carried out in a computer-controlled Tweedy mixer. This is very much a push-button affair with the ingredients pumped in through stainless steel pipes. The flour comes from the tall silos that tower over the factory, each holding as much as fifty tonnes. The yeast is pumped in from large vats in liquid form; the salt arrives already dissolved in warm water; and the milk - for the milk-roll products - in the form of powder. The respective volumes or weights of each ingredient are displayed both digitally and graphically on a TV screen. There is little noise, not a lot of smell - and absolutely no sign of sweaty men with their eyebrows dusted with flour. The mixing is all done in five minutes.

The prepared dough goes through a mechanised divider which cuts it into loaf-sized portions. From there it passes into conical moulders. After about eight minutes' resting the dough is re-moulded before

Peter Bentham Oughtred the Chairman since 1960. "PBO" has steered Jackson's through some exciting yet occasionally difficult times without ever allowing the company to lose sight of its core values.

proving in tins. When risen it is fed by conveyor into the travelling oven. The belts can be set at various speeds according to the product. A bread bun will bake for ten minutes, a standard loaf for about twenty. When the bread emerges it is de-panned automatically and placed in the cooler for two hours.

The finished loaves smell delicious and have a fine crust. Wrapping them in poly-bags keeps the bread moist and fresh but at inevitable expense of the crust. Asked about the supposed public sentiment - or nostalgia - for old-fashioned crusty bread a number of Jackson's bakery staff offer the same response: they pick up the wrapped loaf and squeeze it. "This is a constant challenge we face," says Nigel Snowden, managing director of Jackson's bakeries, "the customer going along the shelf squeezing each loaf in turn to test its softness. That's what people want, and that's what we have to give them. Crusty loaves only remain crusty for a few short hours after purchase. Look at France. They buy their fresh bread two or three times a day, and eat it immediately. If bread is to be kept two or three days - and that's how most people shop - it has to be soft and have the capacity to stay soft. Besides, if you want crusty bread now you can go to one of our in-store bakeries and pick it up hot from the oven!"

Popular views on bread are tied up with a number of misconceptions. One of these has been forcibly underlined by Les Johnson of Stockton, the former factory manager there. He still hears people talking about the loss of the crust being due to modern 'steam ovens' - we have all heard this at one time or another. This is a myth, but a potent one. It goes back to the 1880s and 1890s when bakeries were being mechanised, with steam-powered plant. This was the great age of steam, and manufacturers were naturally proud of their up-to-date equipment. Thus they would advertise their bread as coming from 'a modern steam bakery'. And so the misconception took hold, and is still with us.

In-store bakeries are a comparatively recent innovation, and are often not really bakeries at all. Frozen prepared dough is brought in and baked in small ovens either in a back room or in view of the customers. It is the smell which attracts people, as Vera Owen found out years ago. Back in the sixties and seventies she used to have special deliveries of oven-hot bread made to the Holderness Road shop, a novelty which brought in a rush of mothers as they fetched their children from the nearby school at tea-time. Fragrant, crusty bread - it sells like hot cakes!

In the bakery samples of each batch of bread are taken to a quality control office. Here staff inspect the loaf's appearance for shape and colour, check that it is neither under- nor over-baked, and then sample it for taste and 'mouth feel'. Alongside these test loaves are samples of the day's offerings from Jackson's competitors, bought at local shops. It is not until one sees the various loaves side by side that the considerable variations in quality become evident. A final test in the quality control room is for shelf life. Here loaves are quite literally kept on the shelf until they go mouldy.

Jackson's bakeries' Managing Director, Nigel Snowden, started work with Jackson's in 1965 as a van lad on £2 10s 0d a week, working on the wholesale routes. He vividly remembers the remarkable number of calls made on each round - eighteen shops in Bean Street alone, for example. (Up at Stockton, staff recall one van which had to make forty calls in Middlesbrough's Cannon Street!) Nigel is not alone in having worked his way up from shop floor to boardroom. Ken Hawkridge came to Derringham Street as a casual hand in the early seventies, soon found himself running an entire line, and is now Technical Director for the bakery division.

During Nigel Snowden's time one of the biggest changes has been the withdrawal from confectionery, which took place in the mid-eighties. The writing had been on the wall for some time, Rotherham's confectioners having already gone in the late sixties. The large supermarkets demanded standards of packaging, hygiene and presentation which placed intolerable burdens on all but the most dedicated. Added to this was a string of new regulations brought in by the Health and Safety Executive governing the production process - the strict separation of dairy produce from meat, for example. All of this, allied to hotter competition from well-known national confectioners - and Jackson's growing interest in frozen foods - resulted in confectionery being shut down. Not only did this cause job losses at Derringham Street but it also hit Cottingham Meat very hard. At one point sixty staff there were laid off - although many of these have since found jobs at Tryton Foods. Originally there were five departments - butchery, sliced cooked meat, bacon, bulk cooked meat and sausages. In these, thirty-five varieties were once made and as much as thirty tonnes a week produced. However, during the last few years, before the factory was finally closed in 1994, fourteen varieties totalling fifteen tonnes a week were manufactured, all of which were sold under the NISA label or used in Tryton's ready meals.

Jackson's bread business today falls into three categories: central distribution, where goods go out in bulk to central depots owned by major national supermarket chains for re-distribution nationwide; direct business - that is, goods transported by Jackson's own lorries direct to the stores where they will be sold, anywhere from the Scottish border to Birmingham or Liverpool; and contract business, a growing sector of the bakeries' market: this includes bread specially manufactured for crouton makers, burger buns and the like.

Latterly there have been one or two forays into the export market, for example, a monthly consignment of frozen bread is air-freighted to the expatriate commuity on the Canary Islands. Similiar opportunities are likely to open up now that we have the single European market, and given the proximity of the bakeries to Humberside's European ferry services.

While Derringham Street remains headquarters, Stockton takes the lead in some areas of its own. Quite recently it became the first bakery in the U.K. to be awarded the prestigious BS (British Standard) 5750. This seal of approval assures that a stringent code of rules appertaining to working practices and the production method are known to all staff and rigidly adhered to. Quality is the big issue in food production today, according to the bakeries' sales director Derek Wheeler. Producing the requisite volume of any particular item is not difficult. Maintaining standards of quality and uniformity is what separates the successful from the also-rans in a quality-conscious market-place.

While the bakery has suffered certain cut-backs and Cottingham Meat has effectively ceased to operate since the sale of the Grandways chain, a new division, Tryton Foods, has prospered. Originally it was Tryton Inn Frozen Foods, a name devised by bakery salesman Mike Greenfield in 1974. Around that time Jackson's had built a small freezer unit for certain of its confectionery products in order to help even out the production process. Greenfield saw a market for frozen foods, and began preparing ready meals, marketing them as products of the kitchens of the Triton Inn at Brantingham, one of the company's handful of pubs. His customers were to be caterers.

A major breakthrough came when Jack Allen, a buyer for Butlin's, told Jackson's - who at this time were supplying the firm with bread, cakes and trifles - that their biggest bugbear in mass catering was the humble Yorkshire pudding. At the larger holiday camps such as Pwlhelli and Filey as many as 38,000 cooked meals had to be served each day - and if roast beef was on the menu that meant an awful lot of Yorkshire puds. Could Jackson's help produce one which was proof against the errors of a stressed-out kitchen staff?

The problem wasn't a simple one. An example of the kind of problem faced was that conventional methods of greasing the individual tins didn't work: beef dripping simply turned to glue, and stuck fast. It was indeed some while before a suitable vegetable release agent was developed. The breakthrough in producing a frozen individual pudding was the result of development work by Mike Williamson, son of Joe, the former bakery foreman who had worked under Mr. Mackman.

With the success of the product - initially it only went to Butlin's, and only from April to October - the company decided to invest in some basic plant, and a blast freezer among other things. Meanwhile a solitary Jackson's driver - Gilly Warley - toured the country in a refrigerated lorry dropping off consignments from Ayr to Skegness by way of Bognor Regis.

Peter Hilditch, currently Managing Director of Tryton Foods, arrived in March 1985, around the time that Jackson's was going out of confectionery and putting more resources into frozen foods. By this time, though, the Butlin's market was declining, a reflection of changing holiday habits. In addition United Yeast, one of the firm's biggest customers, ceased to trade with Jackson's. Faced then with an urgent need to find new outlets the Tryton management made a critical decision. With the benefit of hindsight it looks crashingly obvious, although it wasn't at the time. They decided to take this product, which had been going so well at Butlin's, and market it in retail outlets for domestic use.

It was, Peter Hilditch reflects, a well-timed move. The public was now far more freezer-orientated, far keener to buy frozen products and oven-ready meals. Bejam, who had operated a chain of freezer shops where customers generally bought in bulk for the old-fashioned chest freezer, were now taken over by Iceland, and introduced a range of individual products for the fridge-freezer and the microwave.

Tryton approached one of Iceland's buyers and got him to try out their products in a handful of their stores. They went extremely well, and within no time Tryton were being approached by other multiples - Sainsbury, for example - who had seen the product, liked it, and were interested in stocking it.

Tryton staff join managing director Peter Hilditch (centre) to celebrate the production of one million Yorkshire puddings in a single week, summer 1987.

By 1986 the frozen Yorkshire puddings were in all the major multiples. By 1994 the company were making six million two-inch Yorkshire puddings a week. Other sizes were developed and, eventually, a whole family of associated products began to appear: for example, individual toad-in-the-holes, family-sized toads as well as mini-toads for children, with cocktail sausages from Cottingham.

In 1989 Tryton acquired Fridgeway Frozen Foods, a Shipley firm making catering and ready-made meals. This outfit was moved, lock stock and barrel - and owner Bill Ridgeway too! - to the Inglemire Lane site. There they produced the kinds of meals that are on sale in pubs throughout the country - lasagne, casseroles and pasta dishes. However, the Tryton management team decided in 1994 that this market was not one it wished to concentrate on, and the business was subsequently sold.

While Tryton decided early on not to rely exclusively on its core product - the Yorkshire pud - that side of the business continues to dominate. However, other products are tried. One great success has been the French bread pizza, basically a cheese and tomato topping on a French bread rather than a traditional pizza base. Here is an example of the way the company balances the need for each subsidiary to remain competitive with the need for those subsidiaries to contribute to the group's overall progress. When Tryton found that they could actually buy the French bread more cheaply from outside the company production was switched to Stockton where more efficient methods and up-to-date plant brought the price down.

On the back of the success of the original product, Tryton consolidated their market leadership with a series of five- and seven-inch versions, finally developing a seven-inch pudding with an individual dinner inside: roast beef slices, vegetables, roast potatoes and gravy.

Tryton had become a separate business within the bakery division in the mid-eighties. In 1990 it left the bakery division, remaining under the chairmanship of Patrick Farnsworth. Within the next year or two it was felt that not only was the company outgrowing this structure but it was also in danger of becoming something of a one-man band. The board was thus strengthened by drafting in three new directors. Mike Powell, formerly with Heinz, came as production director; David Brewis, the man who put the blue one in the Smarties tube for Rowntrees, came in as marketing director; and Brian Young, formerly with the Bridlington firm Sara Lee, took over finance.

In 1990 the administrative staff moved into their own suite of offices on the Derringham Street site, a modern open-plan arrangement which, according to Peter Hilditch, facilitates communication. "There are no secrets," he says. "If a problem is brewing, we're all aware of it and thus able to sort it out before it overwhelms us."

In the 1970s and particularly the 1980s most businesses of any size spread their wings and ventured into a wide variety of enterprises. Diversification was the name of the game. This was partly born of a self-confidence among that particular generation of executives, partly a protective measure: the further you spread yourself, the less danger of being wiped out as one sector or another suffered decline in a rapidly-changing world. For the nineties the watchword has been 'look after your core interests'.

Jackson's, as we have seen, started as tea-dealers and grocers and diversified as they sought to control all aspects of their business, preferring to hire their own engineers and shopfitters rather than rely on outsiders. Their recent rationalisation - parting company with Services, with their outside catering division, with AIM, even with Cottingham Meat - reflects their concern to protect those interests closest to the heart of the company. To that extent even Grandways proved expendable. Different as the modern company is, it would be in many ways more recognisable to its founder than the company of ten years ago. Bakers and grocers featured prominently in Jackson's early days, and they are still at the centre of it today.

Epilogue

In today's commercial world, it is rare that one has the opportunity to look backwards - normally all of us need to look continually to the future in our business dealings. However, we have told our story within these these pages because we are proud of it - proud of something which William Jackson's has that few of our competitors can copy or invent: namely, a great heritage. Part of understanding where our Business is today comes from knowing where we have come from.

Our story is very much of people who have been a part of William Jackson's along the way. It is the support and loyalty of our employees, customers and suppliers that have made our Company successful.

We have indeed come a long way in the last 143 years and are unusual in being a family business which has been passed successfully down from the founder to the fifth generation. William Jackson was my great-great-grandfather. Our development has always been strongly tied to the City of Hull and its region; indeed all the direct descendants of William Jackson continue to live within a few miles of Hull today.

During the last few years in particular, our Company has undergone some far-reaching changes in order to survive and to succeed in the very competitive fields in which we operate. We have been careful to leave it to a future generation to judge these changes. However, my colleagues and myself are now custodians of a strong and soundly based Business. Our task is to harness the efforts and dedication of previous generations and to take our business forward so that an enviable, reputable and successful company may be available for a sixth generation.

I hope that you have enjoyed reading our story.

Christopher M. Oughtred
September 1994

JACKSON/OUGHTRED FAMILY TREE

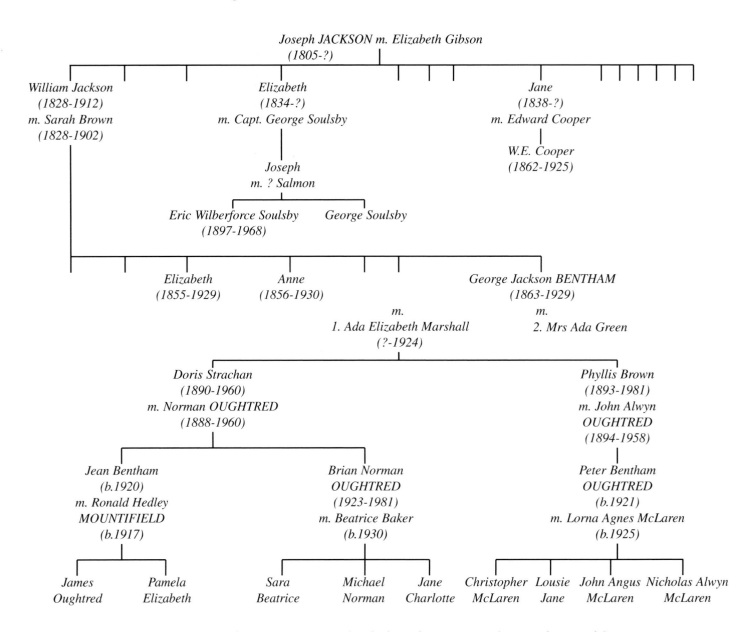

Joseph JACKSON m. Elizabeth Gibson
(1805-?)

William Jackson
(1828-1912)
m. Sarah Brown
(1828-1902)

Elizabeth
(1834-?)
m. Capt. George Soulsby

Joseph
m. ? Salmon

Eric Wilberforce Soulsby
(1897-1968)

George Soulsby

Jane
(1838-?)
m. Edward Cooper

W.E. Cooper
(1862-1925)

Elizabeth
(1855-1929)

Anne
(1856-1930)

George Jackson BENTHAM
(1863-1929)

m.
1. Ada Elizabeth Marshall
(?-1924)

m.
2. Mrs Ada Green

Doris Strachan
(1890-1960)
m. Norman OUGHTRED
(1888-1960)

Phyllis Brown
(1893-1981)
m. John Alwyn
OUGHTRED
(1894-1958)

Jean Bentham
(b.1920)
m. Ronald Hedley
MOUNTIFIELD
(b.1917)

Brian Norman
OUGHTRED
(1923-1981)
m. Beatrice Baker
(b.1930)

Peter Bentham
OUGHTRED
(b.1921)
m. Lorna Agnes McLaren
(b.1925)

James
Oughtred

Pamela
Elizabeth

Sara
Beatrice

Michael
Norman

Jane
Charlotte

Christopher
McLaren

Lousie
Jane

John Angus
McLaren

Nicholas Alwyn
McLaren

Footnote: Vertical line without a name = issue that died in infancy, or not relevant to history of Company.

OUTLINE HISTORY

1828 William Jackson born at Elstronwick, East Yorks

1851 28 Scale Lane, Hull: opened shop as grocer & tea dealer

1878 George Jackson Bentham, his son, entered the business

1885 W.E. Cooper, his nephew & confectioner, joined the firm

1887 G.H. Bompy Hall joined company, director of shops 1913-1935 & on board until death in 1950
16 assistants now up from 3 men & 3 boys in 1861

1891 Clarendon Street, Hull: first bakery & confectioners

1896 J.J.N. Mackman joined company, won over 5,000 awards for bread & confectionery

1904 William Jackson & Son Ltd formed from a partnership

1907 Victoria Street factory opened

1912 William Jackson died

1922 Harry Crawford, Cottingham farmer, joined company, becomes meat director in 1929 until death in 1943

1925 W.E. Cooper, Secretary of company since 1904 died.
John Alwyn Oughtred, "Jack", son in law of Bentham, appointed new Secretary
Farms at Preston & Bilton & Tower Grange nurseries sold

1928 500 staff for first time
Jack Oughtred resigned as company Secretary
Eric Wilberforce Soulsby, great-nephew of Wm Jackson, appointed director & company Secretary

1929 Registered offices moved from Carr Lane to Paragon St
George Jackson Bentham died

1930 J.W. Carmichael appointed chairman & the Oughtred brothers, Jack & Norman, directors

1931 Francis Myers Ltd of Welton bought
Browns Central Supply Stores Ltd of Withernsea bought

Registered offices moved from Paragon Street to 129 Spring Bank, Hull

1932 First shop in York opened

1933 First cafés opened
J.J.N. Mackman, director of bakery, dismissed

1934 Travelling bread oven bought
Automatic bread slicing & wrapping machine experiment & bought one 2 months later

1937 A.W. Cruickshank, company Secretary gaoled because of "defalcations admitted & proved"

1938 Factory meat department moved from Victoria Street to Cottingham slaughterhouse, Inglemire Lane

1939 Registered offices moved to Elloughton Dale, Brough

1940 Slaughterhouse commandeered by Government (returned to company in 1950)

1942 Jack Oughtred appointed Managing Director
T.F. Dodsworth appointed bakery director

1943 Ferguson Fawsitt Arms, Walkington bought

1944/5 T. Swale Ltd, Wakefield; Mitchell (Scunthorpe);
T. Woodhouse (Dudley);
Wilsons (Weaverthorpe);
Harpers (Harrogate); Golden Grain Bakery (Mirfield)
[& H. Adams (Rotherham) in 1940] bought bakeries and retail shops

1945 Gordon Russell appointed stores director
Registered offices moved from Elloughton Dale to 12a Victoria Street, Hull

1946 Crystal Motor, General & Electrical Engineering Co Ltd. incorporated

1947 Barkers (Grocers) Ltd with 10 grocery stores bought

1948 John Cross Ltd, 7 store branches in York bought
Priory Road opened as first self-service store in Hull

1949 Recreation club at 279 Beverley Road opened

1950 Peter Bentham Oughtred (PBO) appointed director

1952 Brian Norman Oughted (BNO) appointed director

1954 First travelling shops
1955 Stockton bakery opened
1958 Jack Oughtred, Managing Director, died
BNO & PBO appointed joint
Managing Directors
1960 J.W. Carmichael retired as Chairman & replaced
by PBO
R.H. Mountifield appointed meat director
Norman Oughtred appointed vice-chairman but
died in May
Primrose Valley, Filey opened grocers & snack bar,
for 7 seasons until 1966
1961 Revolutionary Chorleywood Bread Process
introduced First discount store in Britain opened:
Grandways at New York Road, Leeds
Grafton Street (118/120 Newland Ave) converted
into first "fully-fledged superette"; takings triple!
1963 Public issue of preference shares
1964 Frederick Aitchison appointed bakery director
Richard Hall appointed sales director
R.A. McLaren appointed buying director
Timms of Goole, flour millers: bought half shares
1966 Ordered first computer equipment from ICT
(International Computers & Tabulators Ltd)
E.W. Soulsby, buying director, retired from board
T.F. Dodsworth, bakery director, retired from
executive duties
1968 G.F. Kilburn appointed wholesale director
1969 Beverley race course: sponsor race
1970 Computer Services (Hull) Ltd formed as
computer bureau
Gordon Russell, sales director, retired from
executive duties
Richard Hall appointed group sales director
W.R. Russell resigned as company Secretary &
replaced by G.S. Nurse
Last counter shop, Newland (540/546 Beverley
High Road) converted to supermarket
1971 Wm Jackson & Son (Services) Ltd formed from
Crystal specialized engineering department
1972 £1 million (pre-tax) profits for first time
Martin Russell appointed stores director

1974 Frozen Yorkshire Puddings produced for Butlins
1976 Computer Services (Hull) Ltd renamed AIM Ltd
1979 2 departmental boards of directors formed:
Retail and Bakery & Meat
Fred Aitchison, bakery director, retired
1980 George Kilburn, bakery director, retired
New Recreation club opened on Beverley Road
1981 Christopher Oughtred appointed director
Patrick Farnsworth appointed bakery director
Brian Oughtred, joint Managing Director, died
1982 Rotherham bakery closed
G.S. Nurse retired as company Secretary & is
replaced by Peter Farley
1984 Christopher Oughtred appointed joint
Managing Director
Ron H. Mountifield appointed vice-chairman
Wakefield bakery sold to Warburtons
£1.6 million plant installed at Stockton bakery
1985 Goodfellows Ltd, 16 stores & warehouse bought
1986 Confectionery & savouries production ceased
Richard Hall, retail division chairman, died
1987 8 Hillards stores bought from Tesco
Now 74 Grandways stores
AIM Ltd sold in management buy-out
1988 Melton central distribution centre opened
1990 Giant Grandways at Willerby opened
1991 First Convenient Neighourhood Store opened:
Jackson's of Chanterlands Avenue
Frank Dee appointed Chairman of Retail division
1992-1993 Sold 24 Grandways to Argyll Group &
Kwik Save plc
Frank Dee resigns as Chairman of Retail division
1993 Crystal of Hull Ltd: bought 95% of issued share
capital
1994 "From corner shop to corner shop in five
generations: the history of William Jackson &
Son plc" published!

1851	OPENED	Grocer & tea dealer	28 Scale Lane
1861		Grocer	72 Carr Lane
1863	CLOSED	Grocer	28 Scale Lane
1877	RELOCATED		72 Carr Lane to 37/38 Carr Lane
	OPENED	Grocer	127 Spring Bank
1892		Confectioner	127 Spring Bank
		Grocer	129a Spring Bank
		Grocer	Bright St
			48 Holderness Rd
1899		Confect	63 Holderness Rd
		Confect/Grocer	Severn St/303/5 Holderness Rd
1903		Grocer/Confect	Dairycoates/544/6 Hessle Rd
		Baker/Confect	249/51 Anlaby Rd
1905		Grocer/Confect	45/47 Princes Ave
1907		Confect	Bean St/136a Hessle Rd
1912		Grocer/Confect	614/6 Holderness Rd
		Green fruit	125 Spring Bank
		Green fruit	65 Holderness Rd
		Green fruit	548 Hessle Rd
1913		Confect/Grocer	485a Anlaby Rd
		Grocer/Confect	Grafton St/118/20 Newland Ave
		Confect/Grocer	Stepney/240/2 Beverley Rd
		Grocer	37 Charles St
		Confect	Eton/280 Hessle Rd
1914		Green fruit	301 Holderness Rd
1915		Confect	Brunswick/52 Beverley Rd
		Pork,cooked meats, fruit	East Park/618 Holderness Rd
1916		Grocer	282 Hessle Rd
1919		Pork butchers	278 Hessle Rd
		Green fruit	123 Spring Bank
1920		Stores	59 Charles St
	CLOSED	Grocer	37 Charles St
	OPENED	Stores	130/4 Hessle Rd
1921		Stores	108a Porter St
		Butcher	110 Porter St
1924		Confect,meat	Washington St/430 Beverley Rd
1925		General stores	Gipsyville/821 Hessle Rd
		Green fruit	620 Holderness Rd

Year	Action	Type	Location
1926		Butcher	299 Holderness Rd
		Grocer/Confect/Meat	Newland/540/4 Beverley Rd
1927		Baker	The Square, Hessle
		Baker	309 Hedon Rd
1928		Baker	63 Gordon St
		Grocer/Baker	72/4 Chanterlands Ave
1929		Confect	13 Carr Lane
		Stores	52/3 Paragon St
1930		Baker	112 Argyle St
1931	BOUGHT	Brown's Central Supply Stores	Withernsea
	CLOSED	Grocer	38 Carr Lane
	OPENED	Stores/Cafe	41 Toll Gavel, Beverley
1932		Fish, game & poultry	546 Beverley High Road
		Grocer/Baker	888 Spring Bank West
		Grocer/Baker	71 Goodramgate, York
		Grocer/Baker	490 Inglemire Lane
		Grocer/Baker	Preston Road
1933		Grocer/Baker	6 Newbegin, Hornsea
		Butchers	Queen St/Hull Rd, Withernsea
		Grocer	Park Estate/1022 Anlaby Rd
1934		Grocer/Confect/Butcher	249 Greenwood Ave
		Grocer/Confect/Butcher	Octagon Estate, Willerby
		Grocer/Baker	90 Queen St, Withernsea
		Confect	61 Whitefriargate
	CLOSED	Cafe	41 Toll Gavel, Beverley
		Confect	Queen St South, Withernsea
	OPENED	Stores	Prince/Cliff St, Bridlington
1935	BOUGHT	Grocer/Confect	11 Market Place, Driffield
1936	OPENED	Butchers	Newington/493 Anlaby Rd
		Confect	444 Hessle Road
	CLOSED	Confect	37 Carr Lane
	OPENED	Confect	Gowthorpe, Selby
		Confect	7 St Sepulchregate, Doncaster
1937	CLOSED	Cafe	Prospect Street
	OPENED	Confect	Market Place, Thorne
		Confect	Balby Rd, Doncaster
		Confect	124 Boothferry Rd, Goole
		Restaurant	Cliff St, Bridlington
		Confect	55 High St, Scunthorpe
		Snack bar	Prospect Street

Year	Action	Description	Location
1938	CLOSED	Snack bar	Prospect Street
	OPENED		Confect 128 Kirkgate, Leeds
1939		Confect	Beulah St, Harrogate
		Confect	Station Rd, Stainforth
	REQUISITIONED	Stores	Prince St, Bridlington
1940	OPENED	Confect	14 Charles St
		Confect	Hexthorpe, Doncaster
		Confect	Ashby High St, Scunthorpe
1942	BOUGHT	Grocer	138 Hallgate, Cottingham
		Confect/Post office	Village Rd, Cottingham
	OPENED	Francis Myers	Market Place, South Cave
	BOUGHT	Francis Myers	Skillings Lane, Brough
1944		T. Swale: Confect	Alverthorpe Rd, Wakefield
		Francis Myers: Stores	Onprest, Preston
		Mitchells: Grocer/Confect	24 Cole St, Scunthorpe
		Wilsons: Stores	Weaverthorpe
1945	CLOSED	Confect	Kirkgate, Leeds
	OPENED	Confect	Queen Victoria St, Leeds
	BOUGHT	Harpers: stores	Starbeck, Harrogate
	OPENED	Confect	Otley Rd, Headingley
1946		Francis Myers: Off-licence	Market Place, South Cave
1947	BOUGHT	Barkers (Grocers) Ltd Castleford	Eastmoor, Wakefield
			Methley, Mickleton
			Newton Hill, Wakefield
			Normanton
			Aberford Rd, Oulton
			Leeds Rd, Outwood
			Agbrigg Rd, Sandal
			West Ardsley
		Browne's grocer	Market Place, Pocklington
	OPENED	Barkers: Confect	Station Lane, Featherstone
		Stores	336/8 Priory Rd
1948		First self-service store	336/8 Priory Rd
	BOUGHT	John Cross Ltd, grocer	8 Fossgate, York
			Micklegate, York
			Fulford Rd, York
			Market Place, York
			Walmgate, York
			Petergate, York
			Bootham, York
1949	OPENED	John Cross: stores	New Earswick
	BOUGHT	Barkers: Grocer	Commercial St, Rothwell

Year	Action	Type	Location
1949 *cont...*	OPENED	Willow Plate snack bar	13 Carr Lane
		Stores	Milton Rd, Rotherham
1950		Confect/Off-licence	Netherhall Rd, Doncaster
		Confect	High St, Knaresborough
	CLOSED	Confect	444 Hessle Road
	OPENED	Confect	Frodingham Rd, Scunthorpe
1951		Confect	Carlton St, Castleford
		Mitchells: Confect	Cole St, Scunthorpe
1952		Confect	3 Lane Ends, Castleford
1953	BOUGHT	Linsleys: Grocer/Off-licence	58 Market Place, Driffield
	OPENED	Snack bar	4 Toll Gavel, Beverley
		Butcher	66 Chanterlands Avenue
		Mountains: Butcher	110 Newland Ave
1955		Stores	23 Hull Road, Anlaby
		Grocer/Butcher	Bilton Grange
	CLOSED	Grocer/Confect/Butcher	249/51 Anlaby Road
		Grocer/Confect/Butcher	130/2 Hessle Road
		Confect	309 Hedon Road
		Confect	52a Beverley Road
1956	OPENED	Brown's butchers	Prestongate, Hessle
	CLOSED	Grocer/Confect	61/3 Holderness Rd
		Confect	120 Newland Ave
		Confect	87 Princes Ave
		Barkers	Castleford
		Barkers	Station Lane, Featherstone
		Barkers	Normanton
	BOUGHT	T.A.Scott: Grocer/Confect	Darlington Rd, Ferry Hill
			Osbourne Rd, Ferry Hill
1957	CLOSED	Butcher	65 Holderness Rd
		Confect	High St, Knaresborough
		Confect	Meanwood, Leeds
1958		Willow Plate snack bar	4 Toll Gavel, Beverley
		Butcher/Fruiterer	548/50 Hessle Road
	OPENED	Mays: Confect/Snack parlour	162 High St, Scunthorpe
	CLOSED	Confect	Hexthorpe, Doncaster
1960		John Cross	Fossgate, York
		Confect	73 Hawthorn Ave
	OPENED	Stores	Finkle St, Malton
		Stores/Depot	Commercial St, Norton
1961	CLOSED	Barkers	Commercial St, Rothwell
		Confect	112 Argyle Street
		Grocer/Confect	544/6 Hessle Road

Year	Action	Type	Location
1961 *cont...*		Grocer/Confect	614/6 Holderness Rd
	OPENED	Grandways	New York Rd, Leeds
		Food Hall	Willis Ludlow, Vicar Lane, Leeds
	CLOSED	Bakers	61 Whitefriargate
		Grocer/Confect	821 Hessle Road
		Butcher	618 Holderness Rd
		Francis Myers	Market Hall, Welton
1962	OPENED	Butchers	1020 Anlaby Rd
	CLOSED	Confect	Queen Victoria St, Leeds
		Wilsons	Weaverthorpe
		Barkers: Grocer	Eastmoor, Wakefield
1963		Butcher	493 Anlaby Road
		John Cross	Petergate, York
	SOLD	Grocer/Confect/Post office	Village Rd, Cottingham
	CLOSED	Barkers	Newton Hill, Wakefield
		Confect	7 St Sepulchregate, Doncaster
	OPENED	Discount drapery/Grandways	Boothferry Rd, Goole
1964		Grandways	Albion St, Castleford
	CLOSED	Supermarket	336/8 Priory Road
		Stores	Milton Rd, Rotherham
	BOUGHT	Mostyn's: Butcher	300 Holderness Rd
	CLOSED	Confect	Carlton St, Castleford
		Confect	Ashby High St, Scunthorpe
		Confect	Frodingham Rd, Scunthorpe
		Confect	Balby Rd, Doncaster
1965	OPENED	Foodmarket	Wrawby St, Brigg
	CLOSED	Confect	Goodramgate, York
	BOUGHT	Shop/Warehouse/Garage	Montagu Sq, Mexborough
		Grants: Stores	212/4 Fulford Rd, York
1966	CLOSED	Confect	55 High St, Scunthorpe
		Confect	3 Lane Ends, Castleford
	BOUGHT	Grocers	Farndale Ave, Osbaldwick
	CLOSED	Confect	218 Willerby Road
	OPENED	Grandways Food Hall	Cook Lane, Keithley
	CLOSED	Confect	Market Place, Thorne
	OPENED	Supermarket	Hainton Ave, Grimsby
	BOUGHT	Supermarket	Horsforth, Leeds
	CLOSED	Confect/Grocer	23 Hull Rd, Anlaby
	OPENED	Grandways	42 Hull Rd, Anlaby
	CLOSED	Francis Myers	Onprest, Preston
1967	OPENED	Grandways	Fulford Rd, York
	CLOSED	Confect	Beulah St, Harrogate

Year	Action	Name	Location
1967 *cont...*	OPENED	Grandways	Halton, Leeds
		Grandways	Dewsbury Rd, Leeds
	CLOSED	Confect	Station Rd, Stainforth
		Barkers	Leeds Rd, Outwood
		Grants	Fulford Rd, York
	BOUGHT	Laws supermarket	Driffield
	CLOSED	Linsleys	58 Market Place, Driffield
	OPENED	Grandways	Grimsby Rd, Cleethorpes
	CLOSED	Butcher	66 Chanterlands Ave
		Stores	Finkle St, Malton
		Shop/Depot	Commercial St, Norton
	OPENED	Supermarket	Chapel Allerton, Leeds
	CLOSED	Willow Plate cafe	13 Carr Lane
1968	OPENED	Supermarket	New Lane, Selby
	CLOSED	Grandways	New York Rd, Leeds
		Barkers	Methley, Mickleton
	OPENED	Grandways: Banners	Attercliffe Rd, Sheffield
	CLOSED	Supermarket	Gowthorpe, Selby
		Confect	430 Beverley Road
		Confect	63 Gordon St
		Stores	Anlaby Road
		John Cross: except for off-licence	Micklegate, York
1969		Myers: All except off-licence	South Cave
	OPENED	Food Hall Willis Ludlow	Carr Lane
	RELOCATED		no.6 to 12/16 Newbegin, Hornsea
	OPENED	Grandways	Queen St, Morley
	OPENED	Grandways	Roundhay Rd, Leeds
	CLOSED	John Cross	Market St, York
	OPENED	Grandways	Cromwell Rd, Grimsby
	CLOSED	John Cross	New Earswick
1970		Food Hall Willis Ludlow	Carr Lane
	OPENED	Washeteria	63 Gordon St
	CLOSED	Confect	14 Charles St
	OPENED	Jacksons (Grandways)	Newbegin, Malton
	CLOSED	John Cross: Post office	Walmgate, York
		Supermarket	98 Fountain Rd
	OPENED	Grandways	West St, Boston
	CLOSED	Browns' butchers	Prestongate, Hessle
		Supermarket	14 Charles Street
1971		Mountains butchers	110 Newland Ave
	OPENED	Washeteria	44 Derringham St
		Grandways	Sprotborough Rd, Doncaster

1971 *cont...*	CLOSED	Grandways Food Hall	Cook Lane, Keithley
		Supermarket	Market Place, Pocklington
	OPENED	Jacksons (Grandways)	George St, Pocklington
		Grandways	Eastgate, Louth
1972		Grandways	Prospect Hill, Worksop
		Grandways	Hilderthorpe Rd, Bridlington
	CLOSED	Grandways	Queen St, Morley
	OPENED	Grandways/Petrol station	Balderton, Newark
1974		Grandways	460/2 Holderness Rd
	CLOSED	Myers: Off-licence	South Cave
	OPENED	Grandways	Dinington, Rotherham
	CLOSED	Washeteria	63 Gordon St
	OPENED	Grandways	Ellerburn Ave, Orchard Park
		Grandways	240 Holderness Rd
1975		Grandways	Bottesford, Scunthorpe
		Grandways	Borrowash, nr Derby
	CLOSED	Grandways	Otley Rd, Headingley
1976	OPENED	Grandways	Brecks, Rotherham
	CLOSED	Mostyns	300 Holderness Road
		Supermarket	Preston Road
		Supermarket	316 Southcoates Lane
		John Cross: Off-licence	Micklegate, York
	OPENED	Grandways	Newhall, Burton on Trent
1977		Grandways	Park Rise, Nottingham
1978	CLOSED	Supermarket	Rothwell
1979	OPENED	Grandways	Kirstall Lane, Leeds
1980		Grandways	Old Wainfleet Rd, Skegness
1981		Grandways	Haxby, York
		Grandways	Riverside, Brigg
1982	CLOSED	White Rose Restaurant	52/3 Paragon St
	OPENED	Grandways wet fish shop	446 Holderness Rd
		Grandways	Martongate, Bridlington
1983		Grandways	Boothferry Park
1984	CLOSED	Supermarket	299/305 Holderness Rd
		Supermarket	888 Spring Bank West
		Supermarket	Ashby High St, Scunthorpe
		Supermarket	Cole St, Scunthorpe
		Barkers/Grandways	Barkers/Oulton
1985	BOUGHT	Goodfellows, 16 stores	447/51 Anlaby Road
			71/2 Charles Street
			Coltman Street
			37 Goodhart Road, Bransholme

Year	Action	Type	Location
1985 *cont...*	BOUGHT		23/5 Toll Gavel, Beverley
			101/3 King Street, Cottingham
			4/6 Mariner's Court, Goole
			8a The Weir, Hessle
			Bridlington
			Sharp Street
			Victor Street
			Hessle Rd/Rosamond Street
	CLOSED	Grandways	Chapel Allerton
	OPENED	Grandways	Stainbeck Lane, Leeds
	CLOSED	Supermarket	Octagon Estate, Willerby
	OPENED	Grandways	Kirkella
	CLOSED	Shop/Warehouse/Garage	Montagu Sq, Mexborough
		Supermarket	12/6 Newbegin, Hornsea
	OPENED	Grandways	29/51 Newbegin, Hornsea
	CLOSED	Supermarket	Eton/278/82 Hessle Rd
		Supermarket	Newington/485/a Anlaby Rd
1986		Goodfellows	Bridlington
		Goodfellows	Toll Gavel, Beverley
		Goodfellows	71/2 Charles Street
		Goodfellows	Mariner's Court, Goole
1987	OPENED	Grandways	Norwood, Beverley
	CLOSED	Grandways	Grimsby Rd, Cleethorpes
1988	BOUGHT	Grandways	Heckmondwike
		Grandways	Ossett
		Grandways	Barnsley Rd, Sheffield
		Grandways	Todmorden
		Grandways	Wath-on-Dearne
		Grandways	Wombwell
		Grandways	Hull Rd, York
		Grandways	Barnoldswick
1989	CLOSED	Grandways	Balderton, Newark
	OPENED	New Grandways	Balderton, Newark
1990		Giant Grandways	Willerby
1992	CLOSED	Grandways	Market Place, Driffield
	SOLD	Grandways	460/2 Holderness Rd
		Grandways	The Square, Hessle
		Grandways	George St, Pocklington
		Grandways	Boothferry Park
		Grandways	Ellerburn Ave, Orchard Park
		Grandways	Dinnington, Rotherham
		Grandways	Dewsbury Rd, Leeds

1992 *cont...*		Grandways	Kirkstall Lane, Leeds
		Grandways	Eastgate, Louth
		Grandways	Old Wainfleet Rd, Skegness
		Grandways	Hull Rd, York
		Grandways	King St, Cottingham
		Grandways	Newark
		Grandways	Borrowash, Derby
		Grandways	Cromwell Rd, Grimsby
		Grandways	Armthorpe, Doncaster
		Grandways	Chapel Allerton
		Grandways	Riverside, Brigg
		Grandways	Martongate, Bridlington
		Grandways	Norwood, Beverley
	CLOSED	Grandways	New Lane, Selby
	OPENED	Jacksons	Bricknell Ave
		Jacksons	Spen Lane, Leeds
1993	SOLD	Giant Grandways	Willerby
	CLOSED	Grandways	Willis Ludlow, Leeds
	OPENED	Jacksons	Monk Bretton, Barnsley
		Jacksons	Bishopthorpe Rd, York
		Jacksons	South Elmsall
		Jacksons	Stairfoot, Barnsley
1994		Jacksons	Beckfield Lane, York
		Jacksons	King Edward's Drive, Harrogate
		Jacksons	Cottingham
		Jacksons	Mickleover, Derby
		Jacksons	Woodthorpe, York
		Jacksons	Kings Road, Harrogate

About the Author and Researcher

ALAN WILKINSON *is a Hornsea writer with what has been called a checkered background. He worked as a freight-train guard, immigration officer, cocoa-sifter and rat catcher before coming to Hull in 1984 to take a first class degree in American Studies. In 1989 he took an M.A. in creative writing at the University of East Anglia.*

He has written articles and stories for local and national publications as diverse as the Guardian, What Mortgage?, Yours and the Great Plains Quarterly. He continues to research the history and literature of the American West.

KATHY BEEDHAM *is a Classics scholar and holds an M.A. in Archive Administration. She lives in Hull, but in between working assignments loves to travel. Her recent trips have taken her to South-East Asia and the Pacific Islands. Working on this book has been a great change from her previous project, an in-depth study of voting patterns in eighteenth century Cheshire.*

So far nine-tenths of what she has discovered about Jackson's hasn't seen the light of day: however it has been painstakingly catalogued and listed and forms the basis for the archive she has created for the firm.